Nurse and Spy in the Union Army

S. E. E. Edmonds

S. E. E. Edmonds

H. J.

NURSE AND SPY

IN THE

UNION ARMY:

COMPRISING

The Adventures and Experiences of a Woman in Hospitals, Camps, and Battle-Fields.

By S. EMMA E. EDMONDS.

WITH ILLUSTRATIONS.

Published by Subscription only by
W. S. WILLIAMS & CO., HARTFORD, CONN.
JONES BROS. & CO., PHILADELPHIA AND CINCINNATI.
J. A. STODDARD & CO., CHICAGO, ILL.
1865.

Printed by Wiley, Waterman, & Eaton, Hartford, Conn.

To the

Sick and Wounded Soldiers

of the

Army of the Potomac,

This Volume

IS RESPECTFULLY INSCRIBED

BY

The Author.

EMBELLISHMENTS.

PORTRAIT Engraved on Steel by Geo. E. Perine, N. Y.
Disguises and other Scenes, Drawn and Engraved on Wood by R. O'Brien, New York.

PUBLISHERS' NOTICE.

No apology is necessary for adding one more to the numerous "War Books" which already fill a large space in American Literature; for, to the general reader, nothing connected with the Rebellion can be more interesting than the personal experiences of those who have been intimately associated with the different phases of military life, in Camp, Field, and Hospital.

The "Nurse and Spy" is simply a record of events which have transpired in the experience and under the observation of one who has been on the field and participated in numerous battles—among which are the first and second Bull Run, Williamsburg, Fair Oaks, the Seven days in front of Richmond, Antietam, and Fredericksburg—serving in the capacity of "Spy" and as "Field Nurse" for over two years.

While in the "Secret Service" as a "Spy," which is one of the most hazardous positions in the army—she penetrated the enemy's lines, in various disguises, no less than eleven times; always with complete success and without detection.

Her efficient labors in the different Hospitals as well as her arduous duties as "Field Nurse," embrace many thrilling and touching incidents, which are here most graphically described.

Should any of her readers object to some of her disguises, it may be sufficient to remind them it was from the purest motives and most praiseworthy patriotism, that she laid aside, for a time, her own costume, and assumed that of the opposite sex, enduring hardships, suffering untold privations, and hazarding her life for her adopted country, in its trying hour of need.

In the opinion of many, it is the privilege of woman to minister to the sick and soothe the sorrowing—and in the present crisis of our country's history, to aid our brothers to the extent of her capacity—and whether duty leads her to the couch of luxury, the abode of poverty, the crowded hospital, or the terrible battle field—it makes but little difference what costume she assumes while in the discharge of her duties.—Perhaps she should have the privilege of choosing for herself whatever may be the surest protection from insult and inconvenience in her blessed, self-sacrificing work.

The moral character of the work,—being true to virtue, patriotism, and philanthropy—together with the fine embellishments and neat mechanical execution—will, we trust, render it an interesting and welcome visitor at every fireside.

CONTENTS.

CHAPTER I.

CHAPTER II.

CHAPTER III.

CHAPTER IV.

CHAPTER V.

CHAPTER VI.

CHAPTER VII.

CHAPTER VIII.

CHAPTER IX.

CHAPTER X.

Pages 137–146.

MC CLELLAN'S DESPATCH FROM EWELL'S FARM—CALL FOR REINFORCEMENTS—NEWS FROM NORFOLK—DESCRIPTION OF THE MERRIMAC—THE ENGAGEMENT IN HAMPTON ROADS—FIRST AND LAST FIGHT OF THE MERRIMAC—VICTORY OF THE MONITOR—ADVANCE ON THE PENINSULA—THE BATTLE SONG—A MUDDY MARCH—ON THE CHICKAHOMINY—CRITICAL POSITION OF GENERAL BANKS—THE PRESIDENT'S DESPATCHES—MC-CLELLAN'S REPLY.

CHAPTER XI.

Pages 147–160.

ANOTHER DISGUISE—I BECOME AN IRISH PEDDLER—FEVER AND AGUE—A NIGHT OF SUFFERING IN THE SWAMP—RETROSPECTION—LOST IN THE SWAMP—CANNON MY GUIDES—A SICK REBEL—I FIND SOMETHING TO EAT—MY NEW PATIENT—SYMPATHY FOR SUFFERING—TALK WITH A DYING REBEL—A WILLING DETENTION—EXTEMPORIZING A LIGHT—THE LAST HOUR—SOLDIERS OF CHRIST—THE CHAMBER OF DEATH.

CHAPTER XII.

Pages 161–173.

AM I A STOIC?—SOMEONE'S DARLING—COMPLETING MY DISGUISE—ANOTHER START FOR THE REBEL LINES—PEPPERING MY EYES—CHALLENGED BY A PICKET—A COCKNEY SENTINEL—GETTING INFORMATION—PLENTY OF BEEF, BUT NO SALT—RICE AND CORN MEAL BREAD—PREPARING TO VISIT HEADQUARTERS—INTERVIEW WITH MAJOR MC KEE—THE MAJOR'S MISPLACED CONFIDENCE—RETURN FOR THE BODY OF THE REBEL CAPTAIN—MY LOOK-OUT FOR YANKEES—NEW ORDERS.

CHAPTER XIII.

CHAPTER XIV.

CHAPTER XV.

CHAPTER XVI.

CHAPTER XVII.

CHAPTER XVIII.

CHAPTER XIX.

Pages 249–260.

CHAPTER XX.

Pages 261–273.

CHAPTER XXI.

Pages 273–285.

CHAPTER XXII.

CHAPTER XXIII.

CHAPTER XXIV.

CHAPTER XXV.

CHAPTER XXVI.

CHAPTER XXVII.

CHAPTER XXVIII.

CHAPTER XXIX.

CHAPTER XXX.

HOSPITAL TREE AT FAIR OAKS.—Page 191.

NURSE AND SPY.

CHAPTER I.

COMMENCEMENT OF THE WAR—MY HOME AND MY DUTY—I ENLIST IN THE CAUSE—EXCITEMENT AT THE WEST—TROOPS ON THE MARCH—MOBS AT BALTIMORE—TEMPORARY HOSPITALS—UNAVOIDABLE EVILS—BEGGING FOR COMFORTS—SUPPLIES FOR THE SICK—CAMP HOSPITALS—THUNDER STORMS IN CAMP—A DYING OFFICER—SOLDIERS IN THE PUBLIC BUILDINGS—PREPARATIONS FOR THE ADVANCE.

EARLY in the spring of 1861, I was returning from the far West, and as I sat waiting for the train which was to bear me to my adopted home in New England, and was meditating upon the events which had transpired during the past few months, the record of which was destined to blacken the fair pages of American history, I was aroused from my reverie by a voice in the street crying "New York Herald—Fall of Fort Sumter—President's Proclamation—Call for seventy-five thousand men!" This announcement startled me, while my imagination portrayed the coming struggle in all its fearful magnitude. War, civil war, with all its horrors seemed inevitable, and even then was ready to burst like a volcano upon the most happy and prosperous nation the sun ever shone upon. The contemplation of this sad picture filled my eyes with tears and my heart with sorrow.

It is true, I was not an American—I was not obliged to remain here during this terrible strife—I could return to my native land where my parents would welcome me to the home of my childhood, and my brothers and sisters would rejoice at my coming. But these were not the thoughts which occupied my mind. It was not my intention, or desire, to seek my own personal ease and comfort while so much sorrow and distress filled the land. But the great question to be decided, was, what can I do? What part am *I* to act in this great drama? I was not able to decide for myself—so I carried this question to the Throne of Grace, and found a satisfactory answer there.

Five years previous to the time of which I write, I left my rural home, not far from the banks of the St. John's River, in the Province of New Brunswick, and made my way to the United States. An insatiable thirst for education led me to do this, for I believed then, as now, that the "Foreign Missionary" field was the one in which I must labor, sooner or later. I came here a stranger, with but little to recommend me to the favorable notice of the good people, except a letter from the Pastor of the church to which I belonged, and one from my class-leader—notwithstanding, I found kind friends to help me in all my undertakings, and whether in business, education, or spiritual advancement, I have been assisted beyond my highest expectation. I thank God that I am permitted in this hour of my adopted country's need to express a tithe of the gratitude which I feel toward the people of the Northern States.

Ten days after the President's proclamation was issued, I was ready to start for Washington, having been employed by the Government, and furnished with all the necessary equipments. I was not merely to go to Washington and remain there until a battle had been fought and the wounded brought in, and then in some comfortable hospital sit quietly and fan the patients, after the Surgeon had dressed their wounds; but I was to go to the front and participate in all the excitement of the battle scenes, or in other words, be a "FIELD NURSE."

The great West was stirred to its center, and began to look like a vast military camp. Recruiting offices were filled with men eager to enroll their names as defenders of their country—and women were busily engaged in preparing all the comforts that love and patriotism could suggest, for those who were so soon to go forth to victory or to death, while the clash of arms and strains of martial music almost drowned the hum of industry, and war became the theme of every tongue.

About this time I witnessed the departure of the first western troops which started for Washington. The regiments were drawn up in line—fully equipped for their journey—with their bright bayonets flashing in the morning sunlight. It was on the principal street of a pleasant little village of about a thousand inhabitants, where there was scarcely a family who had not a father, husband, son, or brother in that little band of soldiers who stood there ready to bid them farewell, perhaps for years—perhaps forever. A farewell address was delivered by the village Pastor, and a new Testament presented to each soldier, with the following inscription: "Put your trust in God—and keep your powder dry." Then came the leave-taking—but it is too painful to dwell upon—the last fond word was spoken, the last embrace given, then came the order "march"—and amid the cheers of the citizens—with banners proudly floating, and the bands playing "The Star Spangled Banner," they moved forward on their way to the Capital. On looking back now upon the scenes of that morning, notwithstanding I have looked upon others much more thrilling since then, yet I cannot recall that hour without feelings of deep emotion. While I stood there and beheld those manly forms convulsed with emotion, and heard the sobs of those whom they were leaving behind, I could only thank God that I was free and could go forward and work, and was not obliged to stay at home and weep. A few hours more, and I, too, was on my way to Washington.

When I reached Baltimore I found the city in an uproar—mobs were gathered in the streets and the utmost excitement prevailed: and as the crowded cars moved through the city toward the depot, the infuriated mob threw showers of stones, brickbats, and other missiles, breaking the windows and wounding some of the soldiers. Some of the men could not forbear firing into the crowd—notwithstanding their orders were to the contrary—however, it had a good effect, for the mob soon dispersed; they probably had not forgotten the Sixth Massachusetts and the Pennsylvania troops which had passed through a short time before. The cars soon reached the depot, and started immediately for Washington—where we arrived in due time—weary, and in great need of food and sleep.

Soon after reaching Washington I commenced visiting the temporary hospitals which were prepared to receive the soldiers who arrived there sick. The troops came pouring in so fast, and the weather being extremely warm, all the general hospitals were soon filled, and it seemed impossible to prepare suitable, or comfortable, accommodations for all who required medical attention.

There are many things in connection with this war that we are disposed to find fault with, and we think the blame rests upon such and such individuals—but after investigating the matter, we find that they are all owing to a combination of circumstances entirely beyond the control of those individuals—and it requires time to bring about the desired results. This has been my experience with regard to the hospital department. After walking through the streets for hours on a sultry southern day in search of one of those temporary hospitals, I would find a number of men there delirious with fever—others had been sunstruck and carried there—but no physician to be found in attendance. Then, I would naturally come to the conclusion that the surgeons were all slack concerning their duty—but upon going to the office of the Surgeon in charge of that department, would find that a certain number of surgeons were detailed every morning to visit those hospitals, and were faithfully performing their duty; but that the number of hospitals and patients were increasing so fast that it required all day to make the tour. Consequently the last ones visited were obliged to wait and suffer—without any blame attaching to the surgeons.

Then another great evil was to be remedied—there were thousands of sick men to be taken care of—but for these the Government had made no provision as regards more delicate kinds of food—nothing but hard bread, coffee and pork, for sick and well, alike. The Sanitary Commission had not yet come into operation and the consequence was our poor sick soldiers suffered unspeakably from want of proper nourishment. I was speaking upon this subject one day to Chaplain B. and his wife—my constant companions in hospital labor—when Mrs. B. suggested that she and I should appeal to the sympathies of the ladies of Washington and Georgetown, and try our hand at begging. I agreed to the proposal at once, and wondered why I had not thought of it myself—among all my schemes for alleviating the sufferings of these men, it had never entered into my head to *beg* for them. We decided to go to Georgetown first and if we succeeded there, to canvass Washington. So we started, and commenced operations by calling first upon a clergyman's wife. We made inquiry there with regard to our prospects of success, and the sentiments of the ladies generally upon the war question, and finding that the majority were in our favor, we started again quite hopefully—but not until the lady above mentioned had given us an order on her grocer to the amount of five dollars. I gave Sister B. the credit of that, for I had introduced her as the wife of the Rev. Mr. B., chaplain of the 7th. Then I suggested that we should separate for a few hours—she to take one street and I another, so that we might sooner get through the city. My next call was at a doctor's mansion, but I did not find the lady at home; however, I learned that the doctor in question kept a drug-store near by; she might be there; went, but found no lady; thought fit to make my business known to the doctor, and the consequence was, half a dozen bottles of blackberry wine and two of lemon syrup, with a cordial invitation to call again. So prospered our mission throughout the day, and at the close of it we had a sufficient supply of groceries, brandy, ice, jellies, etc., to fill our little ambulance; and oh, what a change those little delicacies wrought upon our poor sick boys. We were encouraged by that day's work, to continue our efforts in that direction, and finally made Dr. W.'s store a depot for the donations of those kind friends who wished to assist us in restoring to health the defenders of our beloved country.

Typhoid fever began to make its appearance in camp, as the burning sun of June came pouring down upon us, and the hospitals were soon crowded with its victims. It was then that my labors began in earnest, and as I went from tent to tent, ministering to the wants of those delirious, helpless men, I wondered if there ever was a "Missionary Field" which promised a richer harvest, than the one in which I was already engaged; and oh, how thankful I was that it was my privilege to take some small part in so great a work.

I shall notice, briefly, the manner in which the hospitals are conducted in camp. There are large tents furnished for hospital purposes, which will accommodate from twenty to twenty-five men. These tents are usually put up in the most pleasant and shady part of the camp; the inside is nicely leveled, and board floors laid, if boards can be procured, if not, rubber blankets are laid down instead. Sometimes there are straw ticks and cot bedsteads furnished, but not in sufficient quantity to supply all the hospitals. Along each side of the tent the sick are laid, on blankets or cots, leaving room to pass between the beds. In the center of the tent stands a temporary board table, on which are kept books, medicines, et cetera. The hospital corps consists of a surgeon, an assistant surgeon, a hospital steward, a ward-master, four nurses, two cooks, and a man of all work to carry water, cut wood, and make himself generally useful. The immediate care of the sick devolves upon those four nurses, who are generally detailed from the ranks, each one being on duty six hours without intermission. The surgeons visit the patients twice every day, oftener if required; the prescriptions are filled by the hospital steward, and the medicine is administered by the nurses. The nurses are usually very kind to the sick, and when off duty in the hospital, spend much of their time in digging drains around the tents, planting evergreens, and putting up awnings, all of which add much to the coolness and comfort of the hospital. Draining the grounds is a very important part of hospital duty, for when those terrible thunder-storms come, which are so frequent in the south, it is morally impossible to keep the tent floors from being flooded, unless there are drains all around the tents. Great excitement prevails in camp during those tempests—the rain comes down in torrents, while the wind blows a hurricane—lifting the tents from the ground, and throwing everything into wild confusion. I have seen a dozen men stand for hours around one hospital, holding down the ropes and tent poles to prevent the sick from being exposed to the raging elements.

In one of those storms, I saw a tent blown down, in which one of our officers lay suffering from typhoid fever. We did our best to keep him dry until a stretcher could be procured, but all in vain. Notwithstanding we wrapped him in rubber blankets and shawls, yet the rain penetrated them all, and by the time he was carried to a house, a quarter of a mile distant, he was completely drenched. He was a noble fellow and I love to speak of him. Mrs. B. and I remained with him alternately until he died, which was five days from that time. We sent for his wife, who arrived just in time to see him die. He was unconscious when she came, and we were standing around his cot watching every shadow which the sable wing of advancing death cast upon his features, and eagerly looking for a single ray of returning reason. He looked up suddenly, and seeing his wife standing weeping, he beckoned her to come to him. Kneeling beside him, she bent her ear close to the lips of the dying man. He whispered distinctly, "I am going—the way is bright, don't weep—farewell!" A little later he was asked, "What is the foundation of your hope of Heaven?" His face was calm and beautiful in its expression, and his splendid dark eyes lit up with holy confidence and trust, as he replied, "Christ—Christ!" These were his last words. Glorious words for a dying soldier. He lingered a few hours, and then quietly and peacefully breathed out his life. So passed away one of the most exemplary men it has ever been my lot to meet, either in the army or elsewhere. The same day, the sorrowing widow, with the remains of her beloved and noble husband, started for her northern home; and that christian patriot now sleeps in a beautiful little cemetery near the city of Detroit, Michigan, having rendered up his life a willing sacrifice for his country.

Mrs. B. was desirous of visiting some of the public buildings in Washington and wished me to accompany her. I did so, but found that it was almost impossible to get along through the crowded streets. The gallant troops were coming in by thousands from every loyal State in the Union. The Capitol and White House were common places of resort for soldiers. Arms were stacked in the rotunda of the one and the lobbies of the other, while our "noble boys in blue" lounged in the cushioned seats of members of Congress, or reclined in easy chairs in the President's Mansion.

Camps of instruction were prepared near the city, while every hillside and valley for miles around was thickly dotted with snow white tents. Soldiers drilling, fatigue parties building forts, artillery practicing, and the supply trains moving to and from the various headquarters, presented a picture deeply interesting. As I rode from camp to camp and contemplated that immense army concentrating its force on the banks of the Potomac, and saw with what zeal and enthusiasm the soldiers entered upon their duties, I could but feel assured of the speedy termination of the conflict, and look forward with eager anticipation to the day when that mighty host would advance upon the enemy, and like an overwhelming torrent sweep rebellion from the land.

CHAPTER II.

MARCHING ORDERS—REMOVAL OF THE SICK—A YOUNG PATIENT—VISIT FROM HIS MOTHER—MARCH TOWARD MANASSAS—COLLECTING SUPPLIES—FATIGUES OF THE MARCH—PREPARATIONS FOR BATTLE—A CAMP PRAYER MEETING—DIVISIONS DETAILED—MY PLACE ON THE FIELD—"RATHER CLOSE QUARTERS"—A BATTLE SUNDAY—SKULKING FROM THE FIELD.

MARCHING ORDERS received to-day—two days more, and the Army of the Potomac will be on its way to Bull Run. I find this registered in my journal July 15th, 1861, without any comment whatever. But I do not require a journal to refresh my memory with regard to the events of those two days of preparation which followed their announcement. The Army of the Potomac was soon to meet the enemy for the first time—a great battle was to be fought. Oh, what excitement and enthusiasm that order produced—nothing could be heard but the wild cheering of the men, as regiment after regiment received their orders. The possibility of a defeat never seemed to enter the mind of any. All the sick in camp now were to be sent to Washington, clothes changed, knapsacks packed, letters written home, packages sent to the express office, etc. After all was done, everything in readiness, and the sick men tenderly laid in the ambulances, Mrs. B. said:

"Now let us go to every ambulance and bid the boys good-bye." As we passed along from one ambulance to another, speaking words of encouragement to each soldier, many a tear would start from grateful eyes, and many a feeble voice uttered an earnest "God bless you," while others would draw from their bosoms some cherished relic, and give as a token of remembrance. Oh how hard it was to part with those men, with whom we had watched so many weary days and nights—we felt that they had, truly, "become endeared to us through suffering."

There was one patient, however, we did not put into an ambulance, and who was a great source of anxiety to us. He lay there upon a stretcher close by, waiting to be carried to a house not far distant. He was young, not seventeen, with clear blue eyes, curly auburn hair, and a broad, white brow; his mother's pride, and an only son. Two weeks previously he had been attacked with typhoid fever. The surgeon said, "You may do all you can for him, but it is a hopeless case." Mrs. B. had devoted most of her time to him and I was often called to assist her. He was delirious and became quite unmanageable at times, and it required all the strength we possessed to keep him in bed; but now the delirium of fever had passed away and he was helpless as an infant. We had written for his mother to come if possible, and had just received a letter from her, stating that she was on her way to Washington; but would she come before we were obliged to leave? Oh, we hoped so, and were anxiously looking for her.

The ambulances started with their freight of emaciated, suffering men. Slowly that long train wound its way toward the city looking like a great funeral procession, and sadly we turned to our remaining patient, who was deeply affected at the removal of his comrades. He was then carried to the house above mentioned and a nurse left to take care of him, while we were obliged to prepare for our own comfort on the long weary march which was so near at hand. We had just commenced to pack our saddle-bags, when we heard an unusual noise, as of some one crying piteously, and going out to learn the cause of the excitement, whom should we find but the mother of our handsome blue-eyed patient. She had called at the surgeon's tent to inquire for her son, and he had told her that all the sick had been sent to Washington, he having forgotten for the moment, the exception with regard to her son. The first words I heard were spoken in the most touching manner—"Oh, why did you send away my boy? I wrote you I was coming; Oh, why did you send him away!"

I shall never forget the expression of that mother's face as she stood there wringing her hands and repeating the question. We very soon rectified the mistake which the surgeon had made, and in a few moments she was kneeling by the bedside of her darling boy, and we returned rejoicing that it had been our privilege to "deliver him to his mother." Oh, how many, who come to Washington in search of loved ones, are caused unnecessary pain, yes, weeks of torturing suspense and fruitless search, in consequence of some little mistake on the part of a surgeon, a nurse, or some person who is supposed to know just where the sought for are to be found.

The 17th of July dawned bright and clear, and everything being in readiness, the Army of the Potomac took up its line of march for Manassas. In gay spirits the army moved forward, the air resounding with the music of the regimental bands, and patriotic songs of the soldiers. No gloomy forebodings seemed to damp the spirits of the men, for a moment, but "On to Richmond," was echoed and re-echoed, as that vast army moved rapidly over the country. I felt strangely out of harmony with the wild, joyous spirit which pervaded the troops. As I rode slowly along, watching those long lines of bayonets as they gleamed and flashed in the sunlight, I thought that many, very many, of those enthusiastic men who appeared so eager to meet the enemy, would never return to relate the success or defeat of that splendid army. Even if victory should perch upon their banners, and I had no doubt it would, yet many noble lives must be sacrificed ere it could be obtained.

The main column reached Fairfax toward evening and encamped for the night. Col. R.'s wife of the Second ——, Mrs. B. and myself were, I think, the only three females who reached Fairfax that night. The day had been extremely hot, and not being accustomed to ride all day beneath a burning sun, we felt its effects very sensibly, and consequently, hailed with joy the order to encamp for the night. Notwithstanding the heat and fatigue of the day's march, the troops were in high spirits, and immediately began preparing supper. Some built fires while others went in search of, and appropriated, every available article which might in any way add to the comfort of hungry and fatigued men.

The whole neighborhood was ransacked for milk, butter, eggs, poultry, etc. which were found insufficient in quantity to supply the wants of such a multitude. There might have been heard some stray shots fired in the direction of a field where a drove of cattle were quietly grazing; and soon after the odor of fresh steak was issuing from every part of the camp. I wish to state, however, that all "raids" made upon hen-coops, etc. were contrary to the orders of the General in command, for during the day I had seen men put under arrest for shooting chickens by the roadside.

I was amused to hear the answer of a hopeful

young darkey cook, when interrogated with regard to the broiled chickens and beef steak which he brought on for supper. Col. R. demanded, in a very stern voice, "Jack, where did you get that beef steak and those chickens?" "Massa, I'se carried dem cl'ar from Washington; thought I'd cook 'em 'fore dey sp'il'd"; and then added, with a broad grin, "I aint no thief, I aint." Col. R. replied: "That will do, Jack, you can go now." Then the Colonel told us how he had seen Jack running out of a house, as he rode along, and a woman ran out calling after him with all her might, but Jack never looked behind him, but escaped as fast as he could, and was soon out of sight. Said he, "I thought the young rascal had been up to some mischief, so I rode up and asked the woman what was the matter, and found he had stolen all her chickens; I asked her how much they were worth; she "reckoned" about two dollars. I think she made a pretty good hit, for after I paid her, she told me she had had only two chickens." Supper being over, pickets posted, and camp guards detailed, all became quiet for the night.

Early the next morning the reveille beat, the whole camp was soon in motion, and after a slight breakfast from our haversacks the march was resumed. The day was very hot, and we found great difficulty in obtaining water, the want of which caused the troops much suffering. Many of the men were sun-struck, and others began to drop out of the ranks from exhaustion. All such as were not able to march were put into ambulances and sent back to Washington. Toward noon, the tedium of the march began to be enlivened by sharp volleys of musketry, in the direction of the advance guard; but those alarms were only occasioned by our skirmishers, pouring a volley into everything which looked as if it might contain a masked battery, or a band of the enemy's sharpshooters.

Considerable excitement prevailed throughout the day, as we were every hour in expectation of meeting the enemy. Carefully feeling its way, however, the army moved steadily on, investigating every field, building, and ravine, for miles in front and to the right and left, until it reached Centerville, where we halted for the night.

The troops now began to feel the effects of the march, and there was evidently a lack of that pic-nic hilarity which had characterized them the day before. Several regiments had been supplied with new shoes the day before leaving camp, and they found by sad experience, that they were not the most comfortable things to march in, as their poor blistered feet testified; in many cases their feet were literally raw, the thick woolen stockings having chafed the skin off. Mrs. B. and I, having provided ourselves before leaving camp, with a quantity of linen, bandages, lint, ointment, etc.

found it very convenient now, even before a shot had been fired by the enemy.

Our surgeons began to prepare for the coming battle, by appropriating several buildings and fitting them up for the wounded—among others the stone church at Centerville—a church which many a soldier will remember, as long as memory lasts. Late that evening as I was returning from this church, accompanied by Mr. and Mrs. B., I proposed that we should walk through the entire camp to see how the boys were employed, on this, the eve of their first battle. We found many engaged in writing by the glimmering light of the camp-fire—soldiers always carry writing materials on a march; some were reading their bibles, perhaps with more than usual interest; while others sat in groups, conversing in low earnest tones; but the great mass were stretched upon the ground, wrapped in their blankets, fast asleep, and all unconscious of the dangers of the morrow.

We were about to return to our quarters in a log cabin built by the rebel soldiers, and which had been evacuated only a few days previous, when we heard several voices singing in a little grove not far from camp. We turned and walked toward the grove, until we could hear distinctly, the words of the following beautiful hymn :

"O, for a faith that will not shrink,
Though press'd by every foe,
That will not tremble on the brink
Of any earthly woe;

That will not murmur or complain
  Beneath the chastening rod,
But, in the hour of grief and pain,
  Will lean upon its God;

A faith that shines more bright and clear
  When tempests rage without;
That, when in danger, knows no fear,
  In darkness knows no doubt."

"Ah!" exclaimed Mr. B., "I recognize Willie L.'s voice there. I understand now; this is Willie's prayer meeting night, and notwithstanding the fatigue of the march and blistered feet, he has not forgotten it." We drew nearer to listen to and enjoy the exercises unperceived, for no sooner had the last words of the hymn died away on the still midnight air, than Willie's clear voice rose in prayer, filling the grove with its rich, pathetic tones. He prayed for victory on the morrow, for his comrades, for loved ones at home, and his voice grew tremulous with emotion, as he plead with the Saviour to comfort and support his widowed mother, if he should fall in battle.

Then followed a practical talk about being faithful soldiers of Jesus, as well as of their beloved country; of the necessity of being prepared at any moment, to lay down the cross and take up the crown. One after another prayed and spoke, until about a dozen—and that included the whole number present—had addressed the Throne of Grace, and testified to the power of the Gospel of Christ in the salvation of sinners. No one was called upon to pray or speak, no one said he had nothing to say and then talked long enough to prove it, no one excused his inability to interest his brethren, and no time was lost by delay, but every one did his duty, and did it promptly. We retired feeling refreshed and encouraged.

After ascertaining the position of the enemy, Gen. McDowell ordered forward three divisions, commanded by Heintzelman, Hunter and Tyler, Miles being left in reserve at Centerville. Sunday morning before dawn, those three divisions moved forward, presenting a magnificent spectacle, as column after column wound its way over the green hills and through the hazy valleys, with the soft moonlight falling on the long lines of shining steel. Not a drum or bugle was heard during the march, and the deep silence was only broken by the rumbling of artillery, the muffled tread of infantry, or the low hum of thousands of subdued voices.

The divisions separated where three roads branch off toward Bull Run, each taking the road leading to its respective position. Soon the morning broke bright and clear, bringing the two contending armies in plain sight of each other. The enemy was posted on heights that rose in regular slopes from the shore crowned here and there by earthworks. The woods that interfered with his cannon ranges had all been cut away, and his guns had a clean sweep of every approach. On our side the descent was more gradual, and covered with a dense forest. The roar of artillery soon announced that the battle had actually commenced.

Mrs. B. and myself took our position on the field, according to orders, in connection with Gen. Heintzelman's division, having delivered our horses to Jack for safe keeping, with strict orders to remain where he was, for we might require them at any moment. I imagine now, I see Mrs. B., as she stood there, looking as brave as possible, with her narrow brimmed leghorn hat, black cloth riding habit, shortened to walking length by the use of a page, a silver-mounted seven-shooter in her belt, a canteen of water swung over one shoulder and a flask of brandy over the other, and a haversack with provision, lint, bandages, adhesive plaster, etc. hanging by her side. She was tall and slender, with dark brown hair, pale face, and blue eyes.

Chaplain B. sat upon his horse looking as solemn as if standing face to face with the angel of death. The first man I saw killed was a gunner belonging to Col. R.'s command. A shell had burst in the midst of the battery, killing one and wounding three men and two horses. Mr. B. jumped from his horse, hitched it to a tree, and ran forward to the battery; Mrs. B. and I following his example as fast as we could. I stooped over one of the wounded, who lay upon his face weltering in his blood; I raised his head, and who should it be but Willie L. He was mortally wounded in the breast, and the tide of life was fast ebbing away; the stretchers were soon brought, and he was carried from the field.

Seeing the disaster from a distance, Col. R. rode up to the battery, and as he was engaged in giving orders, a solid shot came whizzing by in such close proximity to his head, that it stunned him for a moment; but soon recovering, he turned up the side of his head and shrugged his shoulders, a peculiarity of his, and in his usual nasal twang, said, "rather close quarters," and rode away, apparently as unconcerned as if it had been a humming bird which crossed his path. But not content with admonishing the Colonel, the same shot struck my poor little flask of brandy which lay near me on a drum-head, shattering it as spitefully as if sent by the combined force of the Order of "Good Templars."

Now the battle began to rage with terrible fury. Nothing could be heard save the thunder of artillery, the clash of steel, and the continuous roar of musketry. Oh, what a scene for the bright sun of a holy Sabbath morning to shine upon! Instead of the sweet influences which we associate with the Sabbath—the chiming of church bells calling us to the house of prayer, the Sabbath school, and all the solemn duties of the sanctuary, there was confusion, destruction and death. There was no place of safety for miles around; the safest place was the post of duty. Many that day who turned their backs upon the enemy and sought refuge in the woods some two miles distant, were found torn to pieces by shell, or mangled by cannon ball—a proper reward for those who, insensible to shame, duty, or patriotism, desert their cause and comrades in the trying hour of battle, and skulk away cringing under the fear of death.

CHAPTER III.

WATER FOR THE WOUNDED—COL. CAMERON KILLED—SCENES ON THE BATTLE-FIELD—BURNSIDE'S BRIGADE—CAPTURE OF GRIFFIN'S AND RICKETT'S BATTERIES—REBELS REINFORCED—THE PANIC AND RETREAT—THE WOUNDED AT CENTERVILLE—MY RECONNOISSANCE—AN INSANE WOMAN ON THE FIELD—HIDING FROM THE ENEMY—RETURN TO THE WOUNDED—EXPECTATION OF CAPTURE—ESCAPE FROM THE REBELS—MY WALK TO ALEXANDRIA—FOOTSORE AND WEARY—ARRIVAL IN WASHINGTON—LETTERS FROM DEAD SOLDIERS' FRIENDS.

I WAS hurried off to Centerville, a distance of seven miles, for a fresh supply of brandy, lint, etc. When I returned, the field was literally strewn with wounded, dead and dying. Mrs. B. was nowhere to be found. Had she been killed or wounded? A few moments of torturing suspense and then I saw her coming toward me, running her horse with all possible speed, with about fifty canteens hanging from the pommel of her saddle. To all my inquiries there was but one answer: "Don't stay to care for the wounded now; the troops are famishing with thirst and are beginning to fall back." Mr. B. then rode up with the same order, and we three started for a spring a mile distant, having gathered up the empty canteens which lay strewn on the field. This was the nearest spring; the enemy knew it, and consequently had posted sharpshooters within rifle range to prevent the troops being supplied with water. Notwithstanding this, we filled our canteens, while the Minnie balls fell thick and fast around us, and returned in safety to distribute the fruits of our labor among the exhausted men.

We spent three hours in this manner, while the tide of battle rolled on more fiercely than before, until the enemy made a desperate charge on our troops driving them back and taking full possession of the spring. Chaplain B.'s horse was shot through the neck and bled to death in a few moments. Then Mrs. B. and I dismounted and went to work again among the wounded.

Not long afterwards Col. Cameron, brother of the Secretary of War, came dashing along the line, shouting, "Come on boys, the rebels are in full retreat." The words had scarcely been uttered when he fell, pierced to the heart by a bullet. Surgeon P. was on the ground in an instant, but nothing could be done for him; his wound was mortal, and he soon ceased to breathe. There was no time to carry off the dead; we folded his arms across his breast, closed his eyes, and left him in the cold embrace of death.

Still the battle continues without cessation; the grape and canister fill the air as they go screaming on their fearful errand; the sight of that field is perfectly appalling; men tossing their arms wildly calling for help; there they lie bleeding, torn and mangled; legs, arms and bodies are crushed and broken as if smitten by thunder-bolts; the ground is crimson with blood; it is terrible to witness. Burnside's brigade is being mown down like grass by the rebel batteries; the men are not able to stand that terrible storm of shot and shell; they begin to waver and fall back slowly, but just at the right moment Capt. Sykes comes up to their relief with his command of regulars. They sweep up the hill where Burnside's exhausted, shattered brigade still lingers, and are greeted with a shout of joy, such as none but soldiers, who are almost overpowered by a fierce enemy, and are reinforced by their brave comrades, can give.

Onward they go, close up to the cloud of flame and smoke rolling from the hill upon which the rebel batteries are placed—their muskets are leveled—there is a click, click—a sheet of flame—a deep roll like that of thunder, and the rebel gunners are seen to stagger and fall. The guns become silent, and in a few moments are abandoned. This seems to occasion great confusion in the rebel ranks. Regiments were scattered, and officers were seen riding furiously and shouting their orders, which were heard above the roar and din of battle.

Captain Griffin's and Rickett's batteries are ordered forward to an eminence from which the rebels have been driven. They come into position and open a most destructive fire which completely routs the enemy. The battle seems almost won and the enemy is retreating in confusion. Hear what rebel Gen. Johnson says of his prospects at that time, in his official report: "The long contest against a powerful enemy, and heavy losses, especially of field officers, had greatly discouraged the troops of Gen. Bee and Col. Evans. The aspect of affairs was critical." Another writes: "Fighting for hours under a burning sun, without a drop of water, the conduct of our men could not be excelled; but human endurance has its bounds, and all seemed about to be lost." This goes to prove that it was a desperately hard fought battle on both sides, and if no fresh troops had been brought into the field, the victory would assuredly have been ours.

But just as our army is confident of success, and is following up the advantage which it has gained, rebel reinforcements arrive and turn the tide of battle. Two rebel regiments of fresh troops are sent to make a flank movement in order to capture Griffin's and Rickett's batteries. They march through the woods, reach the top of the hill, and form a line so completely in our rear as to fire almost upon the backs of the gunners. Griffin sees them approach, but supposes them to be his supports sent by Major Barry. However looking more intently at them, he thinks they are rebels, and turns his guns upon them. Just as he is about to give the order to fire, Major B. rides up shouting, "They are your supports, don't fire." "No, sir, they are rebels," replied Capt. Griffin. "I tell you, sir, they are your supports," said Major B. In obedience to orders the guns were turned again, and while in the act of doing so, the supposed supports fired a volley upon the gunners. Men and horses went down in an instant. A moment more and those famous batteries were in the hands of the enemy.

The news of this disaster spread along our lines like wildfire; officers and men were alike confounded; regiment after regiment broke and ran, and almost immediately the panic commenced. Companies of cavalry were drawn up in line across the road, with drawn sabers, but all was not sufficient to stop the refluent tide of fugitives. Then came the artillery thundering along, drivers lashing their horses furiously, which greatly added to the terror of the panic stricken thousands crowded together en masse. In this manner we reached Centerville where order was in some measure restored.

Mrs. B. and I made our way to the stone church around which we saw stacks of dead bodies piled up, and arms and legs were thrown together in heaps. But how shall I describe the scene within the church at that hour. Oh, there was suffering there which no pen can ever describe. One case I can never forget. It was that of a poor fellow whose legs were both broken above the knees, and from the knees to the thighs they were literally smashed to fragments. He was dying; but oh, what a death was that. He was insane, perfectly wild, and required two persons to hold him. Inflammation had set in, and was rapidly doing its work; death soon released him, and it was a relief to all present as well as to the poor sufferer.

I went to another dying one who was bearing patiently all his sufferings. Oh, poor pale face! I see it now, with its white lips and beseeching eyes; and then the touching inquiry, "Do you think I'll die before morning?" I told him I thought he would, and asked: "Has death any terrors for you?" He smiled that beautiful trusting smile which we sometimes see on the lips of the dying saint, as he replied: "Oh no, I shall soon be asleep in Jesus"; and then in a low plaintive voice he repeated the verse commencing,

Asleep in Jesus, blessed sleep.

While I stood beside him thus, some one tapped me on the shoulder. On turning round I was beckoned to the side of one who was laid in a corner, on the floor, with his face toward the wall. I knelt beside him and asked: "What can I do for you, my friend?" He opened his eyes, with an effort, and said, "I wish you to take that," pointing to a small package which lay beside him, "keep it until you get to Washington, and then, if it is not too much trouble, I want you to write to mother and tell her how I was wounded, and that I died trusting in Jesus." Then I knew that I was kneeling beside Willie L. He was almost gone—just ready "to lay down the cross and take up the crown." He signed to me to come nearer; and as I did so, he put his hand to his head and tried to separate a lock of hair with his fingers, but his strength failed; however, I understood that he wished me to cut off a lock to send to his mother with the package. When he saw that I understood him he seemed pleased that his last request was complied with.

Chaplain B. came and prayed with him, and while he was praying, the happy spirit of Willie returned to Him who gave it. Heaven gained in this instance another soul, but there was mourning in that widowed mother's heart. I thought, oh, how appropriate were the words of the poet to that lonely mother:

Not on the tented field,
O terror-fronted War!
Not on the battle-field,
All thy bleeding victims are;

But in the lowly homes
Where sorrow broods like death,
And fast the mother's sobs
Rise with each quick-drawn breath.

That dimmed eye, fainting close—
And she may not be nigh!
'Tis mothers die—O God!
'Tis but we mothers die.

Our hearts and hands being fully occupied with such scenes as these, we thought of nothing else. We knew nothing of the true state of affairs outside, nor could we believe it possible when we learned that the whole army had retreated toward Washington, leaving the wounded in the hands of the enemy, and us, too, in rather an unpleasant situation. I could not believe the stern truth, and was determined to find out for myself. Consequently I went back to the heights, where I had seen the troops stack their guns and throw themselves upon the ground at night-fall, but no troops were there. I thought then that they had merely changed their position, and that by going over the field I should certainly find them. I had not gone far before I saw a camp fire in the distance. Supposing that I had found a clue to the secret, I made all haste toward the fire; but as I drew near I saw but one solitary figure sitting by it, and that was the form of a female.

Upon going up to her I recognised her as one of the washerwomen of our army. I asked her what she was doing there and where the army had gone. Said she: "I don't know anything about the army; I am cooking my husband's supper, and am expecting him home every minute; see what a lot of things I have got for him," pointing to a huge pile of blankets, haversacks and canteens which she had gathered up, and over which she had constituted herself sentinel. I soon found out that the poor creature had become insane. The excitement of battle had proved too much for her, and all my endeavors to persuade her to come with me were unavailing. I had no time to spare, for I was convinced that the army had really decamped.

Once more I started in the direction of Centerville. I had not gone more than a few rods before I heard the clatter of horses' hoofs. I stopped, and looking in the direction of the fire I had just quitted, I saw a squad of cavalry ride up to the woman who still sat there. Fortunately I had no horse to make a noise or attract attention, having left mine at the hospital with the intention of returning immediately. It was evident to my mind that those were the enemy's cavalry, and that it was necessary for me to keep out of sight if possible until they were gone. Then the thought came to me that the woman at the fire knew no better than to tell them that I had been there a few minutes before. Happily, however, I was near a fence, against which there were great piles of brush, and as the night was becoming very dark and it was beginning to rain, I thought I could remain undetected, at least until morning. My suspicions proved to be correct. They were coming toward me, and compelling the woman to come and show them the direction I had taken; I decided to crawl under one of those brush heaps, which I did, and had scarcely done so, when up they came and stopped over against the identical pile in which I was concealed.

One of the men said "See here old woman, are you sure that she can tell us if we find her?" "Oh, yes, she can tell you, I know she can," was the woman's reply. They would go away a little distance and then come back again; by and by they began to accuse the woman of playing a false game; then they swore, threatened to shoot her, and she began to cry. All this was an interesting performance I admit; but I did not enjoy it quite so much, in consequence of being rather uncomfortably near the performers. At last they gave it up as a hopeless case and rode away taking the woman with them, and I was left in blissful ignorance of the mystery which they wished me to unravel, and for once in my life I rejoiced at not having my "curiosity" gratified.

I remained there until the last echo of their retreating footsteps had died away in the distance; then I came forth very cautiously and made my way to Centerville, where the interesting intelligence awaited me that Mr. and Mrs. B. had gone, and had taken my horse, supposing that I had been taken prisoner.

The village of Centerville was not yet occupied by the rebels, so that I might have made my escape without any further trouble; but how could I go and leave those hospitals full of dying men, without a soul to give them a drink of water? I must go into that Stone Church once more, even at the risk of being taken prisoner. I did so—and the cry of "Water," "water," was heard above the groans of the dying. Chaplain B. had told them before leaving that they would soon be in the hands of the enemy—that the army had retreated to Washington, and that there was no possibility of removing the wounded. There they lay, calmly awaiting the approach of their cruel captors, and apparently prepared to accept with resignation any fate which their cruelty might suggest. Oh, how brave those men were! What moral courage they possessed! Nothing but the grace of God and a right appreciation of the great cause in which they had nobly fought, and bled, could reconcile them to such suffering and humiliation.

They all urged me to leave them, and not subject myself to the barbarous treatment which I would be likely to receive if I should be taken prisoner, adding—"If you do stay the rebels will not let you do anything for us." One of the men said: "Dr. E. has only been gone a little while—

he extracted three balls from my leg and arm, and that, too, with his pen-knife. I saw twenty-one balls which he had taken from the limbs of men in this hospital. He was determined to remain with us, but we would not consent, for we knew he would not be allowed to do any more for us after the rebels came; and you must go too, and go very soon or they will be here."

After placing water within the reach of as many as could use their arms, and giving some to those who could not—I turned to leave them, with feelings that I cannot describe; but ere I reached the door a feeble voice called me back—it was that of a young officer from Massachusetts; he held in his hand a gold locket, and as he handed it to me he said—"Will you please to open it?" I did so, and then held it for him to take a last look at the picture which it contained. He grasped it eagerly and pressed it to his lips again and again. The picture was that of a lady of rare beauty, with an infant in her arms. She seemed scarcely more than a child herself; on the opposite side was printed her name and address. While he still gazed upon it with quivering lip, and I stood there waiting for some tender message for the loved ones, the unmistakable tramp of cavalry was heard in the street,—a moment more, and I had snatched the locket from the hands of the dying man and was gone.

The streets were full of cavalry, but not near

enough to discover me, as the night was exceedingly dark and the rain came down in torrents. One glance was sufficient to convince me that I could not escape by either street. The only way was to climb a fence and go across lots, which I immediately did, and came out on the Fairfax road about a mile from the village, and then started for Washington on the "double quick." I did not reach Alexandria until noon the next day—almost exhausted, and my shoes literally worn off my feet. Having walked all the way from Centerville in the rain, without food, together with want of sleep and the fatigue of the past week, caused me to present rather an interesting appearance. I remained there two days before I could persuade my limbs to bear the weight of my body. I then made my way to Washington, where I found my friends quite anxious lest I had fallen into the hands of the enemy. A number of men from whom I had received packages, money, etc., before going into battle, and who reached Washington two days before I did, had come to the conclusion that they had taken a pretty sure way of sending those precious things to Richmond, and therefore my arrival was rather an important event, and I was greeted with a hearty welcome.

My first duty was to attend to those dying soldiers' requests, which I did immediately by writing to their friends and inclosing the articles which I had received from the hands of those loved ones who were now cold in death. The answers to many of those letters lie before me while I write, and are full of gratitude and kind wishes. One in particular I cannot read without weeping. It is from Willie's Mother. The following are a few extracts: "Oh, can it be that my Willie will return to me no more? Shall I never see my darling boy again, until I see him clothed in the righteousness of Christ—thank God I shall see him then—I shall see him then."

> Now with all the mother's heart
> Torn and quivering with the smart,
> I yield him, 'neath the chastening rod,
> To my country and my God.

"Oh, how I want to kiss those hands that closed my darling's eyes, and those lips which spoke words of comfort to him in a dying hour. The love and prayers of a bereaved mother will follow you all through the journey of life." Yes, he is gone to return to her no more on earth, but her loss is his eternal gain.

> Servant of God well done!
> Rest from thy loved employ;
> The battle fought, the victory won,
> Enter thy Master's joy.

He at least had won a victory—notwithstanding the defeat of the federal army. Yes, a glorious victory.

CHAPTER IV.

WASHINGTON AFTER BULL RUN—DEMORALIZATION OF THE ARMY —SICK SOLDIERS—HOSPITAL SCENES—EXTRACTS FROM MY JOURNAL—SYMPATHY OF SOLDIERS—FISHING FOR THE SICK—A FISH-LOVING DUTCHMAN—REORGANIZATION OF THE ARMY—A VISIT TO THE PICKETS—PICKET DUTIES AND DANGERS—THE ARMY INACTIVE—MC CLELLAN'S ADDRESS—MARCHING ORDERS AGAIN—EMBARKATION OF THE ARMY FOR FORTRESS MONROE—THE CROWDED TRANSPORTS—DESCRIPTION OF THE MONITOR—HER BUILD AND ARMAMENT—HER TURRET AND ENGINES.

WASHINGTON at that time presented a picture strikingly illustrative of military life in its most depressing form. To use the words of Captain Noyes—"There were stragglers sneaking along through the mud inquiring for their regiments, wanderers driven in by the pickets, some with guns and some without, while every one you met had a sleepy, downcast appearance, and looked as if he would like to hide his head from all the world." Every bar-room and groggery seemed filled to overflowing with officers and men, and military discipline was nearly, or quite, forgotten for a time in the army of the Potomac. While Washington was in this chaotic condition, the rebel flag was floating over Munson's Hill, in plain sight of the Federal Capital.

When General McClellan took command of the army of the Potomac, he found it in a most lamentable condition, and the task of reorganizing and disciplining such a mass of demoralized men was a Herculean one. However, he proved himself equal to the task, and I think, that even his enemies are willing to admit, that there is no parallel case in history where there has been more tact, energy and skill displayed in transforming a disorganized mob into an efficient and effective army; in fact, of bringing order out of confusion.

The hospitals in Washington, Alexandria and Georgetown were crowded with wounded, sick, discouraged soldiers. That extraordinary march from Bull Run, through rain, mud, and chagrin, did more toward filling the hospitals than did the battle itself. I found Mrs. B. in a hospital, suffering from typhoid fever, while Chaplain B. was looking after the temporal and spiritual wants of the men with his usual energy and sympathy. He had many apologies to offer "for running away with my horse," as he termed it. There were many familiar faces missing, and it required considerable time to ascertain the fate of my friends. Many a weary walk I had from one hospital to another to find some missing one who was reported to have been sent to such and such a hospital; but after reading the register from top to bottom I would find no such name there. Perhaps on my way out, in passing the open door of one of the wards, who should I see, laid upon a cot, but the very object of my search, and upon returning to the office to inform the steward of the fact, I would find that "it was a slight mistake; in registering the name; instead of being Josiah Phelps, it was Joseph Philips; only a slight mistake, but such mistakes cause a great deal of trouble sometimes.

Measels, dysentery and typhoid fever were the prevailing diseases after the retreat. After spending several days in visiting the different hospitals, looking after personal friends, and writing letters for the soldiers who were not able to write for themselves, I was regularly installed in one of the general hospitals. I will here insert an extract from my journal: "Aug. 3d, 1861. Georgetown, D. C. Have been on duty all day. John C. is perfectly wild with delirium, and keeps shouting at the top of his voice some military command, or, when vivid recollections of the battle field come to his mind, he enacts a pantomime of the terrible strife—he goes through the whole manual of arms as correctly as if he were in the ranks; and as he, in imagination, loads and fires in quick succession, the flashing of his dying eye and the nervous vigor of his trembling hands give fearful interest to the supposed encounter with the enemy. When we tell him the enemy has retreated, he persists in pursuing; and throwing his arms wildly around him he shouts to his men—'Come on and fight while there is a rebel left in Virginia!' My friend

Lieut. M. is extremely weak and nervous, and the wild ravings of J. C. disturb him exceedingly. I requested Surgeon P. to have him removed to a more quiet ward, and received in reply—'This is the most quiet ward in the whole building.' There are five hundred patients here who require constant attention, and not half enough nurses to take care of them.

"Oh, what an amount of suffering I am called to witness every hour and every moment. There is no cessation, and yet it is strange that the sight of all this suffering and death does not affect me more. I am simply eyes, ears, hands and feet. It does seem as if there is a sort of stoicism granted for such occasions. There are great, strong men dying all around me, and while I write there are three being carried past the window to the dead room. This is an excellent hospital—everything is kept in good order, and the medical officers are skillful, kind and attentive."

The weary weeks went slowly by, while disease and death preyed upon the men, and the "Soldiers' Cemetery" was being quickly filled with new made graves. The kindness of the soldiers toward each other is proverbial, and is manifested in various ways. It is a common thing to see soldiers stand guard night after night for sick comrades—and when off duty try, to the utmost of their skill, to prepare their food in such a way as to tempt the appetite of those poor fellows whom the surgeons "do not consider sufficiently ill to excuse from duty;" but their comrades do, and do not hesitate to perform their duty and their own also. And when brought to camp hospital, helpless, worn down by disease, and fever preying upon their vitals—those brave and faithful comrades do not forsake them, but come several times every day to inquire how they are, and if there is anything they can do for them. And it is touching to see those men, with faces bronzed and stern, tenderly bending over the dying, while the tears course down their sunburnt cheeks.

There is scarcely a soldier's grave where there is not to be seen some marks of this noble characteristic of the soldier—the tastefully cut sod, the planted evergreen, the carefully carved headboard, all tell of the affectionate remembrance of the loved comrade. You will scarcely find such strong and enduring friendship—such a spirit of self-sacrifice, and such noble and grateful hearts, as among the soldiers. I think this is one reason why the nurses do not feel the fatigue of hospital duty more than they do; the gratitude of the men seems to act as a stimulant, and the patient, uncomplaining faces of those suffering men almost invariably greet you with a smile. I used to think that it was a disgrace for any one, under ordinary circumstances, to be heard complaining, when those mutilated, pain-racked ones bore everything with such heroic fortitude.

I was not in the habit of going among the patients with a long, doleful face, nor intimating by word or look that their case was a hopeless one, unless a man was actually dying, and I felt it to be my duty to tell him so. Cheerfulness was my motto, and a wonderful effect it had sometimes on the despondent, gloomy feelings of discouraged and homesick sufferers. I noticed that whenever I failed to arouse a man from such a state of feeling, it generally proved a hopeless case. They were very likely not to recover if they made up their minds that they must die, and persisted in believing that there was no alternative.

There were a great many pleasant things in connection with our camp hospital duties. I really enjoyed gratifying some of the whims and strange fancies of our poor convalescent boys, with whom I had become quite a favorite. As I would pass along through the hospital in the morning, I would generally have plenty of assistants in helping to make out my programme for the day. For one I had to write letters, read some particular book to another, and for a third I must catch some fish. I remember on one occasion of an old Dutchman, a typhoid convalescent, declaring that he could eat nothing until he could get some fresh fish, and of course I must procure them for him. "But," said I, "the doctor must be consulted; perhaps he will not think it best for you to have any fish yet, until you are stronger." "Vell, I dusn't care for te toctor

—he dusn't know vat mine appetite ish—te feesh I must have. Oh, mine Cot! I must have some feesh." And the old man wept like a child at the thought of being disappointed. "Hunter's Creek" was about a mile and a half from camp, where Mr. and Mrs. B. and I had spent many an hour fishing and shooting at the flocks of wild ducks which frequented it; so, after providing myself with hook, line and bait, I made my way to the creek. Soon after I commenced operations I drew up a monstrous eel, which defied all my efforts to release the hook from its jaws. At last I was obliged to draw it into camp by means of the line—and I was amply repaid for my trouble on seeing the delight of the convalescents, and especially of my old Dutchman, who continued to slap his hands together and say—"Dhat ish coot—dhat ish coot." The eel was handed over to the cook to be prepared for dinner, and to the great satisfaction of the Dutchman he was permitted to enjoy a portion of it.

The army under McClellan began to assume a warlike aspect—perfect order and military discipline were observed everywhere among the soldiers. It was a splendid sight to see those well drilled troops on dress-parade—or being reviewed by their gallant young commander, upon whose shoulders the "stars" sat with so much grace and dignity.

The monotony of camp life began to be broken up by armed reconnoissances and skirmishing between the pickets. Our lines were pushed forward to Lewinsville on the right, and to Munson's Hill in front. The pickets of both armies were posted in plain sight of each other, only separated by the beautiful corn-fields and peach-orchards. Picket firing was kept up all along the lines on both sides, notwithstanding that flags of truce had been sent in by both parties, several times, requesting that this barbarous practice might cease.

As soon as Mrs. B. was so far recovered as to be able to ride, we started one day, accompanied by Mr. B. and Dr. E., for Munson's Hill, to see the pickets on duty. We rode along until we came within a short distance of the rifle pits where our men were, when the rebels fired upon us. We turned and rode back until we came to a clump of trees, where we dismounted, hitched our horses, and proceeded the rest of the way on foot—part of the way having to crouch along on our hands and knees, in order to escape the bullets which were whistling above us. We reached the rifle pits in safety, which were close to a rail fence, the rails of which were perfectly riddled with Minnie balls. While we sat there looking through an opera-glass, whiz! came a ball and struck the rail against which my head rested; glancing, it passed through Dr. E.'s cap and lodged in the shoulder of one of the men. We remained there until the firing ceased, then returned to camp, carrying with us the wounded man.

Picket duty is one of the most perilous and trying duties connected with the service. A clergyman-soldier writing upon this subject, briefly describes it: "Picket duty at all times is arbitrary, but at night it is trebly so. No monarch on a throne, with absolute power, is more independent, or exercises greater sway for the time being, than a private soldier stationed on his beat with an enemy in front. Darkness veils all distinctions. He is not obliged to know his own officers or comrades, or the commanding general, only through the means of the countersign. With musket loaded and capped he walks his rounds, having to do with matters only of life and death, and at the same time clothed with absolute power. It is a position of fearful importance and responsibility, one that makes a man feel solemn and terribly in earnest. Often, too, these posts are in thick woods, where the soldier stands alone, cut off from camp, cut off from his fellows, subject only to the harrassings of his own imagination and sense of danger. The shadows deepen into inky night; all objects around him, even the little birds that were his companions during the day, are gathered within the curtains of a hushed repose; but the soldier, with every nerve and faculty of his mind strained to the utmost tension of keenness and sensibility, speaks only in whispers; his fingers tighten round the stock of his musket as he leans forward to catch the sound of approaching footsteps, or, in absence of danger, looks longingly up to the cold, grey sky, with its wealth of shining stars."

Yes, the picket is exposed to danger constantly, and to various kinds of danger. He knows not what moment a lurking foe may spring upon him from the darkness, or a bullet from a scout or sharpshooter may reach him at any time. Then, too, he is exposed to the raging elements—heat and cold, rain and snow; no matter whether in the depths of the forest, or in the open plain, or in the rifle-pit standing in water knee deep, the poor picket must not heed the storm, but keep both eyes and ears open to catch the slightest sound. After severe marches, when the men are greatly fatigued, and it seems almost impossible to perform any more duty without rest and sleep, some, of course, are sent on picket duty, while the rest are permitted to sleep. Oh, how my heart has ached for those men; and it seemed to me that the persons and regiments in which I was most interested always had the most picket duty to perform.

On the 14th of March General McClellan issued an address to the army of the Potomac, announcing the reasons why they had been so long unemployed. The battle of Bull Run was fought in July, 1861. It was now March, 1862, and during this interval the army of the Potomac, numbering some two hundred and fifty thousand men, had been inactive, excepting their daily drills behind their entrenchments. The flags of the enemy were in sight. Washington was in a state of siege, and not a transport could ascend the river without running the gauntlet of the rebel batteries. In his address General McClellan announced the reasons for their inactivity as follows:

"Soldiers of the Army of the Potomac: For a long time I have kept you inactive, but not without a purpose. You were to be disciplined, armed and instructed. The formidable artillery you now have had to be created. Other armies were to move and accomplish certain results. I have held you back that you might give the death-blow to the rebellion that has distracted our once happy country. The patience you have shown, and your confidence in your General, are worth a dozen victories. These preliminary results are now accomplished. I feel that the patient labors of many months have produced their fruit. The army of the Potomac is now a real army, magnificent in material, admirable in discipline and instruction, excellently equipped and armed. Your commanders are all that I could wish. The moment for action has arrived, and I know that I can trust in you to save our country. The period of inaction has passed. I will bring you now face to face with the rebels, and only pray that God may defend the right."

Marching orders were issued once more to the army of the Potomac. The sick were sent off, camps broken up, and all stood prepared for another encounter with the enemy. The bitter remembrance of the defeat at Bull Run still rankled in the minds of the men, and now they were anxious for an opportunity to retaliate upon the foe, and win back the laurels they had so ingloriously lost upon that disastrous field. Various speculations were indulged in with regard to their destination. One prophesied that they were going to Richmond by way of Fredericksburg, another was positive that they were to go by the way of Manassas, and a third declared that it was down the Shenandoah valley to take Richmond on the flank and rear; but, to the utter astonishment of all, they were ordered to Alexandria to embark for Fortress Monroe. Regiment after regiment was huddled together on board until every foot of room was occupied, and there remained but little prospect of comfort for either officers or men.

As soon as each transport received its cargo of men, horses and provisions, it floated out into the stream, while another steamed up to the wharf in its place, until the whole fleet lay side by side, freighted with over a hundred thousand human lives, and awaiting the signal to weigh anchor. The troops were eager for a campaign; they had lain inactive so long, while "victory" thundered all around them, that they were becoming impatient to strike another blow at rebellion, and blot out the remembrance of the past. Roanoke, Pea

Ridge, Newbern, Winchester and Donelson—were a succession of victories which had been achieved, and the army of the Potomac had not participated in them. The men felt this, and were prepared for anything but inactivity. Everything being in readiness, the signal was given, and the whole fleet was soon moving in the direction of Fortress Monroe, with the stars and stripes floating from every mast-head, and the music of national airs awakening the slumbering echoes as we swiftly glided over the quiet waters of the Potomac.

The first real object of interest which presented itself was the "Monitor" lying off Fortress Monroe. It reminded me of what I once heard a man say to his neighbor about his wife; said he, "Neighbor, you might worship your wife without breaking either of the ten commandments." "How is that?" asked the man; "Because she is not the likeness of anything in heaven above, or in the earth beneath, or in the waters under the earth." So thought I of the Monitor.

There she sat upon the water a glorious impregnable battery, the wonder of the age, the terror of rebels, and the pride of the North. The Monitor is so novel in structure that a minute description will be necessary to convey an accurate idea of her character. "She has two hulls. The lower one is of iron, five-eighths of an inch thick. The bottom is flat, and six feet six inches in depth—sharp at both ends, the cut-water retreating at an angle of about thirty degrees. The sides, instead of having the ordinary bulge, incline at an angle of about fifty-one degrees. This hull is one hundred and twenty-four feet long, and thirty-four feet broad at the top. Resting on this is the upper hull, flat-bottomed, and both longer and wider than the lower hull, so that it projects over in every direction, like the guards of a steamboat. It is one hundred and seventy-four feet long, forty-one feet four inches wide, and five feet deep. These sides constitute the armor of the vessel. In the first place is an inner guard of iron, half an inch thick. To this is fastened a wall of white oak, placed endways, and thirty inches thick, to which are bolted six plates of iron, each an inch thick, thus making a solid wall of thirty-six and a half inches of wood and iron. This hull is fastened upon the lower hull, so that the latter is entirely submerged, and the upper one sinks down three feet into the water. Thus but two feet of hull are exposed to a shot. The under hull is so guarded by the projecting upper hull, that a ball, to strike it, would have to pass through twenty-five feet of water. The upper hull is also pointed at both ends. The deck comes flush with the top of the hull, and is made bomb-proof. No railing or bulwark rises above the deck. The projecting ends serve as a protection to the propeller, rudder and anchor, which cannot be struck. Neither the anchor or chain is ever exposed. The anchor is peculiar, being very short, but heavy. It is hoisted into a place fitted for it, outside of the lower hull, but within the impenetrable shield of the upper one. On the deck are but two structures rising above the surface, the pilot-house and turret. The pilot-house is forward, made of plates of iron, the whole about ten inches in thickness, and shot-proof. Small slits and holes are cut through, to enable the pilot to see his course. The turret, which is apparently the main feature of the battery, is a round cylinder, twenty feet in interior diameter, and nine feet high. It is built entirely of iron plates, one inch in thickness, eight of them securely bolted together, one over another. Within this is a lining of one-inch iron, acting as a damper to deaden the effects of a concussion when struck by a ball—thus there is a shield of nine inches of iron. The turret rests on a bed-plate, or ring, of composition, which is fastened to the deck. To help support the weight, which is about a hundred tons, a vertical shaft, ten inches in diameter, is attached and fastened to the bulk-head. The top is made shot-proof by huge iron beams, and perforated to allow of ventilation. It has two circular port-holes, both on one side of the turret, three feet above the deck, and just large enough for the muzzle of the gun to be run out. The turret is made to revolve, being turned by a special engine. The operator within, by a rod connected with the engine, is enabled to turn it at pleasure. It can be made to revolve at the rate of sixty revolutions a minute, and can be regulated to stop within half a degree of a given point. When the guns are drawn in to load, the port-hole is stopped by a huge iron pendulum, which falls to its place, and makes that part as secure as any, and can be quickly hoisted to one side. The armanent consists of two eleven-inch Dahlgren guns. Various improvements in the gun-carriage enable the gunner to secure almost perfect aim.

"The engine is not of great power, as the vessel was designed as a battery, and not for swift sailing. It being almost entirely under water, the ventilation is secured by blowers, drawing the air in forward, and discharging it aft. A separate engine moves the blowers and fans the fires. There is no chimney, so the draft must be entirely artificial. The smoke passes out of gratings in the deck. Many suppose the Monitor to be merely an iron-clad vessel, with a turret; but there are, in fact, between thirty and forty patentable inventions upon her, and the turret is by no means the most important one. Very properly, what these inventions are is not proclaimed to the public."

CHAPTER V.

ARRIVAL AT FORTRESS MONROE—THE VILLAGE OF HAMPTON—VISITING THE CONTRABANDS—ARRIVAL OF FUGITIVES—A REAL "CAMP MEETING"—FEEDING THE NEGROES—CAMP MISERIES—MULES—MISS PERIWINKLE'S MULES—THE COQUETTISH, THE MORAL, THE HISTRIONIC, AND THE PATHETIC MULE—OUR JACK—LINES OF LOVE—MY BOX AND PRESENTS—A THREE-STORY CAKE—A SERENADE AND SURPRISE PARTY—GOOD AND BAD CHAPLAINS—THE MORALS OF THE ARMY—SLANDERS ABOUT SOLDIERS.

WE arrived at Fortress Monroe in a drenching rain, immediately disembarked, and proceeded at once to Hampton—formerly a beautiful little village containing about five hundred houses, many of them elegant brick buildings, but which now lay a blackened mass of ruins, having been burned a few months previous by order of rebel General Magruder. The village was about three miles from Fortress Monroe, and situated on the west side of a creek, or arm of the sea, called Hampton river, the Yorktown road passing directly through its center. It was a great relief to the troops to disembark from the filthy, crowded transports, notwithstanding they had to march through the mud and rain, and then pitch their tents on the wet ground. Fires were soon built, coffee made, and nice fresh bread served out, which was brought to us by the commissary department at the fort.

As Mrs. B. and I had a little respite at this particular juncture, we set about visiting the contrabands. They occupied a long row of board buildings near the fort. The men were employed in loading and unloading Government vessels, and the women were busily engaged in cooking and washing. No language can describe the joy of these men and women at being liberated from bondage. As the Jews of old were looking for the promised Messiah, so the slaves universally regarded the advent of the northern army as the harbinger of their deliverance.

Mr. A. relates the following anecdote, illustrative of this fact, which took place at the battle of Newbern: "A slaveholder, breathless with terror, spurred his horse to his utmost speed past his own house, not venturing to stop. Just then a shell, with its terrific, unearthly shriek, rushed through the air over his head. A poor slave, a man of unfeigned piety and fervent prayer, in uncontrollable emotions of joy, ran into his humble cabin, shouting: 'Wife, he is running, he is running, and the wrath of God is after him. Glory hallelujah! the appointed time has come; we are free, we are free!'"

With regard to my own visit to the contraband quarters, I give the following extract from my journal: "Visited the contrabands to-day, and was much pleased with their cheerful, happy appearance. They are exceedingly ignorant, yet there is one subject upon which they can converse freely and intelligibly, and that is—Christ—the way of salvation. Almost all with whom I conversed to-day were praying men and women. Oh, how I should like to teach these people! They seem so anxious for instruction, I know they would learn quickly. Some of them are whiter and prettier than most of our northern ladies. There is a family here, all of whom have blue eyes, light hair, fair skin and rosy checks; yet they are contrabands, and have been slaves. But why should blue eyes and golden hair be the distinction between bond and free?"

One bitter, stormy night, about eleven o'clock, a band of these poor fugitives, numbering over forty, presented themselves at the picket line, for admittance to the federal camp, imploring protection. The officer of the picket guard being called, and the case presented, the contrabands were permitted to pass through. But no sooner had their poor torn and bleeding feet touched the federal soil, than they fell upon their knees, and returned thanks to God and to the soldiers for their deliverance. They came into camp about one o'clock in the morning, shouting "Glory! Glory to God!" Notwithstanding the early hour, and the stormy night, the whole camp was aroused; every one rushed out to find out the cause of the excitement. There they were, black as midnight, all huddled together in a little group—some praying, some singing, and others shouting. We had a real "camp meeting" time for a while. Soon the exercises changed, and they began to relate their experiences, not only religious experiences, but a brief history of their lives. Some were husbands and fathers. Their masters had sold them down south, lest they should escape. In their terror they had escaped by night, and fled to the National banner for refuge, leaving all behind that was dear to them.

In conclusion, one old man, evidently their leader, stood up and said: "I tell you, my bred-dern, dat de good Lord has borne wid dis yere slav'ry long time wid great patience. But now he can't bore it no longer, no how; and he has said to de people ob de North—go and tell de slave-holders to let de people go, dat dey may sarve me." There were many there who had listened to the old colored man's speech and believed, as I did, that there was more truth than poetry in it. Many hearts were moved with sympathy towards them, as was soon proved by the actions of the soldiers.

An immense fire was built, around which these poor darkies eagerly gathered, as they were both wet, cold and hungry; then a large camp kettle of coffee was made and set before them, with plenty of bread and meat to satisfy their ravenous appetites—for ravenous they were, not having tasted food for more than two days. Then blankets were provided, and they soon became comfortable, and as happy as human beings could be under such circumstances. Mrs. B. and I returned to our tents feeling very much like indorsing the sentiment of "Will Jones' resolve:"

> Resolved, although my brother be a slave,
> And poor and black, he is my brother still;
> Can I, o'er trampled "institutions," save
> That brother from the chain and lash, I will.

A cold, drizzling rain continued to descend for several days, and our camp became a fair specimen of "Virginia mud." I began to feel the effects of the miasma which came floating on every breeze from the adjacent swamps and marshes, and fever and ague became my daily companions for a time. As I sat in my tent, roasting or shivering as the case might be, I took a strange pleasure in watching the long trains of six mule teams which were constantly passing and repassing within a few rods of my tent. As "Miss Periwinkle" remarks, there are several classes of mules. "The coquettish mule has small feet, a nicely trimmed tail, perked up ears, and seems much given to little tosses of the head, affected skips and prances, and, if he wears bells or streamers, puts on as many airs as any belle. The moral mule is a stout, hardworking creature, always tugging with all his might, often pulling away after the rest have stopped, laboring under the conscientious delusion that food for the entire army depends upon his individual exertions. The histrionic mule is a melo-dramatic sort of quadruped, prone to startle humanity by erratic leaps and wild plunges, much shaking of the stubborn head and lashing of his vicious heels; now and then falling flat, and apparently dying *a la* Forrest, a gasp, a groan, a shudder, etc., till the street is blocked up, the drivers all swearing like so many demons, and the chief actor's circulation becomes decidedly quickened by every variety of kick, cuff and jerk imaginable. When the last breath seems to have gone with the last kick, and the harness has been taken off, then a sudden resurrection takes place. He springs to his feet, and proceeds to give himself two or three comfortable shakes, and if ever mule laughed in scornful triumph it is he, and as he calmly surveys the excited crowd, seems to say: 'A hit! a decided hit!' For once the most stupid of all animals has outwitted more than a dozen of the lords of creation. The pathetic mule is, perhaps, the most interesting of all; for although he always seems to be the smallest, thinnest, and weakest of the six, yet, in addition to his equal portion of the heavy load, he carries on his back a great postillion, with tremendous boots, long tailed coat, and heavy whip. This poor creature struggles feebly along, head down, coat muddy and rough, eye spiritless and sad, and his whole appearance a perfect picture of meek misery, fit to touch a heart of stone.

Then there is another class of mules which always have a jolly, cheer-up sort of look about them—they take everything good naturedly, from cudgeling to carressing, and march along with a roguish twinkle in their eye which is very interesting."

One morning, as I was just recovering from fever and ague, Jack, our faithful colored boy, made his appearance at the door of my tent, touching his hat in the most approved military style, and handed me a letter bearing my address, saying, as he did so, "Dar's a box at de 'spress office for you. May I run and fotch it?" I said, "Oh, yes, Jack, you may bring it, but be careful and keep the cover on, there may be chickens in it." Jack knew the meaning of that allusion to chickens, and so ran off singing:

Massa run, ha, ha!
 Darkies stay, ho, ho!
It must be now dat de kingdom 's cumin
 In de year ob jubilo.

In the meantime I opened my letter, from which I make the following extract: "Having learned your address through Mrs. L——, whose son was killed at the battle of Bull Run, we send you a donation in token of our respect and esteem, and of our gratitude for your faithfulness on the field and in the hospital." The following lines were also inclosed:

In the ranks of the sick and dying, in the chamber where death-dews fall,
Where the sleeper wakes from his trances to leap to the bugle-call,

Is there hope for the wounded soldier? Ah, no! for his heart-blood flows,
And the flickering flames of life must wane, to fail at the evening's close.

Oh, thou who goest, like a sunbeam, to lighten the darkness and gloom,
Make way for the path of glory through the dim and shadowy room;
Go speak to him words of comfort, and teach him the way to die,
With his eyes upraised from the starry flag to the blessed cross on high.

And tell him brave hearts are beating with pulses as noble as thine;
That we count them at home by the thousands—thou sweetest sister of mine;
That they fail not and flinch not from duty while the vials of wrath are outpoured,
And tell him to call it not grievous, but joyous to fall by the sword.

When the hosts of the foe are outnumbered, and the day of the Lord is at hand,
Shall we halt in the heat of the battle, and fall at the word of command?
Oh, no! through the trouble and anguish, by the terrible pathway of blood,
We must bear up the flag of our freedom, on—on through the perilous flood.

And if one should be brought faint and bleeding, though wounded, yet not unto death,
Oh plead with the soft airs of heaven to favor his languishing breath;
Be faithful to heal and to save him, assuaging the fever and pains,
Till the pulse in his strong arm be strengthened and the blood courses free in his veins.

While Mrs. B. and I were speculating with regard to the contents of the box, Jack's woolly head reappeared in the doorway, and the subject of our curiosity was before us. "Dar it be, and mity heavy, too; guess it mus' be from ——." So saying, young hopeful disappeared. The box was soon opened, its contents examined and commented upon. First came a beautiful silk and rubber reversible cloak, which could be folded into such a small compass that it could be put into an ordinary sized pocket, and a pair of rubber boots.

Then came a splendid silver-mounted revolver, belt and miniature cartridge-box. But the greatest piece of perfection I ever saw came in the shape of a "housewife;" it was lined and covered with oil silk, and my name printed on it in gilt letters, above which was an eagle, and below was the following inscription: "A thousand shall fall at thy side, and ten thousand at thy right hand; but it shall not come nigh thee." Then came pocket-handkerchiefs, gloves, and other articles too numerous to mention. But last, not least, was found in the bottom, stowed away in one corner, two bottles of the best currant wine, a nice jar of jelly, and a large loaf of cake, frosted and mottoed in fine style. This cake was certainly a great curiosity. It was a three-story cake, with three doors made to slide back by gently pulling a bell-handle which was made of rosettes of red, white and blue ribbon. To the first bell-cord was attached a splendid gold ring, to the second a ten dollar gold piece, and to the third and last a small sized hunting cased gold watch and chain. At such revelations I began to feel as if my humble tent had become an enchanted palace, and that all I should have to do in future would be to rub that mysterious ring, and the genii would appear, ready to supply all my wants. We then commenced to divide the spoil, Mrs. B. positively asserting that she had no right to any part of the donation, and I telling her that in all probability it was all intended for her, and through one of those "slight mistakes" it was directed to me.

The news of this wonderful box soon spread through camp, and the result was that we had a surprise party as soon as evening came, Chaplain B. taking the opportunity of making some very appropriate remarks on the occasion. Then came the band to serenade us, and the consequence was that our cake and wine disappeared with our numerous friends, for we found that all were willing to obey the scriptural injunction, "Take a little wine," etc. Chaplain B. is a very worthy, zealous, faithful minister, and I have spoken very highly of him, but perhaps in doing so I have given the impression that all chaplains are good and faithful. I am very sorry to state that it is not so. There are some who have no fitness for their work, and some a disgrace to their profession. I think I am safe in saying that one bad chaplain will do more harm in a regiment than a hundred good men can counteract. If there is any place on earth where faithful ministers are needed more than another, it is in the army—it is in the hospital. But may God have mercy upon those who go there, whose object is dollars and cents—who neglect their duty, and fill the places which should be occupied by Christ-like heralds of the cross who love the souls of their fellow men. I think the words of the Saviour are particularly applicable to some of the chaplains of the army when He says: "Woe unto you hypocrites! for ye shut up the kingdom of heaven against men," etc. I have conversed with many in the army upon the subject of religion, who told me that the conduct of certain chaplains had more influence in keeping them away from the Saviour than all the combined forces of the evil one. Such chaplains are there through political influence, regardless of qualifications.

Some persons have tried very hard to get up the general belief that the army is terribly demoralized in its best estate, and all who go there must inevitably plunge into vice; but a greater slander was never propagated. There is, undoubtedly, vice in the army; but where is there a city or community throughout the North where vice is not to be found? notwithstanding the tide of moral and religious influence which is daily brought to bear against it. Although the outer man appears rough, and much drunkenness and other evils exist in the army, yet there is much that is pure, lovely, and of good report in the character of both officers and men. "I can speak of that I do know, and testify of that which I have seen," and I am free to say that I think the morals of the majority of the men are quite as good, if not better than you will find among the same number at home, made up of all classes as we find them in the army.

It is true many have backslidden since they left home; but is equally true that *very* many have been reformed, and are now better men than when they enlisted. Every day's history proves that there are thousands of noble hearted, pure minded christians in our army, and none but traitors and infidels, the enemies of God and man, will deny this fact.

CHAPTER VI.

THE MARCH TO YORKTOWN—SCARCITY OF SUPPLIES—CAMP COOKERY—DIFFERENT CHARACTERS IN THE ARMY—ARRIVAL OF TRAINS—CHANGE OF CAMP—TRYING TO SHELL US OUT—THE OLD SAW-MILL—A CONSTANT TARGET—ASSAULTS ON OUR OUTPOSTS—A REBEL APPEAL—YORKTOWN AND VICINITY—THE SITUATION—BALLOON RECONNOISSANCES—PROF. LOWE ON HIGH—REBEL VIXENS—A CURIOUS VISIT—A STRANGE HOSTESS—SHE TRIES TO KILL ME—I WOUND HER AND CAPTURE A PRISONER—A CONVERSION—THE SECESH WOMAN BECOMES A FEDERAL NURSE.

ON TO RICHMOND once more resounded through the camp, and the army was again in motion. The Yorktown road is one long to be remembered, especially by those who that day had to toil through its mud and mire, or, by making a mis-step, fall into one of the yawning chasms from which some unfortunate mule had been drawn. The rain had continued almost all the time we were encamped at Hampton, "saturating the clayey soil, which soon became a vast bed of mortar under the artillery trains." The distance from Hampton to Yorktown is about twenty-three miles, and it required all the determination and energy of veterans to march half that distance in a day. With two days' rations in their haversacks, the men marched until they arrived in front of Yorktown, where they bivouacked on the ground, over which the water was running like a flood. We remained three days in that condition, and it was the first time I ever saw anything like scarcity of food in the army.

It was scarce indeed, for we were only supplied with two days' rations on starting from Hampton. The fifth day had arrived, but no provisions had yet appeared, and it seemed morally impossible to get a supply train over the road. Mile after mile of corduroy bridge had to be made before a team dare venture to approach. Our horses, too, were as badly off for forage as the men were for provisions. On the fifth day, with several others, I received permission to go out and buy what we could at the houses anywhere within three miles of our encampment.

After procuring a quantity of biscuit, pies, and corn bread, we returned to camp, and were quite surprised to find the boys engaged in cutting up and cooking fresh steak. We thought, of course, our provisions had arrived, but found that it was only a little dash they had just made upon the "chivalry's" cattle, appropriating them to their own use with a sort of earnestness which seemed to say, I firmly believe in the old proverb, *Aide toi, et le ciel t'aidera.*

Oh, what a place the army is for the study of human nature! As I looked around upon that mass of busy men, I thought I could discover almost every trait in the human character depicted upon their countenances. There was the selfish man, only intent upon serving himself, and fearing there would not enough come to his share to satisfy his wants; then there was old churlish Nabal away by himself building a fire for his own especial benefit, and which "no man dare approach unto," no, not within baking, broiling, or roasting distance, not even to get a coal to kindle one for himself. But that class of character, thank heaven, was a very small minority. There, too, was the cheerful, happy man, who had been several hours engaged in cutting up and serving out to others, and had no lot or part in the broiled steaks which were smoking around him; yet he looked as good natured as if he had dined on roast beef and plum pudding. Then there was another phase of character—one who always made it the first duty, under all circumstances, to look after those who were not able to look after themselves.

While the little trials of camp life have a tendency to harden and sour the dispositions of some, they seem to bring to light and develop the cheerful, happy, unselfish spirit of others. One has truthfully said that "there is no other quality so diffusive of joy, both to him who possesses it and to those with whom he has friendly intercourse, as cheerfulness. It is the phase of a soul sitting in its own sunshine. There are luminous planets which are viewed by the aid of their own light, others there are which are seen through borrowed light. So it is with individuals. There seem to be some who have scarcely any light of their own, and who shine by the reflection of the light of others; while others there are who possess an intrinsic and inexhaustible source of sunshine, which renders them not only self-illuminating, but capable of irradiating those around them. Many are cheerful when a sparkling rill of pleasure is gurgling in their hearts, or when prosperity encircles them, or looms up gorgeously in their prospective vision. But few are cheerful when adversity casts its gloomy shadows around them; when sorrow and disappointment dry up their fountains of pleasure and wither their hopes. In such crises cheerfulness is an independent virtue, and in others an accidental mood."

The despondency of the few was soon removed, and the patience and cheerfulness of the many rewarded by the arrival of the provision and baggage trains. We then exchanged our camp for one in a more pleasant locality, where there was more wood and not quite so much water, which added much to the comfort of the troops. The enemy soon found out our position, and did not fail to inform us of the fact by frequently saluting us with an immense shell, or thirty-two pound cannon ball, which would burst over our heads or fall within a few rods—often within a few feet—of our tents. We remained in that camp just one month, and, notwithstanding the enemy shelled us night and day, I never saw a man or beast injured by shot or shell in camp while we remained there.

I presume many of my readers will remember seeing or hearing of the old saw-mill which stood near a peach orchard, and which the soldiers persisted in running, to the great annoyance of the rebels. That old saw-mill deserves to be immortalized in song as well as in history; and if it stood in any other than a christian land, it would undoubtedly become an object of idolatry. There it stood, in perfect range of the enemy's batteries, a target at which they never seemed tired of firing, while our brave soldiers risked their lives in sawing lumber for the purpose of laying board floors in the hospital tents, to secure some degree of comfort for their poor sick comrades.

Time after time the mill was set on fire by the explosion of shells as they passed through it, but up would go some brave young hero, and stand in the very jaws of death while his companions would hand him bucket after bucket of water to quench the flames. As soon as the fire was extinguished the men resumed their labor, and the old mill steamed away with all its might, as if proud of the "stars and stripes" which waved from its summit, and of being permitted to show its patriotism and zeal for the glorious cause of freedom by working for good old "Uncle Sam" and his noble sons. Then it would give vent to its pent up wrath in hisses and shrieks, bidding proud defiance to Jeff. Davis and his minions, who were trying in vain to stop its humane and patriotic efforts. For more than three weeks those brave men kept the steam up in that mill, until their object was accomplished, having to stop almost every half hour to repair the ravages of shot and shell. Notwithstanding the constant fire of the rebel batteries, the dilapidated appearance of the mill from its effects, and the danger of the situation, yet not a man was killed in or about it, and not one wounded, to my knowledge.

I remember one day of passing the mill in a great hurry—and it was well that I was in a hurry, for I had scarcely rode by it when I heard a terrific crash close at hand, which made my horse leap from the ground with terror. Upon turning round I saw that a part of the smoke stack had been carried away, and the mill was on fire. I rode up to the door and inquired if any one was killed or injured; no, not a man was hurt, and the fire was soon subdued by the vigorous efforts of those sturdy soldiers, who looked as jolly over the disaster as if it had really been a good joke.

The rebels were beginning to make some desperate assaults upon our outposts; they were driving in the advance pickets on our left wing, and making similar demonstrations along different parts of the line. They were evidently concentrating a large force behind their fortifications, and were determined to make a desperate resistance. Deserters came in bringing Richmond papers crowded with appeals to the Southern "chivalry," of which the following is a specimen:

"The next few days may decide the fate of Richmond. It is either to remain the Capital of the Confederacy, or to be turned over to the Federal Government as a Yankee conquest. The Capital is either to be secured or lost—it may be feared not temporarily, and with it Virginia. Then, if there is blood to be shed, let it be shed here; no soil of the Confederacy could drink it up more acceptably, and none would hold it more gratefully. Wife, family, and friends are nothing. Leave them all for one glorious hour to be devoted to the Republic. Life, death, and wounds are nothing if we only be saved from the fate of a captured and humiliated Confederacy. Let the Government act; let the people act. There is time yet. If fate comes to its worst, let the ruins of Richmond be its most lasting monument."

General McClellan's despatch to the War Department will best describe the state of affairs at this time in Yorktown and vicinity; he says:

"The whole line of the Warwick, which really heads within a mile of Yorktown, is strongly defended by detached redoubts and other fortifications, armed with heavy and light guns. The approaches, except at Yorktown, are covered by the Warwick, over which there is but one, or at most, two passages, both of which are covered by strong batteries. All the prisoners state that General J. E. Johnson arrived at Yorktown yesterday, with strong reinforcements. It seems clear that I shall have the whole force of the enemy on my hands—probably not less than one hundred thousand men, and possibly more.

"Under the circumstances which have been developed since we arrived here, I feel fully impressed with the conviction that here is to be fought the great battle that is to decide the existing contest. I shall of course commence the attack as soon as I can get up my siege train, and shall do all in my power to carry the enemy's works; but to do this, with a reasonable degree of certainty, requires, in my judgment, that I should, if possible, have at least the whole of the first corps to land upon the Severn river and attack Gloucester in the rear. My present strength will not admit of a detachment sufficient for this purpose without materially impairing the efficiency of this column."

While these preparations were going forward on both sides, Professor Lowe was making balloon reconnoissances, and transmitting the result of his observations to General McClellan by telegraph from his castle in the air, which seemed suspended from the clouds, reminding one of the fabled gods of old looking down from their ethereal abodes upon the conflicts of the inhabitants of this mundane sphere. One of the officers one day playfully remarked: "Professor, I am always sorry when I see you descend with your balloon." "Why are you sorry, Colonel? Would you wish to see me suspended between heaven and earth all the time?" "Oh, no, not that; but when I see you coming down I am afraid you will never get so near heaven again."

I was often sent out to procure supplies for the hospitals, butter, eggs, milk, chickens, etc., and in my rambles I used to meet with many interesting adventures. In some instances I met with narrow escapes with my life, which were not quite so interesting; and the timely appearance of my revolver often rescued me from the hands of the female rebels of the Peninsula. Persons dwelling in regions which slavery has not debased can hardly imagine the malice and ferocity manifested by the rebel vixens of the slave states. Upon this point the testimony from all parts of the South is invariable. The Louisville Journal says: "Thousands have read with astonishment the account which historians give of the conduct of women in Paris during the Reign of Terror. The women are said to have been more fierce and bloodthirsty than even the fiercest and most bloodthirsty of the men. Many of our people have supposed that the accounts given of those things must surely be fictions or exaggerations. They have felt themselves unable to conceive that woman's nature could become a thing so utterly revolting. But if they will look and listen in this region, at the present time, they will find that they have no further reason for incredulity or scepticism. The bitter and ferocious spirit of thousands of rebel women in Kentucky, Tennessee, and other States, is scarcely, if at all, surpassed by the female monsters that shrieked and howled for victims in the French Revolution."

I will here relate a little incident illustrative of the peculiarity of my adventures while on this catering business: One morning I started, all alone, for a five mile ride to an isolated farm-house about three miles back from the Hampton road, and which report said was well supplied with all the articles of which I was in search. I cantered along briskly until I came to a gate which opened into a lane leading directly to the house. It was a large old fashioned two-story house, with immense chimneys built outside, Virginia style. The farm appeared to be in good condition, fences all up, a rare thing on the Peninsula, and corn-fields flourishing as if there were no such thing as war in the land.

I rode up to the house and dismounted, hitched my horse to a post at the door, and proceeded to ring the bell. A tall, stately lady made her appearance, and invited me in with much apparent courtesy. She was dressed in deep mourning, which was very becoming to her pale, sad face. She seemed to be about thirty years of age, very prepossessing in appearance, and evidently belonged to one of the "F. F. V's." As soon as I was seated she inquired: "To what fortunate circumstance am I to attribute the pleasure of this unexpected call?" I told her in a few words the nature of my business. The intelligence seemed to cast a deep shadow over her pale features, which all her efforts could not control. She seemed nervous and excited, and something in her appearance aroused my suspicion, notwithstanding her blandness of manner and lady-like deportment.

She invited me into another room, while she prepared the articles which she proposed to let me have, but I declined, giving as an excuse that I preferred to sit where I could see whether my horse remained quiet. I watched all her movements narrowly, not daring to turn my eyes aside for a single moment. She walked round in her stately way for some time, without accomplishing much in the way of facilitating my depar ture, and she was evidently trying to detain me for some purpose or other. Could it be that she was meditating the best mode of attack, or was she expecting some one to come, and trying to detain me until their arrival? Thoughts like these passed through my mind in quick succession.

At last I rose up abruptly, and asked her if the things were ready. She answered me with an assumed smile of surprise, and said: "Oh, I did not know that you were in a hurry: I was waiting for the boys to come and catch some chickens for you." "And pray, madam, where are the boys?" I asked; "Oh, not far from here," was her reply. "Well, I have decided not to wait; you will please not detain me longer," said I, as I moved toward the door. She began to pack some butter and eggs both together in a small basket which I had brought with me, while another stood beside her without anything in it. I looked at her; she was trembling violently, and was as pale as death. In a moment more she handed me the basket, and I held out a greenback for her acceptance; "Oh, it was no consequence about the pay;" she did not wish anything for it. So I thanked her and went out.

In a few moments she came to the door, but did not offer to assist me, or to hold the basket, or anything, but stood looking at me most maliciously, I thought. I placed the basket on the top of the post to which my horse had been hitched, took my seat in the saddle, and then rode up and took my basket. Turning to her I bade her good morning, and thanking her again for her kindness, I turned to ride away.

I had scarcely gone a rod when she discharged a pistol at me; by some intuitive movement I threw myself forward on my horse's neck and the ball passed over my head. I turned my horse in a twinkling, and grasped my revolver. She was in the act of firing the second time, but was so excited that the bullet went wide of its mark. I held my seven-shooter in my hand, considering where to aim. I did not wish to kill the wretch, but did intend to wound her. When she saw that two could play at this game, she dropped her pistol and threw up her hands imploringly. I took deliberate aim at one of her hands, and sent the ball through the palm of her left hand. She fell to the ground in an instant with a loud shriek. I dismounted, and took the pistol which lay beside her, and placing it in my belt, proceeded to take care of her ladyship after the following manner: I unfastened the end of my halter-strap and tied it painfully tight around her right wrist, and remounting my horse, I started, and brought the lady to consciousness by dragging her by the wrist two or three rods along the ground. I stopped, and she rose to her feet, and with wild entreaties she begged me to release her, but, instead of doing so, I presented a pistol, and told

her that if she uttered another word or scream she was a dead woman. In that way I succeeded in keeping her from alarming any one who might be within calling distance, and so made my way toward McClellan's headquarters.

After we had gone in that way about a mile and a half, I told her that she might ride if she wished to do so, for I saw she was becoming weak from loss of blood. She was glad to accept the offer, and I bound up her hand with my handkerchief, gave her my scarf to throw over her head, and assisted her to the saddle. I marched along beside her, holding tight to the bridle rein all the while. When we were about a mile from McClellan's headquarters she fainted, and I caught her as she was falling from the horse. I laid her by the roadside while I went for some water, which I brought in my hat, and after bathing her face for some time she recovered.

For the first time since we started I entered into conversation with her, and found that within the last three weeks she had lost her father, husband, and two brothers in the rebel army. They had all belonged to a company of sharpshooters, and were the first to fall. She had been almost insane since the intelligence reached her. She said I was the first Yankee that she had seen since the death of her relatives, the evil one seemed to urge her on to the step she had taken, and if I would not deliver her up to the military powers, she would go with me and take care of the wounded. She even proposed to take the oath of allegiance, and seemed deeply penitent. "If thy brother (or sister) sin against thee, and repent, forgive him," are the words of the Saviour. I tried to follow their sacred teachings there and then, and told her that I forgave her fully if she was only truly penitent. Her answer was sobs and tears.

Soon after this conversation we started for camp, she weak and humbled, and I strong and rejoicing. None ever knew from that day to this the secret of that secesh woman becoming a nurse. Instead of being taken to General McClellan's headquarters, she went direct to the hospital, where Dr. P. dressed her hand, which was causing her extreme pain. The good old surgeon never could solve the mystery connected with her hand, for we both refused to answer any questions relating to the wound, except that she was shot by a "Yankee," which placed the surgeon under obligations to take care of the patient until she recovered—that is to say as long as it was convenient for him to do so.

The next day she returned to her house in an ambulance, accompanied by a hospital steward, and brought away everything which could be made use of in the hospitals, and so took up her abode with us. Her name was Alice M., but we called her Nellie J. She soon proved the genuineness of her conversion to the Federal faith by her zeal for the cause which she had so recently espoused. As soon as she was well enough to act in the capacity of nurse she commenced in good earnest, and became one of the most faithful and efficient nurses in the army of the Potomac. But that was the first and the only instance of a female rebel changing her sentiments, or abating one iota in her cruelty or hatred toward the "Yankees;" and also the only real lady in personal appearance, education and refinement, that I ever met among the females of the Peninsula.

CHAPTER VII.

A LOST FRIEND—DEATH OF LIEUTENANT JAMES V.—HIS BURIAL—THE GRAVE BY NIGHT—MY VOW—A SOLDIER-CHAPLAIN—RECOGNITIONS IN HEAVEN—DOUBTS AND DISSATISFACTION—CAPTURE OF A SPY—MY EXAMINATIONS AT HEADQUARTERS—MY DISGUISE AS A SPY—I AM METAMORPHOSED INTO A CONTRABAND—HIRED AS A COOK—BISCUIT MAKING—THE DOCTOR'S TEA.

NOT long after these events, returning one day from an excursion, I found the camp almost deserted, and an unusual silence pervading all around. Upon looking to the right and left to discover the cause of so much quietness, I saw a procession of soldiers slowly winding their way from a peach orchard, where they had just depostted the remains of a comrade. Who could it have been? I did not dare to go and meet them to inquire, but I waited in painful suspense until the procession came up, with arms reversed. With sad faces and slow and measured tread they returned in order as they had gone. I stepped forward and inquired whom they had buried. Lieutenant James V. was the reply.

My friend! They had buried him, and I had not seen him! I went to my tent without uttering a word. I felt as if it could not be possible that what I heard was true. It must be some one else. I did not inquire how, when or where he had been killed, but there I sat with tearless eyes. Mr. and Mrs. B. came in, she sobbing aloud, he calm and dignified, but with tears slowly rolling down his face. Lieutenant V. was thirty-two years of age; he was tall, had black wavy hair, and large black eyes. He was a sincere christian, active in all the duties devolving upon a christian soldier, and was greatly beloved both by officers and men. His loss was deeply felt. His heart, though brave, was tender as a woman's. He was noble and generous, and had the highest regard for truth and law. Although gentle and kind to all, yet he had an indomitable spirit and a peculiar courage and daring, which almost amounted to recklessness in time of danger. He was not an American, but was born of English parents, and was a native of St. John, New Brunswick. I had known him almost from childhood, and found him always a faithful friend.

When we met in the army we met as strangers. The changes which five years had wrought, and the costume which I wore, together with change of name, rendered it impossible for him to recognize me. I was glad that he did not, and took peculiar pleasure in remaining unrecognized. We became acquainted again, and a new friendship sprang up, on his part, for mine was not new, which was very pleasant, at least to me. At times my position became very embarrassing, for I was obliged to listen to a recapitulation of my own former conversations and correspondence with him, which made me feel very much like an eavesdropper. He had neither wife, mother nor sister, and, like myself, was a wanderer from his native land. There was a strong bond of sympathy existing between us, for we both believed that duty called us there, and were willing to lay down even life itself, if need be, in this glorious cause. Now he was gone, and I was left alone with a deeper sorrow in my heart than I had ever known before.

Chaplain B. broke the painful silence by informing me how he had met his fate. He was acting in the capacity of aide-de-camp on General C.'s staff. He was sent to carry an order from headquarters to the officer in command of the outer picket line, and while riding along the line he was struck by a Minnie ball, which passed through the temple, killing him instantly. His remains were brought to camp and prepared for their last resting place. Without shroud or coffin, wrapped in his blanket, his body was committed to the cold ground. They made his grave under a beautiful pear tree, in full bloom, where he sleeps peacefully, notwithstanding the roar of cannon and the din of battle which peal forth their funeral notes over his dreamless bed.

One more buried
  Beneath the sod,
One more standing
  Before his God.

We should not weep
  That he has gone;
With us 'tis night,
  With him 'tis morn.

Night came at last with its friendly mantle, and our camp was again hushed in comparative repose. Twelve o'clock came, but I could not sleep. Visions of a pale face and a mass of black wavy hair, matted with gore which oozed from a dark purple spot on the temple, haunted me. I rose up quietly and passed out into the open air. The cool night breeze felt grateful to my burning brow, which glowed with feverish excitement. With a hasty word of explanation I passed the camp guard, and was soon beside the grave of Lieutenant V. The solemn grandeur of the heavens, the silent stars looking lovingly down upon that little heaped up mound of earth, the death-like stillness of the hour, only broken by the occasional booming of the enemy's cannon, all combined to make the scene awfully impressive. I felt that I was not alone. I was in the presence of that God who had summoned my friend to the eternal world, and the spirit of the departed one was hovering near, although my dim eyes could not penetrate the mysterious veil which hid him from my view. It was there, in that midnight hour, kneeling beside the grave of him who was very dear to me, that I vowed to avenge the death of that christian hero. I could now better understand the feelings of poor Nellie when she fired the pistol at me, because I was "one of the hated Yankees who was in sympathy with the murderers of her husband, father and brothers."

But I could not forgive his murderers as she had done. I did not enjoy taking care of the sick and wounded as I once did, but I longed to go forth and do, as a noble chaplain did at the battle of Pittsburg Landing. He picked up the musket and cartridge-box of a wounded soldier, stepped into the front rank, and took deliberate aim at one rebel after another until he had fired sixty rounds of cartridge; and as he sent a messenger of death to each heart he also sent up the following brief prayer: "May God have mercy upon your miserable soul."

From this time forward I became strangely interested in the fifteenth chapter of first Corinthians·

the doctrine of the resurrection, and the hope of "recognition of friends in heaven" became very precious to me. For I believe with regard to our departed loved ones, that

> When safely landed on that heavenly shore
> Where sighings cease and sorrows come no more—
> With hearts no more by cruel anguish riven,
> As we have loved on earth we'll love in heaven.

And infinitely more than we are capable of loving here. "Few things connected with the great hereafter so deeply concern the heart as the question of personal recognition in heaven. Dear ones of earth, linked to our hearts by the most tender ties, have departed and gone away into the unknown realm. We have carefully and tearfully laid their bodies in the grave to slumber till the great awakening morning. If there is no personal recognition in heaven, if we shall neither see nor know our friends there, so far as we are concerned they are annihilated, and heaven has no genuine antidote for the soul's agony in the hour of bereavement. All the precious memories of toil and trial, of conflict and victory, of gracious manifestations and of holy joy, shared with them in the time of our pilgrimage, will have perished forever. The anxiety of the soul with regard to the recognition of our friends in the future state is natural. It springs from the holiest sympathies of the human heart, and any inquiry that may solve our doubts or relieve our anxiety is equally rational and commendable.

"Tell me, ye who have seen the open tomb receive into its bosom the sacred trust committed to its keeping, in hope of the first resurrection—ye who have heard the sullen rumbling of the clods as they dropped upon the coffin lid, and told you that earth had gone back to earth; when the separation from the object of your love was realized in all the desolation of bereavement, next to the thought that you should ere long see Christ as he is and be like him, was not that consolation the strongest which assured you that the departed one, whom God has put from you into darkness, will run to meet you when you cross the threshold of immortality, and, with the holy rapture to which the redeemed alone can give utterance, lead you to the exalted Saviour, and with you bow at his feet and cast the conqueror's crown before him? And is this hope vain? Shall we not even know those dear ones in the spirit world? Was this light of hope that gilded so beautifully the sad, dark hour of human woe, only a mocking *ignis fatuus*, so soon to go out in everlasting darkness? Is this affection, so deep, so holy, yearning over its object with undying love, to be nipped in the very bud of its being? Nay, it cannot be. There must have been some higher purpose; God could not delight in the bestowal of affections that were to be blighted in their very beginning, and of hopes that were to end only in the mockery of eternal disappointment."

> If fate unite the faithful but to part,
> Why is their memory sacred to the heart?

Oh, thank God for FAITH! for a faith that takes hold of that which is within the veil. There we behold our loved ones basking in the sunshine of the Redeemer's love—there they see Him face to face, and know as they are known. And they speak to us from the bright eternal world, and bid us

> Weep not at nature's transient pain;
> Congenial spirits part to meet again.

Just at this crisis I received a letter from a friend of mine at the North, disapproving in strong terms of my remaining any longer in the army, requesting me to give up my situation immediately, and to meet him in Washington two weeks from date. I regarded that friend's opinions very much, especially when they coincided with my own; but upon this point no two opinions could differ more widely than did ours.

It is true I was becoming dissatisfied with my situation as nurse, and was determined to leave the hospital; but before doing so I thought it best to call a council of three, Mr. and Mrs. B. and I, to decide what was the best course to pursue. After an hour's conference together the matter was decided in my mind. Chaplain B. told me that he knew of a situation he could get for me if I had sufficient moral courage to undertake its duties; and, said he, "it is a situation of great danger and of vast responsibility."

That morning a detachment of the Thirty-seventh New York had been sent out as scouts, and had returned bringing in several prisoners, who stated that one of the Federal spies had been captured at Richmond and was to be executed. This information proved to be correct, and we lost a valuable soldier from the secret service of the United States. Now it was necessary for that vacancy to be supplied, and, as the Chaplain had said with reference to it, it was a situation of great danger and vast responsibility, and this was the one which Mr. B. could procure for me. But was I capable of filling it with honor to myself and advantage to the Federal Government? This was an important question for me to consider ere I proceeded further. I did consider it thoroughly, and made up my mind to accept it with all its fearful responsibilities. The subject of life and death was not weighed in the balance; I left that in the hands of my Creator, feeling assured that I was just as safe in passing the picket lines of the enemy, if it was God's will that I should go there, as I would be in the Federal camp. And if not, then His will be done:

Then welcome death, the end of fears.

My name was sent in to headquarters, and I was

soon summoned to appear there myself. Mr. and Mrs. B. accompanied me. We were ushered into the presence of Generals Mc., M. and H., where I was questioned and cross-questioned with regard to my views of the rebellion and my motive in wishing to engage in so perilous an undertaking. My views were freely given, my object briefly stated, and I had passed trial number one.

Next I was examined with regard to my knowledge of the use of firearms, and in that department I sustained my character in a manner worthy of a veteran. Then I was again cross-questioned, but this time by a new committee of military stars. Next came a phrenological examination, and finding that my organs of secretiveness, combativeness, etc., were largely developed, the oath of allegiance was administered, and I was dismissed with a few complimentary remarks which made the good Mr. B. feel quite proud of his *protege*. This was the third time that I had taken the oath of allegiance to the United States, and I began to think, as many of our soldiers do, that profanity had become a military necessity.

I had three days in which to prepare for my debut into rebeldom, and I commenced at once to remodel, transform and metamorphose for the occasion. Early next morning I started for Fortress Monroe, where I procured a number of articles indispensably necessary to a complete disguise. In the first place I purchased a suit of contraband clothing, real plantation style, and then I went to a barber and had my hair sheared close to my head.

Next came the coloring process—head, face, neck, hands and arms were colored black as any African, and then, to complete my contraband costume, I required a wig of real negro wool. But how or where was it to be found? There was no such thing at the Fortress, and none short of Washington. Happily I found the mail-boat was about to start, and hastened on board, and finding a Postmaster with whom I was acquainted, I stepped forward to speak to him, forgetting my contraband appearance, and was saluted with—"Well, Massa Cuff—what will you have?" Said I: "Massa send me to you wid dis yere money for you to fotch him a darkie wig from Washington." "What the —— does he want of a darkie wig?" asked the Postmaster. "No matter, dat 's my orders; guess it 's for some 'noiterin' business." "Oh, for reconnoitering you mean; all right old fellow, I will bring it, tell him." I remained at Fortress Monroe until the Postmaster returned with the article which was to complete my disguise, and then returned to camp near Yorktown.

On my return, I found myself without friends—a striking illustration of the frailty of human friendship—I had been forgotten in those three short days. I went to Mrs. B.'s tent and inquired if she wanted to hire a boy to take care of her horse.

She was very civil to me, asked if I came from Fortress Monroe, and whether I could cook. She did not want to hire me, but she thought she could find some one who did require a boy. Off she went to Dr. E. and told him that there was a smart little contraband there who was in search of work. Dr. E. came along, looking as important as two year old doctors generally do. "Well, my boy, how much work can you do in a day?" "Oh, I reckon I kin work right smart; kin do heaps o' work. Will you hire me, Massa?" "Don't know but I may; can you cook?" "Yes, Massa, kin cook anything I ebber seen." "How much do you think you can earn a month?" "Guess I kin earn ten dollars easy nuff." Turning to Mrs. B. he said in an undertone: "That darkie understands his business." "Yes indeed, I would hire him by all means, Doctor," said Mrs. B. "Well, if you wish, you can stay with me a month, and by that time I will be a better judge how much you can earn."

So saying Dr. E. proceeded to give a synopsis of a contraband's duty toward a master of whom he expected ten dollars per month, especially emphasising the last clause. Then I was introduced to the culinary department, which comprised flour, pork, beans, a small portable stove, a spider, and a medicine chest. It was now supper time, and I was supposed to understand my business sufficiently to prepare supper without asking any questions whatever, and also to display some of my boasted talents by making warm biscuit for supper. But how was I to make biscuit with my colored hands? and how dare I wash them for fear the color would wash off? All this trouble was soon put to an end, however, by Jack's making his appearance while I was stirring up the biscuit with a stick, and in his bustling, officious, negro style, he said: "See here nig—you don't know nuffin bout makin bisket. Jis let me show you once, and dat ar will save you heaps o' trouble wid Massa doct'r for time to come." I very willingly accepted of this proffered assistance, for I had all the necessary ingredients in the dish, with pork fat for shortening, and soda and cream-tartar, which I found in the medicine chest, ready for kneading and rolling out. After washing his hands and rolling up his sleeves, Jack went to work with a flourish and a grin of satisfaction at being "boss" over the new cook. Tea made, biscuit baked, and the medicine chest set off with tin cups, plates, etc., supper was announced. Dr. E. was much pleased with the general appearance of things, and was evidently beginning to think that he had found rather an intelligent contraband for a cook.

CHAPTER VIII.

MY FIRST SECRET EXPEDITION—MY WORK AMONG CONTRABANDS—PICKAXE, SHOVEL AND WHEELBARROW—COUNTING THE GUNS IN A REBEL FORTIFICATION—A CHANGE OF WORK—CARRYING WATER TO THE REBEL SOLDIERS—GENERALS LEE AND JOHNSON—THE REBEL FORCE AT YORKTOWN—A COUNCIL OF WAR—TURNING WHITE AGAIN—A REBEL SPY—LIEUTENANT V.'S MURDERER—ON PICKET DUTY—MY RETURN TO OUR LINES—I PUT ON UNIFORM AND MAKE MY REPORT.

AFTER supper I was left to my own reflections, which were anything but pleasant at that time; for in the short space of three hours I must take up my line of march toward the camp of the enemy. As I sat there considering whether it was best for me to make myself known to Mrs. B. before I started, Dr. E. put his head in at the tent door and said in a hurried manner: "Ned, I want you to black my boots to-night; I shall require them early in the morning." "All right, Massa Doct'r," said I; "I. allers blacks de boots over night." After washing up the few articles which had taken the place of dishes, and blacking the Doctor's boots, I went to seek an interview with Mrs. B. I found her alone and told her who I was, but was obliged to give her satisfactory proofs of my identity before she was convinced that I was the identical nurse with whom she had parted three days previously.

My arrangements were soon made, and I was ready to start on my first secret expedition toward the Confederate capital. Mrs. B. was pledged to secrecy with regard to her knowledge of "Ned" and his mysterious disappearance. She was not permitted even to tell Mr. B. or Dr. E., and I believe she kept her pledge faithfully. With a few hard crackers in my pocket, and my revolver loaded and capped, I started on foot, without even a blanket or anything which might create suspicion. At half-past nine o'clock I passed through the outer picket line of the Union army, at twelve o'clock I was within the rebel lines, and had not so much as been halted once by a sentinel. I had passed within less than ten rods of a rebel picket, and he had not seen me. I took this as a favorable omen, and thanked heaven for it.

As soon as I had gone a safe distance from the picket lines I lay down and rested until morning. The night was chilly and the ground cold and damp, and I passed the weary hours in fear and trembling. The first object which met my view in the morning was a party of negroes carrying out hot coffee and provisions to the rebel pickets. This was another fortunate circumstance, for I immediately made their acquaintance, and was rewarded for my promptness by receiving a cup of coffee and a piece of corn bread, which helped very much to chase away the lingering chills of the preceding night. I remained there until the darkies returned, and then marched into Yorktown with them without eliciting the least suspicion.

The negroes went to work immediately on the fortifications after reporting to their overseers, and I was left standing alone, not having quite made up my mind what part to act next. I was saved all further trouble in that direction, for my idleness had attracted the notice of an officer, who stepped forward and began to interrogate me after the following manner: "Who do you belong to, and why are you not at work?" I answered in my best negro dialect: "I dusn't belong to nobody, Massa, I'se free and allers was; I'se gwyne to Richmond to work." But that availed me nothing, for turning to a man who was dressed in citizen's clothes and who seemed to be in charge of the colored department, he said: "Take that black rascal and set him to work, and if he don't work well tie him up and give him twenty lashes, just to impress upon his mind that there's no free niggers here while there's a d—d Yankee left in Virginia."

So saying he rode away, and I was conducted to a breast-work which was in course of erection, where about a hundred negroes were at work. I was soon furnished with a pickaxe, shovel, and a monstrous wheelbarrow, and I commenced forth-

DISGUISED AS A CONTRABAND.—Page 113.

with to imitate my companions in bondage. That portion of the parapet upon which I was sent to work was about eight feet high. The gravel was wheeled up in wheelbarrows on single planks, one end of which rested on the brow of the breastwork and the other on the ground. I need not say that this work was exceedingly hard for the strongest man; but few were able to take up their wheelbarrows alone, and I was often helped by some good natured darkie when I was just on the verge of tumbling off the plank. All day long I worked in this manner, until my hands were blistered from my wrists to the finger ends.

The colored men's rations were different from those of the soldiers. They had neither meat nor coffee, while the white men had both. Whiskey was freely distributed to both black and white, but not in sufficient quantity to unfit them for duty. The soldiers seemed to be as much in earnest as the officers, and could curse the Yankees with quite as much vehemence. Notwithstanding the hardships of the day I had had my eyes and ears open, and had gained more than would counterbalance the day's work.

Night came, and I was released from toil. I was free to go where I pleased within the fortifications, and I made good use of my liberty. I made out a brief report of the mounted guns which I saw that night in my ramble round the fort, viz.: fifteen three-inch rifled cannon, eighteen four and a half-inch rifled cannon, twenty-nine thirty-two pounders, twenty-one forty-two pounders, twenty-three eight-inch Columbiads, eleven nine-inch Dahlgrens, thirteen ten-inch Columbiads, fourteen ten-inch mortars, and seven eight-inch siege howitzers. This, together with a rough sketch of the outer works, I put under the inner sole of my contraband shoe and returned to the negro quarters.

Finding my hands would not be in a condition to shovel much earth on the morrow, I began to look round among the negroes to find some one who would exchange places with me whose duty was of a less arduous character. I succeeded in finding a lad of about my own size who was engaged in carrying water to the troops. He said he would take my place the next day, and he thought he could find a friend to do the same the day following, for which brotherly kindness I gave him five dollars in greenbacks; but he declared he could not take so much money—"he neber had so much money in all his life before." So by that operation I escaped the scrutiny of the overseer, which would probably have resulted in the detection of my assumed African complexion.

The second day in the Confederate service was much pleasanter than the first. I had only to supply one brigade with water, which did not require much exertion, for the day was cool and the well was not far distant; consequently I had an opportunity of lounging a little among the soldiers, and of hearing important subjects discussed. In that way I learned the number of reinforcements which had arrived from different places, and also had the pleasure of seeing General Lee, who arrived while I was there. It was whispered among the men that he had been telegraphed to for the purpose of inspecting the Yankee fortifications, as he was the best engineer in the Confederacy, and that he had pronounced it impossible to hold Yorktown after McClellan opened his siege guns upon it. Then, too, General J. E. Johnson was hourly expected with a portion of his command. Including all, the rebels estimated their force at one hundred and fifty thousand at Yorktown and in that vicinity.

When Johnson arrived there was a council of war held, and things began to look gloomy. Then the report began to circulate that the town was to be evacuated. One thing I noticed in the rebel army, that they do not keep their soldiers in the dark as our officers do with regard to the movements and destination of the troops. When an order comes to the Federal army requiring them to make some important movement, no person knows whether they are advancing or retreating until they get to Washington, or in sight of the enemy's guns, excepting two or three of the lead ing generals.

Having a little spare time I visited my sable

friends and carried some water for them. After taking a draught of the cool beverage, one young darkie looked up at me in a puzzled sort of manner, and turning round to one of his companions, said: "Jim, I'll be darned if that feller aint turnin' white; if he aint then I'm no nigger." I felt greatly alarmed at the remark, but said, very carelessly, "Well, gem'in I'se allers 'spected to come white some time; my mudder 's a white woman." This had the desired effect, for they all laughed at my simplicity, and made no further remarks upon the subject. As soon as I could conveniently get out of sight I took a look at my complexion by means of a small pocket looking-glass which I carried for that very purpose—and sure enough, as the negro had said, I was really turning white. I was only a dark mulatto color now, whereas two days previous I was as black as Cloe. However, I had a small vial of nitrate of silver in weak solution, which I applied to prevent the remaining color from coming off.

Upon returning to my post with a fresh supply of water, I saw a group of soldiers gathered around some individual who was haranguing them in real Southern style. I went up quietly, put down my cans of water, and of course had to fill the men's canteens, which required considerable time, especially as I was not in any particular hurry just then. I thought the voice sounded familiar, and upon taking a sly look at the speaker I recognized him at once as a peddler who used to come to the Federal camp regularly once every week with newspapers and stationery, and especially at head-quarters. He would hang round there, under some pretext or other, for half a day at a time

There he was, giving the rebels a full description of our camp and forces, and also brought out a map of the entire works of McClellan's position. He wound up his discourse by saying: "They lost a splendid officer through my means since I have been gone this time. It was a pity though to kill such a man if he was a d—d Yankee." Then he went on to tell how he had been at headquarters, and heard "Lieutenant V." say that he was going to visit the picket line at such a time, and he had hastened away and informed the rebel sharpshooters that one of the headquarter officers would be there at a certain time, and if they would charge on that portion of the line they might capture him and obtain some valuable information. Instead of this, however, they watched for his approach, and shot him as soon as he made his appearance.

I thanked God for that information. I would willingly have wrought with those negroes on that parapet for two months, and have worn the skin off my hands half a dozen times, to have gained that single item. He was a fated man from that moment; his life was not worth three cents in Confederate scrip. But fortunately he did not know the feelings that agitated the heart of that little black urchin who sat there so quietly filling those canteens, and it was well that he did not.

On the evening of the third day from the time I entered the camp of the enemy I was sent, in company with the colored men, to carry supper to the outer picket posts on the right wing. This was just what I wished for, and had been making preparations during the day, in view of the possibility of such an event, providing, among other things, a canteen full of whiskey. Some of the men on picket duty were black and some were white. I had a great partiality for those of my own color, so calling out several darkies I spread before them some corn cake, and gave them a little whiskey for dessert. While we were thus engaged the Yankee Minnie balls were whistling round our heads, for the picket lines of the contending parties were not half a mile distant from each other. The rebel pickets do not remain together in groups of three or four as our men do, but are strung along, one in each place, from three to four rods apart. I proposed to remain a while with the pickets, and the darkies returned to camp without me.

Not long after night an officer came riding along the lines, and seeing me he inquired what I was doing there. One of the darkies replied that I had helped to carry out their supper, and was waiting until the Yankees stopped firing before I started to go back. Turning to me he said, "You come along with me." I did as I was ordered, and he turned and went back the same way he came until we had gone about fifty rods, then halting in front of a petty officer he said, "Put this fellow on the post where that man was shot until I return." I was conducted a few rods farther, and then a rifle was put into my hands, which I was told to use freely in case I should see anything or anybody approaching from the enemy. Then followed the flattering remark, after taking me by the coat-collar and giving me a pretty hard shake, "Now, you black rascal, if you sleep on your post I'll shoot you like a dog." "Oh no, Massa, I'se too feerd to sleep," was my only reply.

The night was very dark, and it was beginning to rain. I was all alone now, but how long before the officer might return with some one to fill my place I did not know, and I thought the best thing I could do was to make good use of the present moment. After ascertaining as well as possible the position of the picket on each side of me, each of whom I found to be enjoying the shelter of the nearest tree, I deliberately and noiselessly stepped into the darkness, and was soon gliding swiftly through the forest toward the "land of the free," with my splendid rifle grasped tightly lest I should lose the prize. I did not dare to approach very near the Federal lines, for I was in more danger of being shot by them than by the enemy; so I spent the remainder of the night within hailing distance of our lines, and with the first dawn of morning I hoisted the well known signal and was welcomed once more to a sight of the dear old stars and stripes.

I went immediately to my tent. Mrs. B. was delighted at my return; she was the only person in camp who knew me. Jack was sent to the quartermaster's with an order for a new suit of soldier's clothes. When he saw they were for me, on his return, he said: "Hi! dat darkie tinks he's some. Guess he don't cook no more for Massa Doct'r." After removing as much of the color as it was possible for soap and water to do, my complexion was a nice maroon color, which my new costume showed off to good advantage. Had my own mother seen me then, it would have been difficult to convince her of our relationship. I made out my report immediately and carried it to General McClellan's headquarters, together with my trophy from the land of traitors. I saw General G. B., but he did not recognize me, and ordered me to go and tell A. to appear before him in an hour from that time. I returned again to my tent, chalked my face, and dressed in the same style as on examination day, went at the hour appointed, and received the hearty congratulations of the General. The rifle was sent to Washington, and is now in the capitol as a memento of the war.

Do my friends wish to know how I felt in such

a position and in such a costume? I will tell them. I felt just as happy and as comfortable as it was possible for any one to be under similar circumstances. I am naturally fond of adventure, a little ambitious and a good deal romantic, and this together with my devotion to the Federal cause and determination to assist to the utmost of my ability in crushing the rebellion, made me forget the unpleasant items, and not only endure, but really enjoy, the privations connected with my perilous positions. Perhaps a spirit of adventure was important—but *patriotism* was the grand secret of my success.

Being fatigued, and the palms of both my hands in raw flesh, I thought it best to wait a few days before setting out upon another adventure.

While I was thus situated I made a point of becoming acquainted with Nellie, my rebel captive. She was trying to make herself useful in the hospital, notwithstanding her hand was very painful—often waiting upon those who were suffering less than she was herself. Her pale, pensive face and widow's weeds seemed to possess peculiar attractions for Doctor E., and her hand was a bond of mutual sympathy between them, and afforded many pretexts for a half hour's conversation.

CHAPTER IX.

EVACUATION OF YORKTOWN—OUR ARMY ON THE DOUBLE QUICK—PURSUIT OF THE FUGITIVES—THE ENEMY'S WORKS—A BATTLE—ON THE FIELD—A "WOUNDED," AND NOT INJURED COLONEL—CARRYING THE WOUNDED—FORT MAGRUDER SILENCED—THE VICTORY WON—BURYING THE DEAD—STORY OF A RING—WOUNDED REBELS—A BRAVE YOUNG SERGEANT—CHRISTIAN SOLDIERS—A SOLDIER'S DEATH-BED—CLOSING SCENES—LAST WORDS.

THE next day the continuous roar of cannon all along the lines of the enemy was kept up incessantly. "Nor did it cease at night, for when darkness settled over the encampment, from the ramparts that stretched away from Yorktown there were constant gushes of flame, while the heavy thunder rolled far away in the gloom." A little after midnight the cannonading ceased, and a strange silence rested upon hill and valley. The first dawn of day which broke peacefully over the landscape discovered to the practiced eye of Professor Lowe that the entrenchments of the enemy were deserted; the rebels had abandoned their stronghold during the night and had fled toward Richmond.

The news spread throughout the Federal army like lightning; from right to left and from center to circumference the entire encampment was one wild scene of joy. Music and cheering were the first items in the programme, and then came the following order: "Commandants of regiments will prepare to march with two days' rations, with the utmost dispatch. Leave, not to return." At about eight o'clock in the morning our advance guard entered Yorktown. There were nearly one hundred guns of different kinds and calibers and a large quantity of ammunition. The road over which the fugitive army passed during the night was beat up into mortar, knee deep, and was strewn with fragments of army wagons, tents and baggage.

The Federal troops were in excellent spirits, and pushed on after the retreating army almost on the double quick. In this manner they kept up the pursuit until toward evening, when the cavalry came up with the rear-guard of the enemy about two miles from Williamsburg, where a sharp skirmish followed. Night came on and firing ceased; the rebels were behind their entrenchments, and our army bivouaced for the night. The cavalry and artillery forces were under command of General Stoneman; Generals Heintzelman, Hooker and Smith were in command of the advance column of infantry, while Generals Kearney, Couch and Casey brought up the rear.

The enemy's works were four miles in extent, nearly three-fourths of their front being covered by the tributaries of Queen's Creek and College Creek. The main works were a large fortification, called Fort Magruder, and twelve redoubts for field guns. The woods around and inside of those works were felled, and the ground was thickly dotted with rifle pits. The battle commenced the next morning at half-past seven o'clock. General Hooker began the attack. The enemy were heavily reinforced, and made a desperate resistance. Hooker lost a great number of men and five pieces of artillery before Kearney, Couch or Casey came up. The roads were a perfect sea of mud, and now it was raining in torrents. The roar of battle sounded all along the lines; the thunder of cannon and the crash of musketry reverberated through the woods and over the plain, assuring the advancing troops that their companions were engaged in deadly strife.

The thick growth of heavy timber was felled in all directions, forming a splendid ambush for the rebel sharpshooters. The Federals moved forward in the direction of the enemy's works, steadily, firmly, through ditch and swamp, mud and mire, loading and firing as they went, and from every tree, bush and covert, which could conceal a man, the rebels poured a deadly fire into the ranks of our advancing troops. I was glad now that I had postponed my second visit to the enemy, for there was plenty of work for me to do here, as the ghastly faces of the wounded and dying testified.

I was subject to all kinds of orders. One moment I was ordered to the front with a musket in my hands; the next to mount a horse and carry an order to some general, and very often to take hold of a stretcher with some strong man and carry the wounded from the field.

I remember one little incident in connection with my experience that day which I shall never forget, viz.: Colonel —— fell, and I ran to help put him on a stretcher and carry him to a place of safety, or where the surgeons were, which was more than I was able to do without overtaxing my strength, for he was a very heavy man. A poor little stripling of a soldier and myself carried him about a quarter of a mile through a terrific storm of bullets, and he groaning in a most piteous manner. We laid him down carefully at the surgeon's feet, and raised him tenderly from the stretcher, spread a blanket and laid him upon it, then lingered just a moment to see whether the wound was mortal. The surgeon commenced to examine the case; there was no blood to indicate where the wound was, and the poor sufferer was in such agony that he could not tell where it was. So the surgeon examined by piecemeal until he had gone through with a thorough examination, and there was not even a scratch to be seen. Doctor E. straightened himself up and said, "Colonel, you are not wounded at all; you had better let these boys carry you back again." The Colonel became indignant, and rose to his feet with the air of an insulted hero and said: "Doctor, if I live to get out of this battle I'll call you to account for those words;" to which Doctor E. replied with decision, "Sir, if you are not with your regiment in fifteen minutes I shall report you to General H."

I turned and left the spot in disgust, mentally regretting that the lead or steel of the enemy had not entered the breast of one who seemed so ambitious of the honor without the effect. As I returned to my post I made up my mind in future to ascertain whether a man was wounded or not before I did anything for him. The next I came to was Captain Wm. R. M., of the — Michigan. His leg was broken and shattered from the ankle to the knee. As we went to lift him on a stretcher he said: "Just carry me out of range of the guns, and then go back and look after the boys. Mc—— and L. have fallen, and perhaps they are worse off than I am." Oh how glad I was to hear those words from his lips. It confirmed the opinion I had formed of him long before; he was one of my first acquaintances in the army, and, though he was a strict disciplinarian, I had watched his christian deportment and kind and affectionate manner toward his men with admiration and interest. I believed him noble and brave, and those few words on the battle-field at such a moment spoke volumes for that faithful captain's heroism and love for his men.

The battle was raging fiercely, the men were almost exhausted, the rebels were fighting like demons, and were driving our troops back step by step, while the space between the two lines was literally covered with dead and wounded men and horses. One tremendous shout from the Federals rent the air and fairly shook the earth. We all knew in an instant, as if by intuition, what called forth such wild cheers from that weary and almost overpowered army. "Kearney!" was shouted enthusiastically along the Federal lines, while the fresh troops were hurled like thunderbolts upon the foe. One battery after another was taken from the enemy, and charge after charge was made upon their works, until the tide of battle was turned, Fort Magruder silenced, and the stars and stripes were floating in triumph over the rebel works.

The battle was won, and victory crowned the Union arms. The rebels were flying precipitately from the field, and showers of bullets thick as hail followed the retreating fugitives. Night closed around us, and a darkness which almost equaled that of "Egypt" settled over the battle-field, and the pitiless rain came down in torrents, drenching alike the living and the dead. There lay upon that crimson field two thousand two hundred and twenty-eight of our own men, and more than that number of the enemy. It was indescribably sad to see our weary, exhausted men, with torches, wading through mud to their knees piloting the ambulances over the field, lest they should trample upon the bodies of their fallen comrades.

All night long we toiled in this manner, and when morning came still there were hundreds found upon the field. Those of the enemy were found in heaps, both dead and wounded piled together in ravines, among the felled timber, and in rifle pits half covered with mud. Now the mournful duty came of identifying and burying the dead. Oh, what a day was that in the history of my life, as well as of thousands both North and South. It makes me shudder now while I recall its scenes.

> To see those fair young forms
> Crushed by the war-horse tread,
> The dear and bleeding ones
> Stretched by the piled-up dead.

Oh, war, cruel war! Thou dost pierce the soul with untold sorrows, as well as thy bleeding victims with death. How many joyous hopes and bright prospects hast thou blasted; and how many hearts and homes hast thou made desolate! "As we think of the great wave of woe and misery surging over the land, we could cry out in very bitterness of soul—Oh God! how long, how long!"

The dead lay in long rows on the field, their ghastly faces hid from view by handkerchiefs or the capes of their overcoats, while the faithful soldiers were digging trenches in which to bury the mangled bodies of the slain. I passed along the entire line and uncovered every face, in search of one who had given me a small package the day before when going into battle, telling me that if he should be killed to send it home; and, said he, "here is a ring on my finger which I want you to send to ——. It has never been off my finger since she placed it there the morning I started for Washington. If I am killed please take it off and send it to her." I was now in search of him, but could find nothing of the missing one. At last I saw a group of men nearly half a mile distant, who also seemed to be engaged in burying the dead. I made my way toward them as fast as I could, but when I reached them the bodies had all been lowered into the trench, and they were already filling it up.

I begged them to let me go down and see if my friend was among the dead, to which the kind hearted boys consented. His body lay there partially covered with earth; I uncovered his face; he was so changed I should not have recognized him, but the ring told me that it was he. I tried with all my might to remove the ring, but could not. The fingers were so swollen that it was impossible to get it off. In life it was a pledge of faithfulness from one he loved, "and in death they were not divided."

The dead having been buried and the wounded

removed to the churches and college buildings in Williamsburg, the fatigued troops sought repose. Upon visiting the wounded rebels I saw several whom I had met in Yorktown, among them the sergeant of the picket post who had given me a friendly shake and told me if I slept on my post he would shoot me like a dog. He was pretty badly wounded, and did not seem to remember me. A little farther on a young darkie lay groaning upon the floor. I went to look at him, and asked if I could do anything for him. I recognized in the distorted face before me the same darkie who had befriended me at Yorktown, and to whom I had offered the five dollar greenback. I assure my friends that I repaid that boy's kindness with double interest; I told Doctor E. what he had done for me when my "hands" turned traitors. He was made an especial object of interest and care.

Some few of the rebel prisoners were gentlemanly and intelligent, and their countenances betokened a high state of moral culture. Many were low, insolent, bloodthirsty creatures, who "neither feared God nor regarded man;" while others there were who seemed not to know enough to be either one thing or the other, but were simply living, breathing animals, subject to any order, and who would just as soon retreat as advance, so long as they did not have to fight. They did not care which way the battle went. On the whole there was a vast contrast between the northern and southern soldiers as they appeared in the hospitals, but perhaps prejudice had something to do in making the rebels appear so much inferior to our men.

In passing through the college building I noticed a young sergeant, a mere boy, who was shot in the temple. He attracted my attention, and I made some inquiry concerning him. He was a Federal, and belonged to the — Massachusetts regiment. An old soldier sitting by him told me the following: "That boy is not sixteen yet; he enlisted as a private, and has, by his bravery and good conduct, earned the three stripes which you see on his arm. He fought all day yesterday like a young lion, leading charges again and again upon the enemy. After we lost our captain and lieutenants he took command of the company, and led it through the battle with the skill and courage of a young brigadier, until he fell stunned and bleeding. I carried him off the field, but could not tell whether he was dead or alive. I washed the blood from his face; the cold water had a salutary effect upon him, for when Hancock and Kearney had completed their work, and the cheers of victory rang over the bloody field, he was sufficiently revived to hear the inspiring tones of triumph. Leaping to his feet, faint and sick as he was, he took up the shout of victory in unison with the conquerers on the field. But he had scarcely uttered the notes of victory and glory when his strength deserted him and he fell insensible to the ground." The old man added: "General —— says if he lives through this he will go into the next battle with shoulder straps on." I went up to him, took his feverish hand, and told him that I was glad that his wound was not mortal. He thanked me, and said with enthusiasm, "I would rather have been killed than to have lost the battle.

There is one thing that I have noticed on the field in every battle that I have witnessed, viz.: that the christian man is the best soldier. Says a minister of the Gospel, writing upon this subject: "It is a common saying among the officers that, as a class, the men who stand foremost when the battle rages are the christian men. Many a time I have talked with them about such scenes, and they have told me that their souls have stood firm in that hour of strife, and that they have been perfectly calm. I have had christian generals tell me this. I have heard General Howard often say that in the midst of the most terrific portion of the battle, when his heart for a moment quailed, he would pause, and lift up his soul to God and receive strength. "And," said he, "I have gone through battles without a particle of fear. I have thought that God sent me to defend my country. I believed it was a christian duty to stand in the foremost of the fight, and why should I be afraid?"

I once heard an eminently pious lady say that she never could reconcile the idea in her mind of a christian going into the army to fight; it was so inconsistent with the christian character that she was tempted to doubt the piety of all fighting men. I respect the lady's views upon the subject, but beg leave to differ from her; for I believe that a man can serve God just as acceptably in fighting the enemies of liberty, truth and righteousness with the musket down South, as he can in the quiet pulpits of the North; in fact I am inclined to think he can do so a little more effectually in the former place. I only wish that there were more of our holy men willing to take up the carnal weapons of warfare, forego the luxuries of home, and, by setting examples worthy of emulation, both in camp and on the battle field, thus strike a fatal blow at this unholy rebellion.

The last night I spent in the hospital before leaving Williamsburg, I witnessed the death of a christian soldier, a perfect description of which I find in the "Memorials of the War:" "It was the hour of midnight, when the chaplain was summoned to the cot of a wounded soldier. He had only left him an hour before, with confident hopes of his speedy recovery—hopes which were shared by the surgeon and the wounded man himself. But a sudden change had taken place, and the surgeon had come to say that the man could live but an hour or two at most, and to beg the chaplain to make the announcement to the dying man. He was soon at his side, but overpowered by his emotions, was utterly unable to deliver his message. The dying man, however, quickly read the solemn truth in the altered looks of the chaplain, his faltering voice and ambiguous words. He had not before entertained a doubt of his recovery. He was expecting soon to see his mother, and with her kind nursing soon to be well. He was therefore entirely unprepared for the announcement, and at first it was overwhelming.

"'I am to die then; and—how long?' As he had before expressed hope in Christ, the chaplain replied: 'You have made your peace with God; let death come as soon as it will, He will carry you safely over the river.' 'Yes; but this is so awfully sudden, awfully sudden!' His lips quivered; he looked up grievingly: 'And I shall not see my mother.' 'Christ is better than a mother,' murmured the chaplain. 'Yes.' The word came in a whisper. His eyes were closed; the lips still wore that trembling grief, as if the chastisement were too sore, too hard to be borne; but as the minutes passed, and the soul lifted itself up stronger and more steadily upon the wings of prayer, the countenance grew calmer, the lips steadier, and when the eyes opened again there was a light in their depths that could have come only from heaven.

"'I thank you for your courage,' he said more

feebly, taking the chaplain's hand; 'the bitterness is over now, and I feel willing to die. Tell my mother'—he paused, gave one sob, dry, and full of the last anguish of earth—'tell her how I longed to see her; but if God will permit me I will be near her. Tell her to comfort all who loved me; to say that I thought of them all. Tell my father that I am glad that he gave his consent. Tell my minister, by word or letter, that I thought of him, and that I thank him for all his counsels. Tell him I find that Christ will not desert the passing soul, and that I wish him to give my testimony to the living, that nothing is of real worth but the religion of Jesus; and now, will you pray with me?' With swelling emotion and tender tones the chaplain besought God's grace and presence; then, restraining his sobs, he bowed down and pressed upon the beautiful brow, already chilled with the breath of the coming angel, twice, thrice, a fervent kiss. They might have been as tokens from the father and mother, as well as for himself.

"So thought, perhaps, the dying soldier, for a heavenly smile touched his face with new beauty, as he said, 'Thank you; I won't trouble you any longer. You are wearied out; go to your rest.' 'The Lord God be with you!' was the firm response. 'Amen,' trembled from the fast whitening lips. Another hour passed, still the chaplain did not go to rest, but retired to an adjoining room; he was about to return to the bedside of the dying when the surgeon met him and whispered softly, 'He is gone.' Christ's soldier had found the captain of his salvation, and received his reward."

Tell my mother, when you see her,
  That I fell amid the strife;
And for freedom and my country
  I have given up my life;
Tell her that I sent this message
  Ere my tongue refused to speak,
And you tell her, comrade, won't you?
  Tell my mother not to weep.

Tell her, comrade, how we battled
  For our country and the right;
How I held the starry banner
  In the thickest of the fight;
Tell her how they struggled for it,
  And, with curses loud and deep,
Took my bosom for their target—
  But tell her not to weep.

Tell her I held up the banner
  'Mid the screaming shot and shell,
Till the fatal leaden missile
  Pierced my side, and then I fell.
Tell her I was ready, waiting,
  When my pulses ceased to beat,
And I longed once more to see her—
  But you tell her not to weep.

Tell her that the truths she taught me
  Nerved my arm and led my feet,
And I trusted in the promise
  'Mid the battle's fiercest heat.
Tell her, while my life was ebbing,
  That I kissed her face so sweet—
Kissed the picture that she gave me—
  And you tell her not to weep.

Tell her, comrade, when you see her,
That my battlefields are o'er,
And I've gone to join an army
Where rebellion comes no more;
Tell her that I hope to greet her,
When together we shall meet,
In that better home in heaven,
Where we never more shall weep.

CHAPTER X.

MC CLELLAN'S DESPATCH FROM EWELL'S FARM—CALL FOR REINFORCEMENTS—NEWS FROM NORFOLK—DESCRIPTION OF THE MERRIMAC—THE ENGAGEMENT IN HAMPTON ROADS—FIRST AND LAST FIGHT OF THE MERRIMAC—VICTORY OF THE MONITOR—ADVANCE ON THE PENINSULA—THE BATTLE SONG—A MUDDY MARCH—ON THE CHICKAHOMINY—CRITICAL POSITION OF GENERAL BANKS—THE PRESIDENT'S DESPATCHES—MCCLELLAN'S REPLY.

ON the tenth of May headquarters were established beyond Williamsburg, and communications were opened between the forces moving by land and water. The following despatch was then sent by General McClellan to Secretary Stanton:

"CAMP AT EWELL'S FARM,
"Three miles beyond Williamsburg,
'*May 10th—5 a. m.*

"From the information reaching me from every source, I regard it as certain that the enemy will meet us with all his force on or near the Chickahominy. They can concentrate many more men than I have, and are collecting troops from all quarters, especially well disciplined troops from the South. Casualties, sickness, garrisons and guards have much reduced our numbers, and will continue to do so. I shall fight the rebel army with whatever force I may have, but duty requires me to urge that every effort be made to reinforce me, without delay, with all the disposable troops in Eastern Virginia, and that we concentrate all our forces, as far as possible, to fight the great battle now impending, and to make it decisive. It is possible that the enemy may abandon Richmond without a serious struggle, but I do not believe he will; and it would be unwise to count upon anything but a stubborn and desperate defense—a life and death contest. I see no other hope for him than to fight this battle, and we must win it. I shall fight them whatever their force may be; but I ask for every man that the department can send me. No troops should now be left unemployed. Those who entertain the opinion that the rebels will abandon Richmond without a struggle are, in my judgment, badly advised, and do not comprehend their situation, which is one requiring desperate measures. I beg that the President and Secretary will maturely weigh what I say, and leave nothing undone to comply with my request. If I am not reinforced it is probable that I will be obliged to fight nearly double my numbers strongly entrenched."

Four days later he writes:

"I will fight the enemy, whatever their force may be, with whatever force I may have, and I believe that we shall beat them; but our triumph should be made decisive and complete. The soldiers of this army love their Government, and will fight well in its support. You may rely upon them. They have confidence in me as their general, and in you as their President. Strong reinforcements will at least save the lives of many of them; the greater our force the more perfect will be our combinations, and the less our loss. For obvious reasons I beg you to give immediate consideration to this communication, and to inform me fully, at the earliest moment, of your final decision."

A few days' rest after the fatigues of the battle, and the glorious news of the evacuation of Norfolk and the total annihilation of the Merrimac, had a wonderful effect upon the spirits of our troops; they seemed inspired with new courage and enthusiasm. Hitherto I have said nothing concerning that great bugbear, the Merrimac. Perhaps some of my "blue-nose" readers are not so well posted with regard to the origin and structure of this formidable rebel battery as the Americans are, and it may be interesting to some to listen to a brief description of it.

"Upon the burning and evacuation of the Norfolk Navy Yard the steam frigate Merrimac was scuttled and sunk, by order of Commodore Macaulay. This was one of the most magnificent ships in the American navy, being rated as a forty-gun frigate, of four thousand tons burden. She was built in Charlestown, Massachusetts, in 1856, and was considered one of the finest specimens of naval architecture then afloat. She was two hundred and eighty-one feet long, fifty-two feet broad, and drew twenty-three feet of water. Her engines were of eight hundred horse power, driving a two-bladed propeller fourteen feet in diameter, and so adjusted as to be raised from the water when the vessel was driven by wind alone. Her armament consisted of twenty-four nine-inch shell guns, fourteen eight-inch, and two one hundred-pound pivot guns. This magnificent structure was raised by the rebels and cut down, leaving only the hull, which was exceedingly massive and solid. Over this they constructed a sloping shield of railroad iron, firmly plaited together, and extending two feet under the water. Its appearance was much like the slanting roof of a house set upon a ship's hull, like an extinguisher, the ends of the vessel, fore and aft, projecting a few feet beyond this roof. The gun-deck was completely inclosed by this shield, and nothing appeared above it but a short smoke-stack and two flag-staffs."

An eye witness gives the following account of the first appearance and conflict of the Merrimac: "About noon of Saturday, the eighth of March, 1862, this monster was seen coming around Craney Island from Norfolk, accompanied by two other war vessels, the Jamestown and Yorktown, and quite a little fleet of armed tugs. The Merrimac, with her imposing retinue in train, headed for Newport News, where there was a national garrison, guarded by the sailing frigates the Cumberland, of one thousand seven hundred and twenty-six tons, and the Congress, of one thousand eight hundred and sixty-seven tons burden. The Merrimac steamed majestically along, as if conscious of resistless strength, and as she passed the Congress discharged a single broadside into the doomed ship, and then, leaving her to the attention of the Jamestown and Yorktown, made directly for the Cumberland. When the Merrimac was within a hundred yards of the two frigates, they both discharged their tremendous broadsides against her armor.

"The mailed monster quivered a moment under the fearful concussion, but every ball glanced from her sloping shield like the wooden arrows of the Indian from the hide of the crocodile. Her ports were all closed. Not deigning to pay any attention to the fierce but harmless assault of the two frigates, she rushed straight forward upon her prey. The formidable national battery at Newport News opened, with all its immense guns, at point-blank range, and these solid shot and shells also glanced harmlessly away. On rushed the silent Merrimac, with not a soul on board to be seen, true as an arrow, and with all the power of her irresistible weight, plunged headlong with a fearful crash into the side of the helpless frigate. The iron prow of the assailant struck the Cumberland amidships, crushing in her side with a mortal gash. Then, reversing her engine, and not even annoyed by the cannon balls rattling against her impervious mail, she retraced her steps a few rods for another butt.

"As she drew back she turned her broadside to the wounded victim, and hurled into her bosom a merciless volley of shot and shells. The ponderous missiles tore through the crowded ship, hurling her massive guns about her decks, and scattering mutilated bodies in all directions. Again gathering headway, she crowded on all steam and made another plunge at the Cumberland. She struck directly upon the former wound, and crushed in the whole side of the ship as if it had been a lattice work of laths.

"Timbers as strong as nature and art could make them, were snapped and crushed like dry twigs. As the sun went down, that night, over Hampton Roads, every Union heart in the fleet and in the fortress throbbed with despair. There was no gleam of hope. The Merrimac was impervious to balls, and could go where she pleased. In the morning it would be easy work for her to destroy our whole fleet. She could then shell Newport News and Fortress Monroe at her leisure, setting everything combustible in flames, and driving every man from the guns.

"'That morrow! How anxiously we waited for it! how much we feared its results! At sundown there was nothing to dispute the empire of the seas with the Merrimac, and had a land attack been made by Magruder then, God only knows what our fate would have been.' All at once a speck of light gleamed on the distant wave; it moved; it came nearer and nearer, and at ten o'clock that night the Monitor appeared. 'When the tale of brick is doubled, Moses comes.' I never more firmly believed in special providences than at that hour. Even skeptics were converted, and said, 'God has sent her.' But how insignificant she looked; she was but a speck on the dark blue wave at night, and almost a laughable object by day. The enemy call her a 'cheese-box on a raft,' and the comparison is a good one." But insignificant as she appeared, she saved the Union fleet, silenced the rebel monster, and eventually caused her to commit suicide. No wonder then that the news of the death of this formidable foe caused great rejoicing among the Union troops.

Orders were issued to continue the advance up the Peninsula; and as the jubilant troops were engaged in striking tents and making the necessary preparations consequent upon a hurried march, "The Battle Song of the Republic" was being sung with enthusiasm throughout the encampment by thousands of manly voices, and every loyal heart seemed inspired by the glorious sentiments which it contained.

Mine eyes have seen the glory of the coming of the Lord;
He is trampling out the vintage where the grape of wrath is stored;
He hath loosed the fateful lightning of his terrible swift sword;
His truth is marching on.
CHORUS—Glory, glory, hallelujah!
Glory, glory, hallelujah!
Glory, glory, hallelujah!
His truth is marching on.

I have seen him in the watch-fires of a hundred circling camps;
They have builded Him an altar in the evening's dews and damps;
I can read his righteous sentence by the dim and flaming lamps;
His day is marching on, etc.

I have read a fiery gospel writ in burnished rows of steel:
As ye deal with my contemners, so with you my grace shall deal;
Let the Hero, born of woman, crush the serpent with his heel,
Since God is marching on, etc.

He has sounded forth the trumpet that shall never call retreat;
He is sifting out the hearts of men before his judgment seat;
O, be swift, my soul, to answer Him! be jubilant, my feet!
Our God is marching on, etc.

In the beauty of the lilies Christ was born across the sea,
With a glory in his bosom that transfigures you and me:
As he died to make men holy, let us die to make men free,
While God is marching on, etc.

The roads were so indescribably bad at this time that the army could make but little progress. I remember it required thirty-six hours for one train to accomplish the distance of five miles. However, after several days wading through mud and water, the troops reached the White House, where a portion of the army remained for a time, while the advance guards pushed on to the Chickahominy River, and established headquarters at Bottom's Bridge—its further progress being impeded by the destruction of the bridge by the rebels.

"The position of the troops were as follows: Stoneman's advance-guard one mile from New Bridge; Franklin's corps three miles from New Bridge, with Porter's corps in advancing distance in its rear; Sumner's corps on the railroad, about three miles from the Chickahominy, connecting the right with the left; Keyes' on New Kent road, near Bottom's Bridge, with Heintzelman's corps at supporting distance in its rear." The ford was in possession of the federal troops, and a reconstruction of the bridge was immediately commenced.

On the 24th of May the two following despatches were received by Gen. McClellan from the President: "I wish you to move cautiously and safely. You will have command of McDowell precisely as you indicated in your despatch to us."

"In consequence of Gen. Banks' critical position, I have been compelled to suspend Gen. McDowell's movement to join you. The enemy are making a desperate push upon Harper's Ferry, and we are trying to throw Gen. Fremont's force, and part of Gen. McDowell's, in their rear!"

On the 25th, the President also sent the following to McClellan: "The enemy is moving north in sufficient force to drive Gen. Banks before him; precisely in what force we cannot tell. He is also threatening Leesburg and Geary on the Manassas Gap Railroad, from north and south; I think the movement is a general and concerted one—such as would not be if he was acting upon the purpose of a very desperate defense of Richmond. I think the time is near when you must either attack Richmond or give up the job, and come to the defense of Washington. Let me hear from you instantly."

To which McClellan replied: "Telegram received. Independently of it, the time is very near when I shall attack Richmond. The object of the movement is probably to prevent reinforcements being sent to me. All the information obtained agree in the statement that the mass of the rebel troops are still in the vicinity of Richmond. I have no knowledge of Banks' position and force, nor what there is at Manassas; therefore cannot form a definite opinion as to the forces against him. I have two corps across Chickahominy, within six miles of Richmond; the others on this side at other crossings, within same distance, and ready to cross when bridges are completed."

CHAPTER XI.

ANOTHER DISGUISE—I BECOME AN IRISH PEDDLER—FEVER AND AGUE—A NIGHT OF SUFFERING IN THE SWAMP—RETROSPECTION—LOST IN THE SWAMP—CANNON MY GUIDES—A SICK REBEL—I FIND SOMETHING TO EAT—MY NEW PATIENT—SYMPATHY FOR SUFFERING—TALK WITH A DYING REBEL—A WILLING DETENTION—EXTEMPORIZING A LIGHT—THE LAST HOUR—SOLDIERS OF CHRIST—THE CHAMBER OF DEATH.

WHILE all these preparations were going forward, I was meditating another visit to the rebel camp. It was not safe for me to attempt to palm myself off again on the rebels as a colored boy. In the first place, I should be in danger of being recognized as the cowardly picket who deserted his post—a crime worthy of death; and in the next place, I should be in imminent danger of blistering my hands again—a thing which I felt particularly anxious to avoid, especially in performing labor that would enable the enemy more successfully to repel the attacks of the Federals. Now a new disguise was necessary, and I decided to abandon the African relation, and assume that of the Hibernian. Having had this in view before leaving Williamsburg, I procured the dress and outfit of an Irish female peddler, following the army, selling cakes, pies, etc., together with a considerable amount of brogue, and a set of Irish phrases, which did much toward characterizing me as one of the "rale ould stock of bog-trotters."

The bridges were not finished across the Chickahominy when I was ready to cross the river, so I packed up my new disguise in my cake and pie basket, and my horse, "Frank," and I took a bath in the cool water of the Chickahominy. After swimming my noble steed across the river, I dismounted, and led him to the edge of the water—gave him a farewell pat, and let him swim back again to the other side, where a soldier awaited his return. It was now evening; I did not know the precise distance to the enemy's picket line, but thought it best to avoid the roads, and consequently I must spend the night in the swamp, as the only safe retreat. It required some little time to don my new disguise, and feel at home in the clothes. I thought the best place for my debut was the "Chickahominy swamp." I did not purpose, this time, to pass the enemy's lines in the night, but to present myself at the picket line, at a seasonable hour, and ask admission as one of the fugitives of that section flying from the approach of the Yankees, which was a usual thing.

In crossing the river I had my basket strapped on my back, and did not know that all it contained was completely drenched, until I required to use its contents. It was, therefore, with feelings of dread and disappointment that I discovered this sad fact, for I had been suffering from slight ague chills during the day, and feared the consequences of spending the night in wet clothing, especially in that malaria-infested region. However, there was no alternative, and I was obliged to make the best of it. I had brought a patch-work quilt with me from the hospital, but that, too, was wet. Yet it kept off some of the chill night air, and the miasmatic breath of that "dismal swamp." The remembrance of the sufferings of that night seem to be written upon my memory "as with a pen of iron." There I was, all alone, surrounded by worse, yes, infinitely worse, than wild beasts—by blood-thirsty savages—who considered death far too good for those who were in the employment of the United States Government.

That night I was attacked by severe chills—chills beyond description, or even conception, except by those who have experienced the freezing sensation of a genuine ague chill. During the latter part of the night the other extreme presented itself, and it seemed as if I should roast alive, and not a single drop of water to cool my parched tongue; it was enough to make any one think of the "rich man" of the Bible, and in sympathy with his feelings cry to "Father Abraham" for assistance. My mind began to wander, and I became quite delirious. There seemed to be the horrors of a thousand deaths concentrated around me; I was tortured by fiends of every conceivable shape and magnitude. Oh, how it makes me shudder to recall the scenes which my imagination conjured up during those dark weary hours! Morning at last came, and I was aroused from the horrible night-mare which had paralyzed my senses through the night, by the roar of cannon and the screaming of shell through the forest.

But there I was, helpless as an infant, equally unable to advance or retreat, without friend or foe to molest or console me, and nothing even to amuse me but my own thoughts. I looked upon the surrounding scenery, and pronounced it very unromantic; then my eye fell upon my Irish costume, and I began to remember the fine phrases which I had taken so much pains to learn, when the perfect absurdity of my position rushed over my mind with overwhelming force, and the ludicrousness of it made me, for the moment, forget my lamentable condition, and with one uncontrollable burst of laughter I made that swamp resound in a manner which would have done credit to a person under happier circumstances, and in a better state of health.

That mood soon passed away, and I began a retrospection of my past life. It certainly had been an eventful one. I took great interest in carefully tracing each link in the chain of circumstances which had brought me to the spot whereon I now lay, deserted and alone, in that notorious Chickahominy swamp. And ere I was aware of it, I was sighing over a few episodes in my past history—and mentally saying, well, only for this intense love of adventure, such and such things "might have been," and I should now be rejoicing in the honorable title of —— ——, instead of "wasting my sweetness on the desert air," in the wilderness of the Peninsula.

> Of all the sad words, of tongue or of pen,
> The saddest are these—"*it might have been.*"

The cannonading was only the result of a reconnoissance, and in a few hours ceased altogether. But not so my fever and chills; they were my constant companions for two days and two nights in succession. At the end of that time I was an object of pity. With no medicine, no food, and consequently little strength; I was nearly in a state of starvation. My pies and cakes were spoiled in the basket, in consequence of the drenching they had received in crossing the river, and now I had no means of procuring more. But something must be done; I could not bear the thought of thus starving to death in that inglorious manner; better die upon the scaffold at Richmond, or be shot by the rebel pickets; anything but this. So I thought and said, as I rallied all my remaining strength to arrange my toilette preparatory to emerging from my concealment in the swamp.

It was about nine o'clock in the morning of the third day after crossing the river, when I started, as I thought, towards the enemy's lines, and a more broken-hearted, forlorn-looking "Bridget" never left "ould Ireland," than I appeared to be that morning. I traveled from that time until five o'clock in the afternoon, and was then deeper in the swamp than when I started. My head or brain was completely turned. I knew not which way to go, nor did I know east from west, or north from south.

It was a dark day in every sense of the word—and I had neither sun nor compass to guide me. At five o'clock the glorious booming of cannon reverberated through the dense wilderness, and to me, at that hour, it was the sweetest and most soul-inspiring music that ever greeted my ear. I now turned my face in the direction of the scene of action, and was not long in extricating myself from the desert which had so long enveloped me.

Soon after emerging from the swamp I saw, in the distance, a small white house, and thither I bent my weary footsteps. I found it deserted, with the exception of a sick rebel soldier, who lay upon a straw-tick on the floor in a helpless condition. I went to him, and assuming the Irish brogue, I inquired how he came to be left alone, and if I could render him any assistance. He could only speak in a low whisper, and with much difficulty, said he had been ill with typhoid fever a few weeks before, and had not fully recovered when General Stoneman attacked the

MAKING HOE-CAKE FOR A SICK REBEL.—Page 153.

rebels in the vicinity of Coal Harbor, and he was ordered to join his company. He participated in a sharp skirmish, in which the rebels were obliged to retreat; but he fell out by the way, and fearing to fall into the hands of the Yankees, he had crawled along as best he could, sometimes on his hands and knees, until he reached the house in which I found him.

He had not eaten anything since leaving camp, and he was truly in a starving condition. I did not dare say to him "ditto"—with regard to poor "Bridget's" case—but thought so, and realized it most painfully. He also told me that the family who had occupied the house had abandoned it since he came there, and that they had left some flour and corn-meal, but had not time to cook anything for him. This was good news for me, and exhausted as I was, I soon kindled a fire, and in less than fifteen minutes a large hoe-cake was before it in process of baking, and a sauce-pan of water heating, for there was no kettle to be found. After searching about the premises, I found some tea packed away in a small basket, with some earthearn ware, which the family had forgotten to take with them. My cake being cooked, and tea made, I fed the poor famished rebel as tenderly as if he had been my brother, and he seemed as grateful for my kindness, and thanked me with as much politeness, as if I had been Mrs. Jeff Davis. The next important item was to attend to the cravings of my own appetite, which I did without much ceremony.

After making my toilet and adjusting my wig in the most approved Irish style, I approached the sick man, and for the first time noticed his features and general appearance. He was a man about thirty years of age, was tall and had a slight figure, regular features, dark hair and large, mournful, hazel eyes; altogether he was a very pleasing and intelligent looking man. I thought him quite an interesting patient, and if I had had nothing more important to attend to, I should have enjoyed the privilege of caring for him until he recovered. It is strange how sickness and disease disarm our antipathy and remove our prejudices. There lay before me an enemy to the Government for which I was daily and willingly exposing my life and suffering unspeakable privation; he may have been the very man who took deadly aim at my friend and sent the cruel bullet through his temple; and yet, as I looked upon him in his helpless condition, I did not feel the least resentment, or entertain an unkind thought toward him personally, but looked upon him only as an unfortunate, suffering man, whose sad condition called forth the best feelings of my nature, and I longed to restore him to health and strength; not considering that the very health and strength which I wished to secure for him would be employed against the cause which I had espoused.

I had a great desire to know more of this man who had so strangely called forth my sympathies, and finding that he had grown stronger since he had partaken of some nourishment, I entered into conversation with him. I found that he was wholly and conscientiously a Confederate soldier, but, strange to say, completely divested of that inveterate hatred of the Yankees which is almost universal among the Southerners. I dared not express my sentiments in very strong terms, but gently interrogated him with regard to the right which he claimed the rebels had to take up arms against the United States Government.

At length I asked him if he professed to be a Soldier of the Cross; he replied with emotion and enthusiasm, "Yes, thank God! I have fought longer under the Captain of my Salvation than I have yet done under Jeff. Davis." My next and last question upon that subject was—"Can you, as a disciple of Christ, conscientiously and consistently uphold the institution of Slavery?" He made no reply, but fixed those mournful eyes on my face with a sad expression, as much as to say—"Ah, Bridget, you have touched a point upon which my own heart condemns me, and I know that God is greater than my heart, and will also condemn me."

In this earnest conversation I had unconsciously forgotten much of my Hibernian accent, and I thought that the sick man began to suspect that I was not what my appearance indicated. It alarmed me for a moment, but I soon recovered my composure after stepping forward and examining his pulse, for he was fast sinking, and the little strength which he seemed to have a short time before was nearly exhausted. After studying my countenance a few moments he asked me to pray with him. I did not dare to refuse the dying man's request, nor did I dare to approach my Maker in an assumed tone of voice; so I knelt down beside him, and in my own natural voice breathed a brief and earnest prayer for the departing soldier, for grace to sustain him in that trying hour, and finally for the triumph of truth and right.

When I arose from my knees he grasped my hand eagerly and said: "Please tell me who you are. I cannot, if I would, betray you, for I shall very soon be standing before that God whom you have just addressed." I could not tell him the truth and I would not tell him a falsehood, so I evaded a direct reply, but promised that when he became stronger I would tell him my history. He smiled languidly and closed his eyes, as much as to say that he understood me.

It was now growing late. I was not far from the rebel lines, but was not able to successfully act a part in my present debilitated condition, and besides, I was glad that I could consistently remain over night with that poor dying man, rebel though he was. I began to look around for something which I might convert into a light, but did not succeed in finding anything better than a piece of salt pork, which I fried, pouring the fat into a dish in which I put a cotton rag, and then lighting the end of the rag I found I had secured quite a respectable light. After making some corn-meal gruel for my patient, I took care to fasten the doors and windows so that no one could enter the house without my knowledge, and screened the windows so that no light might attract the rebel scouts.

Thus with a sort of feeling of security I took my seat beside the sick man. The dews of death were already gathering on his pallid brow. I took his hand in mine, examined his pulse again, and wiped the cold perspiration from his forehead. Oh how those beautiful eyes thanked me for these little acts of kindness! He felt in his heart that I did not sympathize with him as a rebel, but that I was willing to do all that a sister could do for him in this hour of trial. This seemed to call forth more gratitude than if I had been heart and hand with the South. He looked up suddenly and saw me weeping—for I could not restrain my tears—he seemed then to understand that he was really dying. Looking a little startled he exclaimed—"Am I really dying?"

Oh, how often have I been obliged to answer that awful question in the affirmative! "Yes, you are dying, my friend. Is your peace made with

God?" He replied, "My trust is in Christ; He was mine in life, and in death He will not forsake me"—almost the very words I heard a dying Federal soldier say, a few days before, at the hospital in Williamsburg. A few weeks previous these two men had been arrayed against each other in deadly strife; yet they were brethren; their faith and hope were the same; they both trusted in the same Saviour for salvation.

Then he said, "I have a last request to make. If you ever pass through the Confederate camp between this and Richmond inquire for Major McKee, of General Ewell's staff, and give him a gold watch which you will find in my pocket; he will know what to do with it; and tell him I died happy, peacefully." He then told me his name and the regiment to which he had belonged. His name was Allen Hall. Taking a ring from his finger he tried to put it on mine, but his strength failed, and after a pause he said, "Keep that ring in memory of one whose sufferings you have alleviated, and whose soul has been refreshed by your prayers in the hour of dissolution." Then folding his hands together as a little child would do at its mother's knee, he smiled a mute invitation for prayer. After a few moments' agonizing prayer in behalf of that departing spirit, the dying man raised himself up in the bed and cried out with his dying breath, "Glory to God! Glory to God! I am almost home!"

He was almost gone. I gave him some water, raised the window, and using my hat for a fan, I sat down and watched the last glimmering spark of light go out from those beautiful windows of the soul. Putting his hand in mine he signed to me to raise his head in my arms. I did so, and in a few moments he ceased to breathe.

He died about twelve o'clock—his hand clasping mine in the painful grip of death, my arm supporting him, and his head leaning on my bosom like a wearied child. I laid him down, closed his eyes, and straightened his rigid limbs; then folding his hands across his breast, I drew his blanket close around him and left him in the silent embrace of death. The beautiful, calm expression of his face made me think he looked

> Like one who wraps the drapery of his couch
> About him, and lies down to pleasant dreams.

This was rather a strange position for me to occupy at midnight—alone with death! Yet I thanked God that it was my privilege to be there; and I thanked Him for the religion of Jesus which was the strength of my heart in that trying hour. Yes, I could then rejoice in the providence which had detained me in the Chickahominy swamp, and had thus brought me to the bedside of that suffering stranger. Profound silence reigned supreme, and there was naught to chase away the darkness of that gloomy midnight hour save the consciousness that God was there.

I felt it good thus to be drawn away from the tumult of war, and there, in the presence of the angel of death, hold communion with my own heart and drink deep from the well of holy meditation. I thought there were happy spirits hovering round the lifeless form of him who was so lovable in life and lovely in death. Yes, I imagined the shining host had returned from escorting the triumphant spirit to the Throne of God, and were now watching the beautiful casket which had encased the bright spirit whose companionship had made some southern home bright and joyous.

I thought, too, of the loved ones who had gone and left me to finish my journey alone, and who would soon come to bear me away to that bright eternal world, if I only proved faithful unto death. "How impressively sad, how thrillingly beautiful, the lesson we glean from this silent spirit communion! Our physical nature starts and shudders at the thought of joining the silent numbers of the dead; but our spiritual nature catches a glimpse of that spirit-life beyond the portals of the tomb, where life, pure, free and joyous, shall be ours."

A lesson sad, but fraught with good—
A tearful one, but strengthening food—
Thou givest me;
We learn that "dust returns to dust,"
Anew in God we put our trust,
And bow the knee.

CHAPTER XII.

AM I A STOIC?—SOMEONE'S DARLING—COMPLETING MY DISGUISE—ANOTHER START FOR THE REBEL LINES—PEPPERING MY EYES—CHALLENGED BY A PICKET—A COCKNEY SENTINEL—GETTING INFORMATION—PLENTY OF BEEF, BUT NO SALT—RICE AND CORN MEAL BREAD—PREPARING TO VISIT HEADQUARTERS—INTERVIEW WITH MAJOR MC KEE—THE MAJOR'S MISPLACED CONFIDENCE—RETURN FOR THE BODY OF THE REBEL CAPTAIN—MY LOOK-OUT FOR YANKEES—NEW ORDERS.

PERHAPS some of my readers will pronounce me a stoic, entirely devoid of feeling, when I tell them that two hours after I wrapped the unconscious form of my late patient in his winding-sheet, I enveloped myself in my patchwork quilt, and laid me down not far from the corpse, and slept soundly until six o'clock in the morning. Feeling much refreshed I arose, and after spending a few moments by the side of my silent companion, contemplating the changes which the King of Terrors had wrought, I cut a lock of hair from his temple, took the watch and a small package of letters from his pocket, replaced the blanket reverently, and bade him farewell.

Kiss him once for somebody's sake
  Murmur a prayer soft and low;
One bright curl from its dark mates take,
  They were somebody's pride, you know:

Somebody's hand hath rested there—
Was it a mother's, soft and white?
And have the lips of a sister fair
Been baptized in their waves of light?

God knows best! He was sombebody's love;
Somebody's heart enshrined him there;
Somebody wafted his name above,
Night and morn, on the wings of prayer.
Somebody wept when he marched away,
Looking so handsome, brave and grand;
Somebody's kiss on his forehead lay,
Somebody clung to his parting hand.

Somebody 's waiting and watching for him,
Yearning to hold him again to her heart;
And there he lies with his dark eyes dim,
And the smiling, childlike lips apart.
Tenderly bury the fair young dead,
Pausing to drop in his grave a tear;
Carve on the wooden slab at his head
"Somebody's darling slumbers here."

After hastily partaking of a slight repast, which I could scarcely term breakfast, I commenced immediate preparations to leave the house. Upon examining the basket in which I had found the tea on my arrival, I found a number of articles which assisted me much in assuming a more perfect disguise. There was mustard, pepper, an old pair of green spectacles, and a bottle of red ink. Of the mustard I made a strong plaster about the size of a dollar, and tied it on one side of my face until it blistered it thoroughly. I then cut off the blister and put on a large patch of black court-plaster; with the ink I painted a red line around my eyes, and after giving my pale complexion a deep tinge with some ochre which I found in a closet, I put on my green glasses and my Irish hood, which came over my face about six inches.

I then made the tour of the house from garret to cellar, to find all the household fixings which an Irishwoman would be supposed to carry with her in such an emergency—for I expected to be searched before I was admitted through the the lines. I packed both my baskets, for I had two now, and was ready for another start. But before leaving I thought best to bury my pistol and every article in my possession which could in any way induce suspicion. Then taking a farewell look at the beautiful features of the dead, I left the house, going directly the nearest road to the rebel picket line. I felt perfectly safe in doing so, for the rebel soldier's watch was a sufficient passport in daylight, and a message for Major McKee would insure me civility at least.

I followed the Richmond road about five miles before meeting or seeing any one. At length I saw a sentinel in the distance, but before he observed me I sat down to rest and prepare my mind for the coming interview. While thus waiting to have my courage reinforced, I took from my basket the black pepper and sprinkled a little of it on my pocket handkerchief, which I applied to my eyes. The effect was all I could have desired, for taking a view of my prepossessing countenance in the small mirror which I always carried with me, I perceived that my eyes had a fine tender expression, which added very much to the beauty of their red borders. I was reminded of poor Leah of old who failed to secure the affection of her husband in consequence of a similar blemish, and thought myself safe from the slightest approach to admiration on the part of the chivalry.

I now resumed my journey, and displayed a flag of truce, a piece of a cotton window curtain which I brought from the house at which I had stopped over night. As I came nearer the picket-guard signaled to me to advance, which I did as fast as I could under the circumstances, being encumbered with two heavy baskets packed full of earthenware, clothing, quilts, etc. Upon coming up to the guard, instead of being dismayed at his formidable appearance, I felt rejoiced, for there stood before me an immense specimen of a jolly Englishman, with a bland smile on his good-natured face, provoked, I presume, by the supremely ludicrous figure I presented.

He mildly questioned me with regard to my hopes and fears, whence I came and whither I was going, and if I had seen any Yankees. My sorrowful story was soon told. My peppery handkerchief was freely applied to my eyes, and the tears ran down my face without the least effort on my part. The good-natured guard's sympathy was excited, more especially as I was a foreigner like himself, and he told me I could pass along and go just wherever I pleased, so far as he was concerned, adding in a sad tone, "I wish I was hat 'ome with my family, hand then Jeff. Davis hand the Confederacy might go to 'ell for hall me. Hinglishmen 'ave no business 'ere."

I mentally exclaimed, "Good for you—you are one after my own heart," but I replied to the Englishman's patriotic speech after the following manner: "Och, indade I wish yez was all at home wid yer families, barrin them as have no families; an sure its we poor craythurs of wimen that's heart-broken intirely, an fairly kilt wid this onnathral war;" and here my eyes were again carefully wiped with my handkerchief.

After thanking the picket-guard for his kindness, I went on my way toward the rebel camp. I had not gone far when the guard called me back and advised me not to stay in camp over night, for, said he, "One of our spies has just come in and reported that the Yankees have finished the bridges across the Chickahominy, and intend to attack us either to-day or to-night, but Jackson and Lee are ready for them." He went on to tell me how many masked batteries they had prepared, and said he, "There is one," pointing to a brush-heap by the roadside, "that will give them fits if they come this way."

Feeling somewhat in a hurry, I started once more for camp. I concluded after getting through the lines that I could dispense with one of my baskets, so setting one of them down under a tree I felt much more comfortable, and was not quite so conspicuous an object going into camp. I went directly to headquarters and inquired for Major McKee. I was told that he would not be there before evening, and my informant drawled out after me, "He 's gone to set a trap for the d—d Yankees."

I made up my mind at once that I must find out as much as possible before night, and make my way back before the impending battle came on. Upon looking around the camp I saw a shanty where some negro women were cooking meat. I went and told them that I was hungry and would like to have something to eat. "Oh yes, honey, we'se got lots o' meat and bread, but haint got no salt; but reckon ye can eat it without." So saying an old auntie brought me a piece of boiled fresh beef and some bread; but I could not make out what the bread was made of; as near as I could guess, however, it was made of boiled rice and corn-meal, and that also was without salt.

I thought it would be well to look a little smarter before I presented myself at headquarters again, lest I might not meet with that confidence which I felt it was important for me to secure. My patched and painted face made it impossible for any one to define the expression of my countenance. My blistered cheek was becoming very painful in consequence of the drawing of the court-plaster. I took off my glasses and bathed my face in clear, cold water, which did not remove much of the color, but made me a shade more like myself; then I succeeded in getting one of the colored women to go to the doctor's quarters and get me some unguent, or simple cerate, with which I dressed the blister. My eyes were sufficiently disfigured by this time to dispense with the glasses, so putting them in my basket I laid them aside for another occasion. There was no difficulty in finding out the force of the enemy or their plans for the coming battle, for every one, men and women, seemed to think and talk of nothing else.

Five o'clock came, and with it Major McKee. I lost no time in presenting myself before his majorship, and with a profound Irish courtesy I made known my business, and delivered the watch and package. I did not require any black pepper now to assist the lachrymal glands in performing their duty, for the sad mementoes which I had just delivered to the major so forcibly reminded me of the scenes of the past night that I could not refrain from weeping. The major, rough and stern as he was, sat there with his face between his hands and sobbed like a child. Soon he rose to his feet, surveyed me from head to foot, and said, "You are a faithful woman, and you shall be rewarded."

He then asked: "Can you go direct to that

house, and show my men where Allen's body is?" I answered in the affirmative—whereupon he handed me a ten dollar Federal bill, saying, as he did so: "If you succeed in finding the house, I will give you as much more." I thanked him, but positively declined taking the money. He did not seem to understand the philosophy of a person in my circumstances refusing money, and when I looked at him again his face wore a doubtful, puzzled expression, which alarmed me. I was actually frightened, and bursting into a passionate fit of weeping, I exclaimed vehemently: "Oh, Gineral, forgive me! but me conshins wud niver give me pace in this world nor in the nixt, if I wud take money for carying the dyin missage for that swate boy that's dead and gone—God rest his soul. Och, indade, indade I nivir cud do sich a mane thing, if I im a poor woman." The major seemed satisfied, and told me to wait until he returned with a detachment of men.

When he returned with the men, I told him that I did not feel able to walk that distance, and requested him to let me have a horse, stating the fact that I had been sick for several days, and had slept but little the night before. He did not answer a word, but ordered a horse saddled immediately, which was led forward by a colored boy, who assisted me to mount. I really felt mean, and for the first time since I had acted in the capacity of spy, I despised myself for the very act which I was about to perform. I must betray the confidence which that man reposed in me. He was too generous to harbor a suspicion against me, and thus furnished me the very means of betraying him.

This feeling did not last long, however, for as we started on our mission he said to his men: "Now, boys, bring back the body of Captain Hall, if you have to walk through Yankee blood to the knees." That speech eased my conscience considerably. I was surprised to hear him say "Captain Hall," for I did not know until then that he was an officer. There was nothing about his uniform or person to indicate his rank, and I had supposed he was a private soldier.

We made our way toward the house very cautiously, lest we should be surprised by the Federals. I rode at the head of the little band of rebels as guide, not knowing but that I was leading them into the jaws of death every step we advanced, and if so it would probably be death for me as well as for them. Thus we traveled those five miles, silently, thoughtfully, and stealthily. The sun had gone down behind the western hills, and the deepening shadows were fast gathering around us as we came in sight of the little white cottage in the forest, where I had so recently spent such a strangely, awfully solemn night.

The little detachment halted to rest, and to make arrangements before approaching the house.

This detachment consisted of twenty-four men, under a sergeant and a corporal. The men were divided into squads, each of which was to take its turn at carrying the body of their late Captain upon a stretcher, which they had brought for that purpose. As we drew near, and saw no sign of an approaching enemy, they regretted that they had not brought an ambulance; but I did not regret it, for the present arrangement suited me exactly. Having settled things satisfactorily among themselves, we again resumed our march and were soon at the gate. The sergeant then ordered the corporal to proceed to the house with a squad of men and bring out the corpse, while he stationed the remaining men to guard all the approaches to the house.

He then asked me to ride down the road a little way, and if I should see or hear anything of the Yankees to ride back as fast as possible and let them know. I assented, and joyfully complied with the first part of his request. This was a very pleasant duty assigned me, for which I mentally thanked the sergeant a thousand times. I turned and rode slowly down the road, but not "seeing or hearing anything of the Yankees," I thought it best to keep on in that direction until I did. I was like the zouave, after the battle of Bull Run, who said he was ordered to retreat, but not being ordered to halt at any particular place, he preferred to keep on until he reached New York. So

I preferred to keep on until I reached the Chickahominy, where I reported progress to the Federal general.

I had no desire to have that little escort captured, and consequently said nothing about it in my report; so the sergeant, with his men, were permitted to return to the rebel camp unmolested, bearing with them the remains of their beloved captain. After getting out of sight of the rebel guards, I made that horse go over the ground about as fast, I think, as he ever did before—which seemed to give him a bad impression of Yankees in general, and of me in particular, for ever after that night, it was as much as a person's life was worth to saddle him; at every attempt he would kick and bite most savagely.

The next day the following order was issued: "Upon advancing beyond the Chickahominy the troops will go prepared for battle at a moment's notice, and will be entirely unencumbered, with the exception of ambulances. All vehicles will be left on the eastern side of the Chickahominy, and carefully packed.

"The men will leave their knapsacks, packed, with the wagons, and will carry three days rations. The arms will be put in perfect order before the troops march, and a careful inspection made of them, as well as of the cartridge-boxes, which in all cases will contain at least forty rounds; twenty additional rounds will be carried by the men in their pockets. Commanders of batteries will see that their limber and caisson-boxes are filled to their utmost capacity.

"Commanders of Army Corps will devote their personal attention to the fulfillment of these orders, and will personally see that the proper arrangements are made for packing and properly guarding the trains and surplus baggage, taking all the steps necessary to insure their being brought promptly to the front when needed; they will also take steps to prevent the ambulances from interfering with the movements of any troops. Sufficient guards and staff-officers will be detailed to carry out these orders. The ammunition-wagons will be in readiness to march to their respective brigades and batteries at a moment's warning, but will not cross the Chickahominy until they are sent for. All quarter-masters and ordnance officers are to remain with their trains.

"In the approaching battle the general commanding trusts that the troops will preserve the discipline which he has been so anxious to enforce, and which they have so generally observed. He calls upon all the officers and soldiers to obey promptly and intelligently all the orders they may receive; let them bear in mind that the Army of the Potomac has never yet been checked, and let them preserve in battle perfect coolness and confidence, the sure forerunners of success. They must keep well together, throw away no shots, but aim carefully and low, and, above all things, rely upon the bayonet. Commanders of regiments are reminded of the great responsibility that rests upon them; upon their coolness, judgment and discretion, the destinies of their regiments and success of the day will depend."

CHAPTER XIII.

OUR COMMUNICATIONS WITH THE CHICKAHOMINY—PORTER'S SUCCESSES—DESPATCHES TO THE PRESIDENT—HIS REPLY—HANOVER COURT HOUSE—TERRIBLE STORM AND FLOOD—HOPES OF THE ENEMY—A SUDDEN AND STRONG ATTACK—I ACT AS AN ORDERLY—THROUGH THE FLOOD—MY RETURN AND REPORT—JOYFUL NEWS—MY OWN DISASTER—SCENES IN THE OLD MILL—WAITING ON THE WOUNDED—MY SUFFERINGS BY THE ROADSIDE—A HARD-HEARTED CHAPLAIN—A STUMBLING BLOCK.

FOR several days the enemy had been concentrating a large force on the right flank of the Federals, with the intention of cutting off their communications with the river. A portion of Fitz John Porter's corps was detailed to dispose of this force, and also to cut the Virginia Central, Richmond and Fredericksburg railroads. The communication was cut off, and after two severe engagements the enemy retreated, leaving behind them several hundred prisoners, their cannon and camp equipage. On the same day the following despatch was sent to the Secretary of War by the commanding general:

"Camp near New Bridge, May 28th. Porter has gained two complete victories over superior forces; yet I feel obliged to move in the morning with reinforcements to secure the complete destruction of the rebels in that quarter. In doing so I run some risk here, but cannot help it. The enemy are even in greater force than I had supposed. I will do all that quick movements can accomplish, but you must send me all the troops you can, and leave me to full latitude as to choice of commanders. It is absolutely necessary to destroy the rebels near Hanover Court House before I can advance."

To which the President replied: "I am very glad of General Porter's victory. Still, if it was a total rout of the enemy, I am puzzled to know why the Richmond and Fredericksburg railroad was not seized again, as you say you have all the railroads but the Richmond and Fredericksburg. I am painfully impressed with the importance of the struggle before you, and shall aid you all I can consistently with my view of due regard to other points."

Two days later McClellan telegraphs again: "From the tone of your despatches I do not think that you appreciate the value and magnitude of Porter's victory. It has entirely relieved my right flank, which was seriously threatened, it has routed and demoralized a considerable portion of the rebel forces, taken over seven hundred and fifty prisoners, killed and wounded large numbers; one gun, many small arms, and much baggage taken. It was one of the handsomest things in the war, both in itself and in its results. Porter has returned, and my army is again well in hand. Another day will make the probable field of battle passable for artillery. It is quite certain that there is nothing in front of McDowell at Fredericksburg. I regard the burning of South Anne bridge as the least important result of Porter's movement."

The battle of Hanover Court House was certainly a splendid affair, and a very important victory to the Army of the Potomac. Three days after this battle, while the army was divided by the river, a portion of the troops having crossed over the day before, a most fearful storm swept over the Peninsula, accompanied with terrible exhibitions of lightning and explosions of thunder. The water came down all night and all day in perfect floods, completely inundating the valley through which the Chickahominy flows, turning the narrow stream into a broad river, converting the swamps into lakes, and carrying away one bridge and rendering the other unsafe. And still the rain came pouring down in torrents, reminding one of that crisis in the world's history when "the fountains of the great deep were broken up, and the windows of heaven were opened." Had it not been for McClellan's faith in the bible and in God's covenant with Noah, he would no doubt have seriously contemplated building an ark, in order to save himself and his army from destruction. The rebels seemed to think this flood was sent as a judgment from the Almighty upon their hated enemies, and was a direct interposition of Providence in their behalf, which would enable them to visit wholesale destruction upon the Yankees.

On the thirtieth of May the enemy, taking advantage of this terrible state of things caused by the disastrous storm, came rushing down upon our troops in immense force. A battle opened at about one o'clock in the afternoon, and after three hours' desperate fighting, General Casey's division, occupying the first line, was compelled to fall back in considerable disorder upon the second line, causing temporary confusion; but the rapid advance of Generals Heintzelman and Kearney with their divisions soon checked the rebels. Sumner, Sedgwick, Couch, Keyes and the other commanders also labored valiantly to retrieve the injury effected by the unfortunate retirement of Casey's command.

The enemy, led by Hill and Longstreet, advanced in massive columns, with threefold lines, and came boldly on like an overwhelming wave, as if determined to crush all opposition by the suddenness and fierceness of the attack. Total annihilation seemed to be their motto, and the determined and reckless daring of the fierce and bloodthirsty rebels in such overpowering numbers carried conviction to many loyal hearts that they would succeed in driving that devoted fragment of an army into the Chickahominy, before it would be possible for reinforcements to arrive.

At this time I was in military uniform, mounted upon my rebel horse, and was acting orderly for General K. Several aides and orderlies had been sent with messages and despatches, but no reinforcement had yet arrived, and, taking a Federal view of it, the picture presented a gloomy appearance. General K. reined in his horse abruptly, and taking from his pocket an envelope, he hastily wrote on the back of it with a pencil—"In the name of God bring your command to our relief, if you have to swim in order to get here—or we are lost." Handing it to me he said—"Go just as fast as that horse can carry you to General G., present this with my compliments, return immediately, and report to me."

I put poor little "Reb" over the road at the very top of his speed until he was nearly white with foam, then plunged him into the Chickahominy and swam him across the river. I met General G. about a hundred rods from the river making the best of his way toward the bridge. Engineers were at once set to work strengthening the crazy structure, which was swaying to and fro with the rushing tide. The eager, excited troops dashed into the water waist deep, and getting upon the floating planks went pouring over in massive columns. I preferred to swim my horse back again rather than risk myself upon such a bridge, for I looked every moment to see it give way and engulf the whole division in the turbid waters of the swollen creek. However, all reached the other side in safety, and started along the flooded road on the double quick. This was cheering news to carry back to General K., so I started again for the field in order to claim the reward of "him who bringeth good tidings."

I found General K. in the thickest of the fight, encouraging his men and shouting his orders distinctly above the roar and din of battle. Riding up to him and touching my hat, I reported—"Just returned, sir. General G., with his command, will be here immediately." It was too good to keep to himself, so he turned to his men and shouted at the top of his voice—"Reinforcements! reinforcements!" then swinging his hat in the air he perfectly electrified the whole line as far as his voice could reach, and the glorious word "reinforcements" was passed along until that almost exhausted line was reanimated and inspired with new hope.

While I was thus watching with delight the effects of this joyful news upon the soldiers, my attention was directed to another object. General H., who had made himself conspicuous by his gal-

ACTING ORDERLY.—Page 178.

lant conduct, was struck by a ball which shattered his arm badly. He was only a few rods from me, and there was none near to help him. I asked General K. if I might go to him, and after obtaining permission I rode up to him, leaped from my horse, and hitched him near by. I then removed the clothing from his arm, gave him some water, poured some on the wound, and went to my saddle-bags to get some bandages, when my rebel pony laid hold of my arm with his teeth and almost tore the flesh from the bone. Not content with that, he turned his heels in an instant and kicked with both feet, sending me about a rod. My arm was now almost as bad as General H.'s, and I could do but little to help him, for in ten minutes it was swollen terribly, and I could not raise it to my head; finally I was ordered back to an old saw-mill about a mile and a half from the field, where were considerable quantities of quartermasters' and commissary stores, with orders to have them removed further to the rear; and all who were able to come to the front, together with the surgeon and a portion of the hospital corps who had been left there in charge of the sick, were to lose no time in reporting themselves for duty on the field.

Upon arriving at the old saw-mill I found it crowded with wounded men who had crawled there from the battle-field, to have their wounds dressed if possible, and if not to lie down and suffer where the shot and shell could not reach them. I delivered my orders. In a few moments more there was not a soul left to minister to those poor fellows who were huddled together in that mill by the score; all had gone to the front, and I was left there in a sad plight.

I put my vicious little "Reb" in a building near the mill, where there was plenty of hay and corn, but did not dare to unsaddle him. I then examined the extent of the injury done to my arm, and found it was worse than I had supposed. It was badly mangled by the horse's teeth, and in one place a large piece of flesh was torn from the arm and hung by small shreds. But the arm was not the worst; he had kicked me in the side, which had lamed and bruised me sadly. Yet this was no time to groan over a slight kick from a horse, when so many lay around me with shattered limbs and ghastly saber wounds, some of them even now in the very agonies of death. So, resolutely saying to pain and lameness, "Stay thou here while I go yonder," I bound up my arm in a sling, and set about removing the blood-clotted clothing from the wounds of those who needed it most; but having neither knife or scissors, I was obliged in many instances to use my teeth in order to tear the thick woolen garments stiffened and saturated with blood, the very remembrance of which now makes me feel rather uncomfortable in the gastric region; but then there was no unpleasant sensation.

The next thing to be thought of was, how I could procure some bandages; but as to getting them from the saddle-bags, I would as soon have thought of bearding a lion in his den, as of tempting the jaws of that ferocious animal again. However, there were two houses within a mile, and I decided to try my fortune in that direction. First of all I went among the sick, who were left there by the surgeon, and inquired if there were any who were able to assist me in dressing wounds. Yes, I found two; one a little mail-carrier, and the other a commissary sergeant, both of whom were scarcely able to stand alone. These two I set to work pouring cold water upon the wounded limbs occasionally, and giving the men water to drink until I returned.

At the first house I went to they would not let me in at all, but raised the window and wished to know what was wanted. I told them, anything that would admit of tearing up for bandages. No, they had nothing of the kind, and closed the window again. I limped along to the next house. A man came to the door, holding it, to prevent my attempting to get in. The same question was asked, and a similar answer returned. By this time my patience and strength were both exhausted, and my mind was made up with regard to the course I should pursue. Therefore, drawing both my pistols from my belt, I demanded some cotton, new or old—sheets, pillow-cases, or any other article which would answer the purpose for bandages. The man trembled from head to foot, and called his wife to know if she could let me have anything of the sort; yes, she could, if I would pay her for it; and of course I was willing to pay her; so she brought me an old sheet, a pair of pillow-cases, and three yards of new factory cotton cloth, for which she demanded five dollars. Happening to have only three dollars in change, I told her I thought that would be sufficient; and so saying, I left immediately.

I did not know, until I had proceeded some distance, that the blood was running from my arm in a perfect stream. In my excitement and determination, I had grasped one of my pistols with the lame hand and started those terrible gashes bleeding afresh. I grew faint and dizzy, and sat down by the road-side to gather a little strength before proceeding further. While I sat there I saw a horseman coming in the distance, but could not tell whether it was friend or foe, for it was growing dark. I waited until he came nearer, when I was rejoiced to see that it was a chaplain; not Mr. B., but of course he was a good man, being a chaplain and a Federal. So I felt that relief was at hand. But imagine my disappointment and chagrin when he came up and, priest-like, looked upon me, "and passed by on the other side." Well, after all, I did not care so much for myself, but I thanked heaven that he had come on the poor men's account, for he would, no doubt, do much during the night to relieve their sufferings.

Taking courage, I made my way slowly toward the mill, where I found, on my arrival, the chaplain dismounted, coat off, and wisp in hand, rubbing and brushing every speck of mud from his horse. After performing this important duty, he then went to the nearest house, ordered supper, and after partaking of a warm meal, he returned to the mill. Oh how glad I was that all these preliminaries were gone through with, for now he would at once enter upon the care of the wounded, and my heart ached for those two sick boys, who were still attending to the wants of such as they could assist, notwithstanding they required waiting upon themselves.

The wounded were coming in faster than ever, and I was busy tearing up the cotton in strips, and trying to bind up some of the poor mangled limbs, the little sick sergeant being my right hand man. I looked around for the chaplain, but he was no where to be seen. I hobbled out to the building where I had seen him put his horse, to see if he had really gone away; no, he had not gone. There he lay on the floor, upon which was a quantity of hay, wrapped up in his blanket, apparently unconscious that there was any such thing as suffering in the world. Oh how I wanted to go to him, quietly lay my hand on him, and say:

"Chaplain, will you be so kind as to take the saddle from my horse; it has been on since early morning, and I am not able to take it off." Not that I cared particularly for having the saddle removed, but just for sake of having "Reb" bring the chaplain to his senses, and give him a little shaking up, so that he might realize that these were war times, and that consequently it was out of the question for chaplains in the army, especially in time of battle, to

Be carried to the skies
 On flowery beds of ease;
While others fought to win the prize,
 And sailed through bloody seas.

But instead of doing so, I sat down and wept bitter tears of disappointment and sorrow, and then, with a heavy heart and aching limbs, I returned again to the mill.

All that weary night my heart burned with indignation, and I seemed endowed with supernatural powers of endurance, for when morning came and found me still at my post, without having tasted food for twenty-four hours, I felt stronger and fresher than I had done the day before. My two young sick friends had been persuaded to lie down, and were now fast asleep, side by side with the wounded. But where was the chaplain? What had become of him? He had escaped with the earliest dawn, without so much as inquiring whether the men were dead or alive. This was the conduct of a man who professed to be a faithful follower of Him who went about doing good! This was a man whom I had reverenced and loved as a brother in Christ. Oh, what a stumbling-block that man was to my soul; for weeks and months Satan took occasion to make this a severe temptation and trial to me. I was tempted to judge every christian by that unholy example, and to doubt the truth of every christian experience which I heard related from time to time. But, thank God, I had the example of my faithful friend, Mr. B., to counterbalance this, and by God's grace I was enabled to rise above this temptation. My doubts were gradually removed, and my faith in christians re-established—but I never sufficiently recovered from my feelings of disgust towards that particular chaplain, to ever again be able to persuade myself to listen to a sermon delivered by him, or to attend any religious meeting at which he presided. I always looked upon him afterwards, as "one who had stolen the livery of heaven to serve the devil in;" a mere whited sepulchre, and unworthy the sacred name of a minister of the Gospel.

Oh, may our sympathizing breasts
That generous pleasure know;
Kindly to share in others' joy,
And weep for others' woe.

When poor and helpless sons of grief
In deep distress are laid;
Soft be our hearts their pains to feel,
And swift our hands to aid.

On wings of love the Saviour flew,
To bless a ruined race;
We would, O Lord, thy steps pursue,
Thy bright example trace.

CHAPTER XIV.

RENEWAL OF THE BATTLE—VICTORY FOR THE FEDERAL ARMS—ADDRESS TO THE ARMY—MORE DESPATCHES—MY BATTLE TROPHY—PONY REB'S PERFORMANCES—THE HOSPITAL TREE—TOUCHING SCENES—BISHOP SIMPSON—THE CROSS AND THE FLAG—AFTER THE BATTLE—DELAYS BY STORMS, FLOODS AND MUD—MC CLELLAN'S CALL FOR MORE MEN—IN READINESS TO MARCH—PROMISED REINFORCEMENTS.

NIGHT brought a cessation of hostilities to the weary troops, but to neither side a decided victory or defeat. Both armies bivouaced on the bloody field, within a few rods of each other. There they lay waiting for the morning light to decide the contest. The excitement and din of battle had ceased; those brief hours of darkness proved a sweet respite from the fierce struggle of the day, and in the holy calm of that midnight hour, when silence brooded over the blood-washed plain, many brave soldiers lay down on that gory field—

The weary to sleep, and the wounded to die.

Sunday, the first of June, dawned beautifully, a day of hallowed rest and promise to the millions who rose to their devotions, ere the bell called them to the house of prayer, but not of rest to the weary, broken armies the drum-beat called from their wet and muddy beds to renew the contest. At a quarter-past seven o'clock the battle again commenced, and raged fiercely until about noon. Both armies fought with determination and heroic bravery until the rebels were compelled to yield, and victory once more perched upon the banners of the National troops.

I came on the field about ten o'clock, and remained until the close of the battle, but could do little more than look upon the terrible scene. General McClellan was on the field when I arrived. I saw him ride along the entire battle-front, and if I had not seen him, I could not have long remained in ignorance of his presence—for the cheers from all parts of the Federal lines told as plainly as words could express that their beloved commander was with them, amid that desperate struggle for victory. It was a terrible slaughter—more than fifteen thousand lay upon the field. It was enough to make angels weep, to look down upon that field of carnage. The dead and wounded of the enemy fell into the hands of the Unionists, which added fearfully to the labors of that exhausted, battle-worn army.

On the evening of the third of June, General McClellan issued the following address to his troops, which was read on dress parade, and was received with tremendous cheering:

"Soldiers of the Army of the Potomac! I have

fulfilled at least a part of my promise to you. You are now face to face with the rebels, who are held at bay in front of their capital. The final and decisive battle is at hand. Unless you belie your past history, the result cannot be for a moment doubtful. If the troops who labored so faithfully at Yorktown, and fought so bravely, and won the hard fights at Williamsburg, West Point, Hanover Court-house and Fair Oaks, now prove themselves worthy of their antecedents, the victory is surely ours. The events of every day prove your superiority; wherever you have met the enemy, you have beaten him; wherever you have used the bayonet, he has given way in panic and disorder.

"I ask of you, now, one last crowning effort. The enemy has staked his all on the issue of the coming battle. Let us meet him, crush him here, in the very centre of the rebellion. Soldiers! I will be with you in this battle, and share its dangers with you. Our confidence in each other is now founded upon the past. Let us strike the blow which is to restore peace and union to this distracted land. Upon your valor, discipline and mutual confidence, the result depends."

Every battle fought on the Peninsula fearfully reduced the strength of the Army of the Potomac, and proved to a demonstration that the enemy far outnumbered the Union forces. Still there were no reinforcements, notwithstanding McClellan's daily urgent despatches to the President and Secretary of War, and the great impending battle in front of the rebel Capital so near at hand.

The next day McClellan sent another despatch, as follows:

"Please inform me at once what reinforements, if any, I can count upon having at Fortress Monroe or White House, within the next three days, and when each regiment may be expected to arrive. It is of the utmost importance that I should know this immediately. The losses in the battle of the thirty-first and first will amount to seven thousand. Regard this as confidential for the present. After the losses in our last battle, I trust that I shall no longer be regarded as an alarmist. I believe we have at least one more desperate battle to fight."

The day after the battle of Fair Oaks, a splendid sword was presented to me. It had been struck from the hand of a rebel colonel, while in the act of raising it to strike one of our officers after he had fallen from his horse. Oh, how proud I felt of that beautiful silver-mounted trophy, from the bloody field of Fair Oaks, which had so recently been wielded by a powerful arm, but powerless now, for he lay in the agonies of death, while his splendid sword had passed into my feeble hands. I presume if he had known this, it would have added another pang to his already agonized spirit. The sword was presented by General K., to whom I gave my rebel pony, with the comforting assurance that he was only intended for ornament, and not for use; for generals were too scarce on the Peninsula to risk their precious lives by coming in contact with him. The General was delighted with him, and without paying the slightest attention to my suggestion deliberately walked up to the pony and commenced patting him and handling his limbs as if he were the most quiet creature in the world, while "Reb" stood eyeing his new master with apparent satisfaction, and seemed to rejoice that he had passed from my insignificant hands, and was henceforth to be the honored bearer of. shoulder-straps. After thoroughly examining him he said: "He is certainly a splendid horse, and worth three hundred dollars of any man's money; all he requires is kind treatment, and he will be as gentle as any one could desire."

But "Reb" very soon gave him to understand decidedly that he was overrating his good qualities; for no sooner had the General turned his back toward him than he struck him between the shoulders with both hind feet, sending him his full length upon the ground; and as soon as he attempted to rise he repeated the same performance until he had knocked him down four or five times in succession. By that time the General was pretty thoroughly convinced that "Reb's" social qualities were somewhat deficient, his bump of combativeness largely developed, and his gymnastics quite impressive.

On the evening of the same day in which the victory was won I visited what was then, and is still called, the "hospital tree," near Fair Oaks. It was an immense tree under whose shady, extended branches the wounded were carried and laid down to await the stimulant, the opiate, or the amputating knife, as the case might require. The ground around that tree for several acres in extent was literally drenched with human blood, and the men were laid so close together that there was no such thing as passing between them; but each one was removed in their turn as the surgeons could attend to them. I witnessed there some of the most heart-rending sights it is possible for the human mind to conceive. Read what a Massachusetts chaplain writes concerning it:

"There is a large tree near the battle-ground of Fair Oaks, the top of which was used as an observatory during the fight, which stands as a memento of untold, and perhaps never to be told, suffering and sorrow. Many of the wounded and dying were laid beneath its branches after the battle, in order to receive surgical help, or to breathe their last more quietly. What heart-rending scenes did I witness in that place, so full of saddened memories to me and to others. Brave, uncomplaining men were brought thither out of the woodland, the crimson tide of whose life was ebbing away in the arms of those who carried them. Almost all who died met death like heroes, with scarcely a groan. Those wounded, but not mortally—how nobly they bore the necessary probings and needed ampðtations! Two instances of this heroic fortitude deserve to be specially mentioned. One of them is that of William C. Bentley, of the Second Rhode Island regiment, both of whose legs were broken by a bomb-shell, whose wrist and breast were mangled, and who yet was as calm as if he suffered no pain. He refused any opiate or stimulant that might dim his consciousness. He asked only that we should pray for him, that he might be patient and submissive, and dictated a letter to be sent to his mother. Then, and not till then, opiates were given him, and he fell gently asleep, and for the last time.

"The other case was that of Francis Sweetzer, of Company E, of the Sixteenth Massachusetts Regiment, who witnessed in death, as he had uniformly done in life, a good confession of Christ. 'Thank God,' he said, 'that I am permitted to die for my country. Thank God more yet that I am prepared to die;' and then after a moment's thought he modestly added, 'at least I hope I am.' When he died he was in the act of prayer, and in that position his limbs grew rigid, and so remained after the spirit had left his body."

Oh, who that has witnessed such triumphant deaths on the battle-field will presume to doubt that the spirit of that patriot who falls amid the terrible clash of arms and the fierce surge of battle, is prepared to go from that scene of blood and strife, and to enter into that rest that God has prepared for them that love Him? Yes, the noble men who have gone from under the sheltering wings of the different evangelical churches throughout the land, have gone in the strength of God, and with the full assurance that if they should fall fighting for the God-given rights of humanity, there, amid the shock of battle, the still, small voice of Jesus would be heard speaking peace to the departing soul, and that their triumphant spirits would go home rejoicing to be forever with the Lord! When I see a man first lay himself upon the altar of God, and then upon the altar of his country, I have no fear for that man's happiness in time or in eternity.

Good Bishop Simpson, of the Methodist Episcopal Church, soon after the outbreak of the great rebellion, delivered a sermon on the National crisis, at Chicago. It is represented as one of the ablest efforts of this clergyman, so distinguished for his power in the pulpit. As it was one of the anniversaries of the denomination, thousands were present to hear the discourse. Suddenly, at one point in the sermon, and as the fitting close of a most impassioned paragraph, he gave utterance to the following noble sentiment: "We will take our glorious flag, the flag of our country, and nail it just below the cross! That is high enough. There let it wave as it waved of old. Around it let us gather: first Christ's; then our country's." Oh, that the sentiments of the following beautiful lines were the sentiments of every heart in the United States:

O Lord of Hosts! Almighty King!
Behold the sacrifice we bring!
To every arm thy strength impart,
Thy spirit shed through every heart!

Wake in our breasts the living fires,
The holy faith that warmed our sires;
Thy hand hath made our nation free;
To die for her is serving Thee.

Be Thou a pillar'd flame to show
The midnight snare, the silent foe,
And when the battle thunders loud,
Still guide us in its moving cloud.

God of all nations! sovereign Lord!
In thy dread name we draw the sword,
We lift the starry flag on high
That fills with light our stormy sky.

No more its flaming emblems wave
To bar from hope the trembling slave;
No more its radiant glories shine
To blast with woe one child of Thine!

From treason's rent, from murderer's stain,
Guard Thou its folds till peace shall reign,
Till fort and field, till shore and sea,
Join our loud anthem, Praise to Thee!

I cannot better describe the state of affairs after the battle of Fair Oaks than by giving the following despatch from McClellan, dated June 7th: "In reply to your despatch of 2 p. m. to-day, I have the honor to state that the Chickahominy river has risen so as to flood the entire bottoms to the depth of three or four feet; I am pushing forward the bridges in spite of this, and the men are working night and day, up to their waists in water, to complete them. The whole face of the country is a perfect bog, entirely impassable for artillery, or even cavalry, except directly in the narrow roads, which renders any general movement, either of this or the rebel army, entirely out of the question until we have more favorable weather. I am glad to learn that you are pressing forward reinforcements so vigorously. I shall be in perfect readiness to move forward and take Richmond the moment McCall reaches here and the ground will admit the passage of artillery. I have advanced my pickets about a mile to-day, driving off the rebel pickets and securing a very advantageous position. The rebels have several batteries established, commanding the debouches from two of our bridges, and fire upon our working parties continually; but as yet they have killed but few of our men."

Again, June 10th, he says: "I am completely checked by the weather. The roads and fields are literally impassable for artillery—almost so for infantry. The Chickahominy is in a dreadful state. We have another rain storm on our hands. I wish to be distinctly understood that whenever the weather permits I will attack with whatever force I may have, although a larger force would enable me to gain much more decisive results. I would be glad to have McCall's infantry sent forward by water at once, without waiting for his artillery and cavalry."

The next day the Secretary of War replied: "Your despatch of 3.30 p. m. yesterday has been received. I am fully impressed with the difficulties mentioned, and which no art or skill can avoid, but only endure. Be assured, General, that there never has been a moment when my desire has been otherwise than to aid you with my whole heart, mind and strength, since the hour we first met; and whatever others may say for their own purposes, you never have had, and never can have, any one more truly your friend, or more anxious to support you, or more joyful than I shall be at the success which I have no doubt will soon be achieved by your arms."

The above despatch has the appearance of the genuine article—but I am inclined to think it a clever counterfeit. While McClellan's requests were cheerfully complied with, as far as promises were concerned, little was done to strengthen his weakened forces in view of the coming struggle with an overwhelming force in front, and the flooded Chickahominy in the rear. By unreliable promises he was filled with delusive hopes, and lead on to more certain destruction—to disaster and failure, at least.

CHAPTER XV.

LEAVE OF ABSENCE—VISIT TO THE WILLIAMSBURG HOSPITALS—EFFECTIVE PREACHING—YORKTOWN REVISITED—LONGINGS—WHITE HOUSE LANDING—TIRED OF IDLENESS—PREPARATIONS TO RETURN TO DUTY—STUART'S CAVALRY RAID—A TRAIN FIRED INTO—FAIR OAKS GROVE—THE STRENGTH OF THE ENEMY—TRYING TIMES ON THE PENINSULA—THE ENDURANCE OF OUR SOLDIERS—LABORS OF MR. ALVORD.

WHILE preparations were going on for the great battle in front of Richmond, I obtained leave of absence for a week, and recruited my shattered health, lame side and arm. Mr. and Mrs. B. were both gone home on furlough, and Nellie was at the Williamsburg Hospital. I thought I should like to visit the different hospitals, while I was thus riding round from place to place in search of something of interest. I visited Williamsburg Hospitals, both Union and rebel, and found many things amusing and interesting.

Nellie was delighted to see me, and told me much of her experience since the battle of Williamsburg. Her hand was still in a sling, which reminded me of my first shot at a rebel female. She was a most faithful nurse, and had endeared herself to all the boys by her kindness and patience toward them. She introduced me to several of her favorites, calling each by some pet name, to which they seemed to answer as a matter of course. I spent a day and a night there, and attended a meeting in the evening, which was held by a minister from the Christian Commission for the benefit of the wounded soldiers. Oh, what a sermon was that! The tender mercies of the Father, the love of the Son of God, were described; the wailings of the lost and the raptures of the redeemed were portrayed in the most powerful and touching manner. I have never heard the sinner invited to the cross in more persuasive strains than flowed from his lips.

His countenance was pleasing, his manners courteous, and his deportment unassuming. He did not preach one of those high-toned, intellectual discourses which we so often hear, and which almost invariably fail to reach the heart. But he preached Christ with such winning simplicity, such forgetfulness of self, and with such an eager yearning after souls, that even the most depraved were melted to tears. How soul-refreshing is this simple mode of preaching! I seem to see him standing before me now, with uplifted hands, glowing cheeks and streaming eyes—and though I have forgotten much of the discourse, yet I can distinctly remember the impression which it made upon me then. It was good, humbling, purifying. He was evidently not a highly educated man, yet he proclaimed the unsearchable riches of Christ in such a way as to make the proudest eloquence and the most profound philosophy, seem in comparison, "like sounding brass or tinkling cymbal."

Often, when hearing a certain class of ministers preach, I am reminded of the saying of a good Baptist clergyman with regard to A. and B., two ministers of his own denomination: "When I hear Brother A. preach, I am in love with the man; but when I hear Brother B. preach, I am in love with Jesus." This is the kind of preaching we want—that which makes us fall in love with Jesus, instead of the preacher. Oh, that there were more of Christ, and less of self, preached.

After leaving Williamsburg, I kept on down the Peninsula until I came to Yorktown. After visiting the hospitals there, I then went to the old camp where I had spent so many weeks. There were the dear old familiar places, but all that gave them interest were gone now. The old saw-mill, too, was gone, and all that remained was a heap of ruins, to tell where it once stood. But there was a spot undisturbed, away in the corner of the peach orchard, under an isolated pear tree, a heaped up mound, underneath which rested the noble form of Lieutenant V. It was sweet to me to visit this spot once more. I knew that in all probability it would be the last time; at least for a long period, perhaps forever.

When this frail body shall be done with earth,
And this heart shall be free from care;

When my spirit enters that other world,
Oh, say, shall I know thee there?

When the last hours of life are closing around
And death's summons cometh to me;
Will God send an angel messenger down?
Shall I know the bright spirit as thee?

Rest weary heart, rest patient and wait,
Till thy happiness cometh to thee;
Thou'lt meet and thou'lt know when thou gainest that shore
Which opes to eternity.

From Yorktown I went to the White House Landing, where everything looked neat, orderly, peaceful and happy, as a quiet little country village. The grounds were laid out in broad streets and squares, which were swept clean as a floor, and there were long rows of snow-white tents, with their neatly printed cotton sign-boards, "to guide the traveler on his way" to the different head-quarters, provost marshal, hospital, sutlers, blacksmith, etc.

After spending a day there, and beginning to feel tired of idleness, I made up my mind to return to camp again. So going to Colonel Ingalls, I procured transportation for myself and horse, and stepping aboard of a provision train destined for Fair Oaks Station, I anticipated a pleasant ride, but, as usual, was blessed with quite a little adventure before I reached my destination. The train started, and, after steaming over the road for some time at its usual rate, had reached the vicinity of Tunstall's Station, when we heard the down train whistle, and immediately after a sharp volley of musketry was fired in the same direction. The engineer switched off the track, and awaited the other train. It came thundering on as if the engineer was possessed by the *sauve qui peut* spirit, and, as it passed, the wildest confusion was visible on board, and the groans of the wounded could be heard above the screaming of the engine. On it went, like a streak of lightning, signaling for our train to follow.

There was no time to be lost; our train was immediately in hot pursuit of the other, and both were soon at the White House. Among those I saw taken from the cars wounded, was the spy whom I had met in the rebel camp in front of Yorktown, and heard haranguing his fellow countryman upon the important service he had rendered the Confederate Government, and confessing himself to be the cause of Lieutenant's V's death.

Everything was thrown into wild confusion by the arrival of the trains and the news of the attack. The troops at the White House were immediately called out under arms to protect the depot. All this excitement had been produced by a detachment of Stuart's cavalry, consisting of about fifteen hundred men, and which resulted in the slight disaster to the train; the burning of two schooners laden with forage, and fourteen Government wagons; the destruction of some sutler's stores; the killing of several of the guard and teamsters; some damage done to Tunstall's Station; and the tearing up of a portion of the railroad. There was but little damage done to the train, considering that there were three hundred passengers. Some military officers of high rank were on board, who would have been a rich prize for the rebels if they had succeeded in capturing the train; but it had eluded their grasp by the admirable conduct and presence of mind of the engineer, who crowded on all possible steam, and escaped with his freight of human life with only a loss of fourteen in killed and wounded.

As soon as the wounded were taken care of I visited the provost marshal, and made known the fact that there was among the wounded a rebel spy who required immediate attention. He sent a guard with me, who searched his person and found satisfactory proof that my statement was correct. He was only slightly wounded, and by the time the railroad was repaired he was able to bear the fatigue of a journey to headquarters, and I returned to camp.

On the twenty-fifth of June the battle of Fair Oaks Grove was fought. Hooker's command had been ordered to occupy a new and important position, when they were suddenly attacked while passing through a dense thicket and almost impassable swamp. The foe was gradually pushed back until he was obliged to seek safety behind his rifle-pits. About noon General McClellan, who had remained at headquarters to communicate with the left wing, rode upon the field and, to the joy of his soldiers, ordered them again to advance. The order was cheerfully obeyed, and after renewed desperate fighting, at sunset the day was won by the Federal arms.

At this time it was not necessary for me to use any stratagem in order to visit the rebel encampment, for all that was necessary to be known of the rebel force and movements had been already ascertained. Consequently I was quietly awaiting further developments, and while waiting was trying to make myself generally useful in the hospitals. A singular case came under my notice there: that of a man being stunned by the near approach of a cannon-ball. It did not come in contact with even his clothing, and yet he was knocked down senseless, and for several days he could neither hear nor speak.

I think the most trying time that the Army of the Potomac ever had on the Peninsula was in front of Richmond, just before the seven days' battle—that is to say, if anything could be worse than the seven day's battle itself. A heavy and almost incessant firing was kept up day and night, along the entire left wing, and the men were kept in those rifle pits, (to say in water to the knees is a very moderate estimate), day after day, until they looked like fit subjects for the hospital or lunatic asylum, and those troops in camp who were not supposed to be on duty, but were kept in reserve, were often called out ten times in one night. The firing would become so alarmingly hot that it was supposed a general engagement was at hand; but on going out to the front, perhaps it would cease for a moment, then they would be ordered back to camp again. In that manner I have known the entire force to be kept in motion almost all night, and sleep for any one was a thing out of the question.

It soon became evident that there was some movement on foot which was not understood by the great mass of the army, and I have no doubt it was a good thing that the troops did not even imagine that a retreat was already being planned by their commander. The men endured all these hardships most uncomplainingly; yes, cheerfully; and every day was supposed to be the last ere they would walk the streets of Richmond triumphantly, and thus reap the fruits of their summer's campaign.

The constant fire kept up along the entire line, and the frequent charges made upon rifle-pits, rapidly increased the numbers in the hospital, and kept the surgeons and nurses busy night and day, and then they could not attend to all who required assistance. Just at this particular juncture I remember the timely aid afforded by the members of the Christian Commission and Tract Society.

They brought relief not only in one sense, but in many. Spiritual food for the hungry, dying soldier—consolation for the worn out and discouraged—delicacies for the sick and feeble—warm-gushing heart sympathy for the suffering, and actual assistance with their own hands in cases of amputations, and the removal of the sick from one place to another. Rev. Mr. Alvord gives a very modest account of the services which he rendered, when he says: "I went to the hospitals, where I worked hour after hour with the surgeons. Men were brought in with all sorts of wounds. Surgeons were scarce and were engaged in amputations, so you know I could attend to minor matters. Where the bullet had gone through body or limb, I could dress it perhaps as well as any one; also, all sorts of flesh wounds. I cannot tell you of the variety of operations I performed. The wounds had been stiffening since the day before, not having been dressed. I enjoyed the work, as in every case such relief was given. Then I could carry water to the thirsty, and speak words of comfort to the dying; for, as you may suppose, there were many in this state."

Again he says: "Just now, by my side, lies a Philadelphia zouave, a fine boy to whom I have been ministering. I gave him some hot tea, with the charming crackers Mr. Broughton sent; he is now sitting up, looking more cheerful. I mention this in detail, that you may have a specimen of the work which occupies one every moment through the day and night, who is able or willing to work in this department. On the other side of me, as I write here on my knees, lies a colored boy, haggard and sick, to whom I have given medicine and similar food. His dark face is full of gratitude."

Many an hour I have worked and watched in hospitals by the side of Mr. Alvord, and marked his cheerful christian spirit and warm sympathies for the sufferers. And often, on a march, I have gone to him, and asked if he would let some weary sick soldier ride in his carriage, who had fallen out by the way—and my request was never refused, although to do so he would sometimes have to walk through the mud himself, his horse being frequently heavily loaded. I have also distributed publications for him, and have stood by the cot of many a dying soldier where he has ministered consolation to the departing spirit. He is one of those who will have many stars in his crown of rejoicing when eternity unfolds the results of his faithful labors.

CHAPTER XVI.

CHANGE OF BASE ACROSS THE PENINSULA—EVACUATION OF WHITE HOUSE—THE MOVEMENT—BATTLE OF MECHANICSVILLE—GAINES' MILL—A REPULSE—MC CLELLAN'S DESPATCH—HOSPITALS IN DANGER—CONVALESCENT OFFICERS—LENDING MY HORSE—A LOTTERY—INSPECTING FARM STOCK—CATCHING A COLT—DANGER OF CAPTURE—RIDING FOR LIFE—BETWEEN TWO FIRES.

THE employment of General McDowell's force in the defense of Washington, and its failure to co-operate by land with McClellan, necessitated on the part of the Army of the Potomac an immediate change of base across the Peninsula. Such a change in the face of a powerful enemy is considered one of the most hazardous undertakings in war. But McClellan had no doubt of the ability of his army to fight its way, even against superior numbers, through to the James River, and thus secure a new position for an advance against Richmond.

The entire energy of the army was now directed to this object. A despatch was sent by General Van Vliet, chief quartermaster of the Army of the Potomac, to Colonel Ingalls, quartermaster at White House, as follows:

"Run the cars to the last moment, and load them with provision and ammunition. Load every wagon you have with subsistence, and send them to Savage's Station, by way of Bottom's Bridge. If you are obliged to abandon White House, burn everything that you cannot get off. You must throw all our supplies up the James River as soon as possible, and accompany them yourself with all your force. It will be of vast importance to establish our depots on James River, without delay, if we abandon White House. I will keep you advised of every movement so long as the wires work; after that you must exercise your own judgment."

All these commands were obeyed. So excellent were the dispositions of the different officers in command of the troops, depots and gunboats, and so thorough was the warning of the approach of the enemy, that almost everything was saved, and but a small amount of stores was destroyed to prevent them from falling into the hands of the enemy. General Stoneman's communications with the main army being cut off, he fell back upon White House Station, thence to Yorktown, when White House was evacuated.

On the twenty-sixth instant orders were sent to all the corps commanders on the right bank of the Chickahominy to be prepared to send as many troops as they could spare on the following day to the left bank of the river. General Franklin received instructions to hold General Slocum's division in readiness by daybreak on the twenty-seventh, and if heavy firing should at that time be heard in the direction of General Porter, to move at once to his assistance without further orders. At noon, on the twenty-sixth, the approach of the enemy, who had crossed above Meadow Bridge, was discovered by the advanced pickets at that point, and at half-past twelve in the afternoon they were attacked and driven in. All the pickets were now called in, and the regiment and battery at Mechanicsville were withdrawn.

About three o'clock in the afternoon the enemy formed his line of battle, and came down upon our troops like a torrent—attacking the entire line. McClellan, anticipating a fierce onset, was prepared for such an event, and gave him a warm reception. Our artillery occupied positions commanding all the roads and open ground. Timber had been felled, rifle-pits dug, and the infantry were under cover of the thick woods. All remained quiet until the rebel mass came rushing on—yelling as they came—within a short distance of our line, when every battery and division opened simultaneously a most destructive fire, which drove the enemy back with tremendous slaughter. Several other attacks were made on our lines during the afternoon, which proved disastrous to the enemy. At nine o'clock in the evening the firing ceased, the action having lasted six hours.

During the night the heavy siege guns and wagons were removed to the right bank of the Chickahominy, and most of the troops withdrawn, unknown to the enemy. About noon the next day another general engagement came on, and after seven hours hard fighting the left flank of the Federal line was turned, and they were driven from their position.

General McClellan says: "About seven o'clock in the evening they threw fresh troops against General Porter with still greater fury, and finally gained the woods held by our left. This reverse, aided by the confusion that followed an unsuccessful charge by five companies of the Fifth Cavalry, and followed as it was by more determined assaults on the remainder of our lines, now outflanked, caused a general retreat from our position to the hill in rear overlooking the bridge. French's and Meagher's brigades now appeared, driving before them the stragglers who were thronging toward the bridge. These brigades advanced boldly to the front, and by their example, as well as by the steadiness of their bearing, reanimated our troops and warned the enemy that reinforcements had arrived. It was now dusk. The enemy, already repulsed several times with terrible slaughter, and hearing the shouts of the fresh troops, failed to follow up their advantage. This gave an opportunity to rally our men behind the brigades of Generals French and Meagher, and they again advanced up the hill, ready to repulse another attack. During the night our thinned and exhausted regiments were all withdrawn in safety, and by the following morning all had reached the other side of the stream."

A despatch from General McClellan to Secretary Stanton, on the twenty-eighth, tells a sad story, a part of which I quote:

"Had I twenty thousand, or even ten thousand fresh troops to use to-morrow, I could take Richmond; but I have not a man in reserve, and shall be glad to cover my retreat, and save the material and *personnel* of the army. If we have lost the day, we have yet preserved our honor, and no one need blush for the Army of the Potomac. I have lost this battle because my force was too small. I again repeat that I am not responsible for this, and I say it with the earnestness of a General who feels in his heart the loss of every brave man who has been needlessly sacrificed to-day.

"In addition to what I have already said, I only wish to say to the President that I think he is wrong in regarding me as ungenerous, when I said that my force was too weak. I merely intimated a truth which to-day has been too plainly proved. If, at this instant, I could dispose of ten thousand fresh men, I could gain the victory to-morrow. I know that a few thousand more men would have changed this defeat to a victory. As it is, the Government must not and cannot hold me responsible for the result.

"I feel too earnestly to-night. I have seen too

many dead and wounded comrades to feel otherwise than that the Government has not sustained this army. If you do not do so now, the game is lost. If I save this army now, I tell you plainly that I owe no thanks to you, or to any other persons in Washington. You have done your best to sacrifice this army."

While the battle of Gaines' Mill was in progress, I was despatched to several hospitals remote from the direct line of communication, with orders to the surgeons, nurses, and such of the patients as could walk, to take care of themselves as best they could, for no ambulances could reach them; that the army was retreating to the James River, and if they remained longer they would fall into the hands of the enemy.

At one of the hospitals, about eight miles distant, I found a captain and three lieutenants with whom I was acquainted. They were just recovering from fever and unable to endure much fatigue, but could probably reach the James River if they should try. I was beset on every side to give up my horse to one and to another of them until I knew not what to say or do. I did not feel unwilling to give my horse to assist them in escaping from the rebels, and walk all the way myself, but I knew I was expected to return immediately and report to the officer in command of the ambulance corps, and undoubtedly would be required to perform other missions during the day. But all such excuses as these were thrown into the shade by the powerful oratory of the convalescent captain, who poured forth a vehement torrent of overwhelming arguments which would have made a less experienced messenger believe that the horse was for the captain individually, had been sent for his especial benefit, and was consequently entirely at his disposal.

His eloquence had not quite this effect upon me, notwithstanding I decided to give up my horse and to take the consequences. I did not feel so particularly drawn toward Captain A. as to let him have the horse entirely to himself, and to leave the other three poor fellows to live or die. Upon coming to the conclusion, after mature deliberation, to part with my faithful horse, the same one I rode on the Bull Run battle-field, I informed those officers of my intention. But, said I, not for the benefit of any one of you in particular, but for the mutual benefit of all four; then I proceeded to make arrangements that two of them should ride alternately, and not faster than the other two could walk. Then I took two slips of paper and told them to cast lots to see who should ride first.

After they had drawn the lots to settle this matter, and the poor captain was doomed to foot it the first part of the journey, and I saw that he looked rather maliciously at me, as much as to say that I had assisted fate in deciding that he should walk instead of ride, the thought struck me that there would probably be some trouble when it came his turn to ride. So I delivered the following brief lecture, which was especially intended for his ear: "Gentlemen, you are aware that by giving you my horse I am running the risk of incurring Major N.'s displeasure, and am exposing myself to the very danger from which I am assisting you to escape. Now, in return, I make one request of you, that is that you all do as you have agreed to; don't play false one with the other. Those who ride are not to go faster than the others can walk, and you are to ride equal distances as near as you may be able to judge, unless otherwise arranged among yourselves. The horse you are to have taken care of when you arrive at your destination. I trust these matters to your honor, but if honor should forget to assert its rights, the case will be reported at headquarters."

There were several others in the same hospital, but some were unconscious of the state of affairs around them; others were conscious, but unable to help themselves in the least. One of the noble hearted nurses refused to leave those helpless men, whom he had taken care of so long, and was taken prisoner. I marked that noble boy's countenance, dress and general appearance, and by making inquiry afterwards I found out that his name was J. Robbins, of the Second Michigan Regiment, and after he had undergone the hardships of imprisonment and had been exchanged, I had the honor of meeting and congratulating him, I felt that it was a greater honor than to converse with many of our major generals.

As I turned to retrace my steps I began to think over the lottery busines; and wondered if I had not introduced a species of gambling into my charitable deed. I did not feel clear on this point until I thought of reading in the Bible something about casting lots. Yes, it must be right, for there were instances of it in the Bible. I tried to remember an instance to find out in what connection I had read it, but my mind was quite confused, and it required some time to recall one of those passages. After a while, however, I thought of the one where the Roman soldiers cast lots for the vestments of the Saviour, but this text did not bring much comfort to my mind; I was somehow reminded of the woman who had named her child Beelzebub because it was a Scripture name, and I concluded to leave the further discussion of the subject until a more convenient season.

I remembered now of having noticed a farm house when I came that way in the morning, around which were a number of horses, mules, or something of that sort, and I thought it would be well to investigate the matter. Moving along in that direction as fast as possible, I soon came to the house and saw the animals there, feeding as before. Whatever I intended to do must be done quickly, for the near approach of the cannonading warned me that the army was fast retreating and I would soon be cut off from the James river road. I went at once to examine the stock on the farm for the purpose of ascertaining whether there was anything worth appropriating.

There were four splendid mules and a colt, but whether the colt was a two year old or ten I could not tell, for it was very small and very handsome, looking much like an Indian pony, and it might be a dozen years old. But the all absorbing questions in my mind were how was I going to secure this colt, and if I should catch him what was I going to do with him, having neither saddle nor bridle? I went to the barn, looked around and found an old halter that, for want of something better, would be of service. Now was the time to catch the colt, but this was easier said than done, for upon going towards it I found that it was about as wild as a young buffalo. Not discouraged, however, I started it, together with the mules, in the direction of the barn, and opened a door leading into a long shed connected with the barn. This plan succeeded admirably, for they all ran into the shed without the least trouble. But the greatest difficulty was to put the halter on the colt and get on his back; however, I at length succeed, and, mounting it, started toward James river.

The enemy had by this time succeeded in driving the Federals from their first position, and

RIDING FOR LIFE.—Page 217.

were now between them and me. Turning off from the main road, I struck out into the woods and rode as fast as possible. The woods were open and clear so that I could see a long way ahead. On I went until I came near a little thicket so dense that I could not see anything beyond its border. Not daring to go into any place which looked suspicious, I turned to go round it, when my ear caught the click, click of a dozen rifles, and a shower of Minnie balls came round me thick as hailstones, but not one of them pierced even my clothing. My colt took fright at this unexpected salute, and plunged into the woods in another direction with the speed of lightning.

I soon came to an open field and saw in the distance a large number of soldiers. One glance convinced me that they were Federals, for they wore United States uniform. Bounding over the field in an instant I had come within a hundred yards of them before I noticed that they were prisoners, guarded by a band of rebels. The first thing that caused me to discover this fact was one of the prisoners waving his hand for me to go in another direction, upon seeing which one of the rebel guards sprang forward and struck the prisoner with the butt of his musket.

This little demonstration revealed to me at once my position, and turning I fled in the direction indicated by the prisoner, when another volley followed me which proved as harmless as the first.

I began now to think that I was about as safe inside the rebel lines as anywhere, for their bullets seemed quite harmless so far as I was personally concerned. I remembered that when I was a child, I heard my mother once tell a Scotch Presbyterian clergyman she was afraid I would meet with some violent death, for I was always in some unheard of mischief, such as riding the wildest colt on the farm, firing off my father's shot-gun, and climbing to the highest point of the buildings. To which the good old predestinarian replied: "Ah weel, my guid woman, dinna fret; it is an auld saying, an' I believe a true one, 'A wean that's born to be hung 'ill ne'er be droon'd.'" Then turning to me and laying his hand on my head, he said: "But, me wee lassie, ye mauna tempt Providence wi' your madcap antics, or ye may no live oot half your days." I did not know after all but that the fates were reserving me for a more exalted death on the scaffold at Richmond—for the old minister's words would occasionally ring in my ears: "If the wean is born to be hung it will ne'er be droon'd"—and, I added, or be shot either. I was now outside of the rebel lines, but I was just between two fires, and tremendous hot ones at that, for the whole lines were a perfect blaze both of musketry and artillery. Nothing but the power of the Almighty could have shielded me from such a storm of shot and shell, and brought me through unscathed. It seems to me now that it was almost as much of a miracle as that of the three Hebrew children coming forth from the fiery furnace without even the smell of fire upon them.

CHAPTER XVII.

WITHDRAWAL TO MALVERN HILL—THE SOLDIER'S LAST WATCH—TROWBRIDGE'S GRAVE—SCENES IN A HOSPITAL—CAPTURE OF THE WOUNDED—A NOBLE SURGEON—LINE OF BATTLE—HARD FIGHTING—THE ENEMY REPULSED—HUNTING FOR FOOD—IN A FARM-HOUSE—PERILOUS POSITION—SECURING THE SPOILS—RELIEF OF THE FAMISHING—SUBLIME SCENE—ON THE MARCH—GENERAL KEYES—GUN-BOATS—ARRIVAL AT HARRISON'S LANDING—SAD CONDITION OF TROOPS—OUR LOSSES—MC CLELLAN'S ADDRESS TO THE ARMY.

WHEN I reached the main army the troops had gained a new position, and were driving the enemy back. The troops were well nigh exhausted, yet fighting bravely and determinedly. Night came and put an end to that day's battle, but instead of spending the night in taking care of our poor wounded men, we were obliged to retreat, under cover of darkness, to Malvern Hill, and leave our wounded in the hands of the enemy.

Of the many who died from exhaustion, as well as wounds, during our retreat from the vicinity of Richmond, I know of none more worthy of record than that of a young man of my acquaintance who died on the field the night after this battle. He was not wounded, but died at his post from sheer exhaustion. In the course of the evening, I had seen and offered him some brandy from my flask, which I had for the wounded. He was then scarcely able to stand on his feet, yet he refused to take the brandy, saying, "that others needed it more than he did; and besides," said he, "I never take any intoxicating liquor under any circumstances."

A notice of his death by an eye-witness, given under the heading, "the Soldier's Last Watch," says: "A lonely grave, a little apart from others, stands on the ground of one of the battles fought in the retreat from Richmond, in the summer of 1862, which bears on its wooden head-board simply the name, TROWBRIDGE.

"The turf covers the remains of a youthful soldier who was not only brave and patient, but exemplary as a christian. Those battles renewed from day to day, and attended by so many hardships, destroyed many lives in addition to those lost in conflict with the enemy. Hundreds and thousands of our gallant men, worn out by marches, fighting, hunger, and loss of sleep, became discouraged, and either recklessly threw themselves into the jaws of death, or fell into the hands of the enemy, because they were unable to keep up with their more robust, though not braver companions.

"The circumstances of the death of one of these silent martyrs to their country were taken down from the lips of a soldier who was with him in his last hours. It is all that may be known, save to a few bleeding hearts, of one who, alas! like so many others, sleeps in that saddest of all places, a battle-field. The worn-out soldier, the day before his death, said to his lieutenant, 'I am so weak and helpless, I do not know what I can do further.' He was told to lie down, and get what rest he could on the battle-field. About ten at night, said his companion, as we were talking together, an officer of the company came up, and told us we should retreat at two o'clock in the morning. He ordered us to stand guard till then, two hours each in turn. We took straws, and drew lots to decide who should stand first. The lot fell on Trowbridge. I threw myself on the ground, under a tree, with my blanket drawn over me, and was soon fast asleep. At twelve I was aroused, but said, 'you must be mistaken; it cannot be five minutes since I lay down.' We had been ordered not to speak aloud, or to have a light; and he replied in a whisper, 'Feel the hands of my watch—it is twelve.'

"I took his place, and he was soon asleep, or seemed to be. At half-past one o'clock the order came to move. I went to awake Trowbridge, but had no answer, except that he groaned heavily once and again. I tried to soothe him, and awake him gently, but he turned aside his head, groaned once more, and was gone I struck a match, and looked upon his features; they were set, and ghastly in death. I placed his hand on my cheek, and asked him if he was still conscious to press it. There was no response; life was evidently extinct.

"I made an attempt to find the surgeon, or chaplain, but they had both gone forward with the army. So I searched his pockets, and taking from them six dollars for his mother, and a letter directed to himself, I replaced the envelope, that his name, at least, might be known to those who should find the body. Several days after this, I was one of the number detailed to go back to that spot and bury the dead. On searching near the place where Trowbridge died, I found a grave with a wooden tablet, bearing his name. Not far distant was a house at which I called, and asked the inmates if they knew anything of that grave. The woman of the family then brought forward an envelope, (the very one that I had replaced), and said they had buried a soldier there, from whose pocket it was taken. It was a relief to know what had become of the body. Of course I wrote to his mother, sending the money, and giving an account of her son's last moments, and his burial."

This is only a solitary instance of the bravery and faithfulness of the men who fought those terrible battles, day after day, many of whom died with their muskets in their hands, and without receiving a wound, died from hunger, thirst, and fatigue.

There was a farm-house near the battle-field, to which the wounded were carried, and the surgeons of the Union Army made it their head-quarters during the battle. I will not attempt to describe the scenes which I witnessed in that building, for it beggars all description. The poor fellows seemed to know that they could not be removed, and would inevitably fall into the hands of the enemy. One man asked a surgeon, who had just performed an operation on one of his arms, "Doctor, is there no alternative—must I be taken prisoner?" The doctor was only a boy in appearance, a little Scotchman, and as noble-hearted a man as ever amputated a limb. He replied, in broad Scotch, "No, my man, there is no alternative; but keep up a good heart, I am not going to leave you, I shall be a prisoner for your sakes, and will take care of you as long as I can." He did so, and was really taken prisoner, but was not permitted to do much for those for whom he had made such a noble sacrifice. He was Doctor Cleland, of Detroit, Michigan.

When the order was given to retreat that night, I started with my colt, having a good saddle and bridle on him now, which I had taken off a dead horse on the battle-field, and reached Malvern Hill about two o'clock in the morning. After hitching my horse, and unstrapping a small bag of oats and my blanket from the saddle, I fed him, and proceeded to take a glance around, to see how things looked. The artillery was already in position, and the weary troops were in line of battle, but flat on the ground and fast asleep—all except the guards, who were pacing backward and forward in front of the line, ready to arouse the sleepers at any moment. Feeling safe to consign myself to the arms of Morpheus after this reconnoissance, I returned, wrapped myself in my blanket, and slept until the thundering of cannon awoke me in the morning.

Malvern Hill is an elevated plateau, about a mile and a half by three-fourths of a mile in area, nearly cleared of timber, and with several converging roads running over it. In front there are numerous ravines. The ground slopes gradually toward the northeast to the wooded plain beyond, giving clear ranges for artillery in different directions.

The batteries were advantageously posted on those hills, while the reserve troops were sheltered as much as possible by the ravines. The artillery of the reserve was placed in position so as to bring the concentrated fire of sixty guns to bear upon the enemy's front and left, approaching from Richmond or White Oak Swamp. The brave Colonel Tyler, First Connecticut, with great exertion succeeded in getting ten of his siege guns in position on the highest point of the hill; the men having to haul many of them up by hand. Commodore Rodgers, commanding the flotilla on

James river, placed his gun-boats in position to protect the left flank and to command the approaches from Richmond.

The battle commenced about nine o'clock in the morning, and raged all day with terrible fury. At three in the afternoon the enemy attacked our right and center with tremendous force both of artillery and infantry. The artillery was replied to with good effect, but our infantry lay upon the ground and withheld their fire until the advancing column was within short musket range, when they sprang to their feet and poured in a deadly volley which entirely broke the attacking force, and drove the rebels back some eight hundred yards in great confusion.

The battle raged most furiously hour after hour, the enemy advancing in massive column, often without order, but with perfect recklessness; and the concentrated fire of our gun-boats, batteries and infantry mowing down the advancing host in a most fearful manner, until the slain lay in heaps upon the field.

At four o'clock the firing ceased along the rebel line, and it was supposed the battle was over; but it proved only a calm before a more terrible storm.

At six o'clock the enemy suddenly opened upon the left of our line with the whole strength of his artillery, and fiercely pushed forward his column of attack to carry the hill. His infantry in immense force formed under cover of the woods, and starting on a run across the open space, charging almost up to the muzzle of the guns of our advance batteries, came rushing on with yells and imprecations—but in a moment the whole hill was one blaze of light—those terrible siege guns had belched forth a murderous fire, and a simultaneous volley from the gun boats, infantry and numerous batteries, sent the enemy reeling back to shelter, leaving the ground covered with their dead and wounded. Then our men dashed forward with the bayonet, with wild shouts and cheers, capturing prisoners and colors, and driving the routed rebels in confusion from the field.

At a little past four in the afternoon, when there was a lull in the terrible storm of grape and cannister, I ventured to go to a house which stood about half way between our line of battle and that of the enemy. I found a large quantity of flour, bacon, smoked ham, etc. The appearance of everything in the house indicated that the family had left suddenly, without disturbing anything. The dishes were on the table, as if the family had risen from dinner; the beds and bedding too remained undisturbed; the late inhabitants seemed to have thought of nothing but of saving their lives and escaping from the Yankees.

I was not long in searching cupboard, pantry and store-room, and appropriating tea, baking-soda, cream-of-tartar, et cetera. But in order to reach the house unobserved by the rebels I had been obliged to crawl there on my hands and feet, and now the question arose how was I to carry anything back with me? Taking a bed-quilt I spread it on the floor and commenced selecting the most important articles, such as a small bag of flour, ham, an iron spider, a large coffee-pot, and some other things; after tying these up in the quilt I attached a long bed-cord to the bundle, intending to drag it along the ground. Just as I was completing my arrangements, a shell came crashing through the side of the house, and passing through the window on the opposite side, it made the house tremble as if shaken by an earthquake. Then another and another came in quick succession until I was obliged to seek refuge in the cellar. The rebels evidently thought that the house contained a band of our sharpshooters, and were determined to dislodge them if possible, for they brought three pieces to bear upon it for about twenty minutes, until they succeeded in setting it on fire. Before the echo of the last shot had died away I heard the crackling of the fire above my head, and thought it prudent to make an attempt to escape. I did not find it very difficult to do so, as the fire was principally confined to the upper part of the house. So taking my precious burden of provisions, which still lay unharmed on the floor, I began my retreat in the same manner in which I had advanced, drawing my pack after me by means of the cord. I could not make much progress, however, for I found it very difficult to drag that immense weight over the rough ground. But I at length succeeded in reaching the lines, and was hailed by hearty cheers from those who were anxiously awaiting the result of my hazardous mission. Several of the boys caught up the spoil and carried it to the rear, where we built a fire and commenced cooking immediately. An hour later we had a nice lot of hot bread, fried ham and tea ready for disposal.

Oh, I shall never forget the thrill of pleasure which I experienced when I carried this food and set it before those famishing men, and saw them eat it with a sort of awe and reverence as if it had fallen from heaven. One of the men looked up, with moistened eyes, and said: "Bob, do you know that this food has been sent us by our heavenly Father, just as much as the manna was sent to the Children of Israel? That boy risked his life in procuring it for us, but he never would have returned from that burning building if God had not shielded him from the bursting shell. I believe it has just come in time to save me from sharing the fate of poor Trowbridge."

The battle of Malvern Hill presented, by far, the most sublime spectacle I ever witnessed. All the battles I had seen before, and those which I have seen since, were nothing to be compared to it. The elevated position which the army occupied, the concentration of such an immense force in so small compass, such a quantity of artillery on those hills all in operation at the same time, the reflection of the flashes of fire from hundreds of guns upon the dense cloud of smoke which hung suspended in the heavens, turning it into a pillar of fire which reminded one of the camp of the Israelites and of God's dealings with His people of old, the vivid flashes of lightning, the terrific peals of thunder mingled with the continuous blaze of musketry, sudden explosions of shell and the deafening roar of cannon, combined to make a scene which was *awfully grand.* My soul was filled with the sublimity and grandeur of the scene, notwithstanding the ghastly wounds and piteous groans of the mangled, helpless ones around me. Thus it continued from seven to nine in the evening, the most thrilling picture which the imagination can conceive.

As soon as the firing ceased the rear of the army began to move off in the direction of Harrison's Landing, and the exhausted troops in front threw themselves upon the ground to rest.

The greater portion of the transportation of the army having been started for Harrison's Landing during the night, the order was at once issued for the movement of the army upon the final repulse of the enemy at Malvern Hill. The troops were to move by the left and rear; General Keyes' corps being ordered to remain in position until all had moved off—then to cover the retreat.

General McClellan, in his official report, awards great credit to General Keyes for the manner in which he carried out these orders. He took every advantage of the ground to open new avenues to aid the movement, and made preparations to obstruct the roads as soon as the army had withdrawn.

In this way the march to Harrison's Landing was continued; the bridges were all destroyed and timber felled across the roads immediately after the army passed, thus rendering any rapid pursuit by the enemy impossible. The trains were kept in the middle of the road, leaving room for the infantry on each side, so as to be in good position to repel any attack which might be made during the march. His dispositions were so successful that, to use his own words: "I do not think more vehicles or any more public property were abandoned on the march from Turkey bridge than would have been left, in the same state of the roads, if the army had been moving toward the enemy instead of away from him; and when it is understood that the carriages and teams belonging to the army, stretched out in one line, would extend not far from forty miles, the energy and caution necessary for their safe withdrawal from the presence of an enemy in vastly superior numbers will be appreciated."

"High praise," says the commanding general, "is also due to the officers and men of the First Connecticut Artillery, Colonel Tyler, for the manner in which they withdrew all the heavy guns during the seven days and from Malvern Hill. Owing to the crowded state of the roads the teams could not be brought within a couple of miles of the position; but these energetic soldiers removed the guns by hand for that distance, leaving nothing behind."

The enemy followed the army with a small force, and occasionally threw a few shells at the rear-guard, but were quickly dispersed by our batteries and gun-boats, and on the evening of the third of July the entire army reached the Landing.

The troops presented a most distressing appearance as they drew up in line, and stacked their guns at Harrison's Bar. The rain had been pouring down most of the night, and was still drenching the poor battle-worn, foot-sore soldiers, and turning the roads into beds of mortar, and the low marshy ground at the Landing into such a condition that it was impossible to get along dry shod, except for those who rejoiced in the possession of high boots.

The aggregate of our entire losses in the seven days' battles, from the twenty-sixth of June to the first of July, inclusive, was ascertained, after arriving at Harrison's Landing, to be fifteen thousand two hundred and forty-nine, namely: fifteen hundred and eighty-two killed; seven thousand seven hundred and nine wounded, and five thousand nine hundred and fifty-eight missing.

On the fourth of July the following address was issued to the troops by General McClellan:

"HEADQUARTERS, ARMY OF THE POTOMAC,
Camp near Harrison's Landing, July 4, 1862.

"Soldiers of the Army of the Potomac:—Your achievements of the last ten days have illustrated the valor and endurance of the American soldier. Attacked by superior forces, and without hope of reinforcements, you have succeeded in changing your base of operations by a flank movement, always regarded as the most hazardous of military expedients. You have saved all your material, all your trains and all your guns, except a few lost in battle, taking in return guns and colors from the enemy. Upon your march, you have been assailed day after day, with desperate fury, by men of the same race and nation, skillfully massed and led. Under every disadvantage of number, and necessarily of position also, you have in every conflict beaten back your foes with enormous slaughter. Your conduct ranks you among the celebrated armies of history. No one will now question that each of you may always with pride say: 'I belong to the Army of the Potomac.' You have reached the new base, complete in organization and unimpaired in spirit. The enemy may at any moment attack you. We are prepared to meet them. I have personally established your lines. Let them come, and we will convert their repulse into a final defeat. Your Government is strengthening you with the resources of a great people. On this, our nation's birth-day, we declare to our foes, who are enemies against the best interests of mankind, that this army shall enter the capital of the so-called confederacy; that our national constitution shall prevail, and that the Union, which can alone insure internal peace and external security to each State, 'must and shall be preserved,' cost what it may in time, treasure, and blood."

CHAPTER XVIII.

RETURN OF OLD ACQUAINTANCES—THE WOUNDED COLONEL—I VISIT WASHINGTON—MILITARY DISPLAY—EPAULETS—ARISTOCRACY—SPIRIT OF JOHNNY BULL—SOLDIERS' FREE LIBRARY—CONTRABAND CAMP—NEGRO TESTIMONY—PATIENT CHARLEY—PAINFUL POSITION—BROTHER'S LAST CONVERSATION—RETURN TO THE ARMY—CHRISTIAN COMMISSION—GENERAL HOWARD'S SPEECH.

ABOUT a week after we arrived at Harrison's Landing a number of our absent ones joined us, among whom were Mr. and Mrs. B., Nellie, Jack, my wounded darkie friend from Williamsburg Hospital, and last and least of all came that pusillanimous coward, Colonel ——, whom I had assisted in carrying from the field at the battle of Williamsburg, and whom Doctor E. had ordered back to his regiment under penalty of being reported to his superior officer. The next day after the arrival of this individual I received a message requesting me to appear at the headquarters of the — regiment. I started immediately, and found to my astonishment that it was this Colonel who desired an interview with me.

He had been gone on furlough ever since the battle of Williamsburg, and had played his cards so well that he had been promoted to the command of a brigade. He had also managed, by false representations, to have the following notice inserted in the leading newspapers of his native State, viz.: "Colonel —— was severely wounded at the battle of Williamsburg, while gallantly leading a desperate charge on the enemy's works, and was carried from the field, but no sooner had the surgeons bound up his wound than the noble and patriotic colonel returned again to his command and led his men again and again upon the foe, until the day was won; when he sank upon the ground, exhausted from loss of blood and fatigue, and was carried the second time by his men from the field."

The paper in which this false statement was published found its way to camp, and Doctor E. replied to it, somewhat changing the editor's sentiments with regard to the conduct of the "noble and patriotic colonel." He, the colonel, had now returned to wreak vengeance upon Doctor E.

Going to his tent I found the colonel alone. He arose as I entered, and in rather an excited manner spoke as follows: "I am informed that you are one of the persons who carried me off the field when I was wounded at Williamsburg, and witnessed the infamous conduct of Doctor E., and heard the insulting language which he used toward me." I did not reply, but stood gazing at the man before me. He looked me in the face for the first time since I entered, and discovering the smile of contempt which I could not suppress, he seized me roughly by the arm and exclaimed: "See here boy, what do you mean? Why do you not answer me?" I replied with provoking coolness and the same sarcastic smile: "Pardon me, sir, I was not aware that you asked me a direct question; I understood you to say that you were informed that I was one of the persons who carried you off the battle-field at Williamsburg. I have the honor to inform you that thus far your informant was correct."

"Then you saw the treatment which I received, and heard the abusive language which Doctor E. made use of on that occasion?"

"I saw Doctor E. examine you carefully and thoroughly, and when he could discover no cause for your being brought there, I heard him say—'Colonel, you are not wounded at all. You had better let these boys carry you back to your regiment;' and when you so suddenly recovered your strength and sprang to your feet, making use of threats and profane language, he said: 'If you do not return to your regiment within fifteen minutes I will report you to General ——.'"

Suddenly relaxing his grasp of my arm, he assumed a fawning tone and manner, and taking a paper from his pocket he asked me to put my name to it, and he would reward me handsomely. I took the document from his hand and read it carefully. It was drawn up, as near as I can remember after the following manner: "This is to certify that Colonel —— has been infamously treated and maliciously slandered by Doctor E., while said colonel was suffering from a wound received at Williamsburg battle. Two of the undersigned carried him bleeding from the field, and witnessed the cruel treatment and insulting language of Doctor E."

After reading the document, I said very calmly and decidedly, "Colonel, I must decline signing this paper."

By this time I had become indignant, and determined to cut short the interview; so touching my hat in mock respect, I left him to his own reflections.

Now it came my turn to visit Washington—and the very next boat that left the landing bore me over the quiet waters of the James river. In due time I reached the Capital, and spent three days in visiting the hospitals in Washington, Georgetown and Alexandria, and various other places of interest.

I was commissioned with numerous orders and had any amount of messages to deliver for officers and others; as many of our men were in the different hospitals in those cities, and I was expected to find them and deliver letters, packages, etc.

The military display made in Washington is certainly astonishing, especially to those who are accustomed to see major generals go round in slouched hats and fatigue coats, without even a star to designate their rank. But cocked and plumed hats, scarlet lined riding cloaks, swords and sashes, high boots and Spanish spurs, immense epaulets, glittering stars, and gaily caparisoned horses, are to be seen by the hundred around Willard's hotel and other places of resort.

I noticed that some in particular wore painfully tight uniforms and very small caps, kept on by some new law of gravitation, as one portion rested on the bump of self esteem and the other on the bridge of the nose. "Miss Periwinkle" says of this class of military heroes: "They look like stuffed fowls, and ride as if the safety of the nation depended upon their speed alone."

Chaplain A. H. Quint manfully defends the multiplicity of epaulets in Washington, and very appropriately remarks: "Willard's is the news depot. Consider how easily a hundred, interested to read the bulletin there, could assemble. First, the general-in-chief is in Washington, and has a staff necessarily. Secondly, the quartermaster general,

not ... military governor, the
I w... surgeon-general, have
S... military force there is
sum... fourthly, there is a mul-
pap... mistaken for army officers,
man... Add to these the conva-
I to ... to move about, and you
car... ...ly in Washington. And
men... epaulets is great."
cert... "troublous times," there
treat... at the Capital. Levees
while... are frequent, except during
ceiv... when some bold dash of rebel
sign... the devoted city, and then
with... panic for a short time.
guag... think there is as much of the
A... you will find in the United
and... are respected and graded
this... uniform; everything is regu-
By... caste, and it is as David Crock-
term... ...: common people dine at
my... clerks in departments at one,
refl... representatives at three, heads
N... four, senators at five, ambassa-
and... the President—well, he doesn't
me... day.
du... ...les I visited the Senate cham-
day... occupied, except by a few speci-
G... America, who were playing leap-
pla... ...s and desks. I leisurely sur-

veyed every item of interest—sat in Sumner's chair, and recalled the scene enacted there a few years previous, and in imagination thrashed Brooks until he was a fit subject for a hospital—then giving him a farewell *coup de pied*, I betook me to the picture galleries.

After admiring Pocahontas sufficiently, and gazing at expiring heroes, who all "appeared to be quitting their earthly tabernacles in convulsions," ruffled shirts, and a tremendous shower of bombshell, until my head ached; I then turned for relief to the noble form of "The Father of his Country," which looked out from the canvas in all the princely majesty which characterized that *great* and *good* man. I stood wrapped in profound reverence, when a friend drew my attention to two paintings which I had not noticed before. They represented the surrender of Lord Cornwallis and General Burgoyne. I felt a warm current of blood rush to my face, as I contemplated the humiliating scene—the spirit of Johnny Bull triumphed over my Yankee predilections—and I left the building with feelings of humiliation and disgust.

Next in order, I visited the "Soldier's Free Library," in Fifth street, under the superintendence of John A. Fowle, Esq. He has accumulated over two thousand five hundred volumes of well selected historical, biographical and religious works. The soldiers in the different hospitals have the free use of the library, which is open daily. The room is nicely furnished, and the pictures hanging on the walls give it a cheerful home-look, and the soldiers come there by the score. It is an excellent arrangement. Thanks to the benevolent hearts and hands that have provided such a luxury for the soldier.

An hour's walk through the contraband camp was amusing and instructive. Here were specimens of all grades of the negro character, from the genuine pious, cheerful trusting christian, to the saucy, lazy, degraded creature, which generations of slavery has made almost on a level with the beasts of the field. But all of them kind-hearted, merry-tempered, and quick to feel and accept the least token of kindness.

Their cheerfulness is proverbial: old women, with wool white with age, bent over the wash-tub, grinned and gossiped in the most cheerful manner—girls romped with their dusky sweethearts, and mothers tossed their babies with that tender pride and mother-love which beautifies the blackest and homeliest face.

All were happy, because they were free—and there seemed to be no room for anything like gloom or despondency in their hearts. Men, women, and children sang, whistled and laughed together—and whether their songs were of heaven, or of hoe-cakes, they were equally inspiring.

I found a young lady there, from the North, who had come to Washington with the intention of nursing the sick soldiers, but her sympathies being divided between sick America and down-trodden Africa, she decided to teach the contrabands instead. She seemed delighted with her employment, and the little black faces were beaming with joy as they gathered around her to receive instruction.

One colored man stood listening to the questions which were being asked and answered, and looked as if he would like to give in his testimony. I turned to him, and asked: "How is it with you? do you think you can take care of yourself, now that you have no master to look after you?" "Gosh a-mighty, guess I can! Ben taking car' of self and massa too for dis fifteen year. Guess I can take car' of dis nig all alone now."

While at one of the hospitals in Alexandria, the head steward told me the following touching incident, which occurred in that hospital. Said he:

"A young man had been placed under our care, who had a severe wound in the thigh. The ball passed completely through, and amputation was necessary. The limb was cut up close to the body, the arteries taken up, and he seemed to be doing well. Subsequently, one of the small arteries sloughed off; an incision was made, and it was taken up. 'It is well it was not the main artery,' said the surgeon, as he performed the operation. 'He might have bled to death before it could have been taken up.' But the patient, (Charley, as we

16

room is nicely furnished, and t' a time.
on the walls give it a cheerful,
soldiers come there by the se ne night.
lent arrangement. Thanks was
hearts and hands that have p ——, my leg
for the soldier. bedclothes.
An hour's walk through the main artery
was amusing and instruct
mens of all grades of th to do: and in an
the genuine pious, che n the place, and
the saucy, lazy, degrad o close to the body
tions of slavery has m r my thumb, but I
the beasts of the fie e, and arousing one
hearted, merry-temp n for the surgeon,
accept the least tok
Their cheerful e, as he saw me, 'that
with wool white to do, for otherwise
grinned and g before I could have
ner—girls ro
and mothers he case, he looked ex-
pride and m for other surgeons.
est and hon reach, and a consulta-
All wer er fellow. One conclu-
there see There was no place to
gloom or my thumb was placed;
men, and er my thumb, and if I
gether— to death before the
or of h There was no way to
I fo
who h was very calm when they

told him, and he requested that his brother, who was in the same hospital, might be called up. He came and sat down by the bedside, and for three hours I stood, and by the pressure of my thumb kept up the life of Charley, while the brothers had their last conversation on earth. It was a strange position for me to occupy, to feel that I held the life of a fellow mortal in my hands, and stranger yet to feel that an act of mine must cause that life to depart. Loving the poor fellow as I did, it was a hard thought; but there was no alternative. The last words were spoken. Charley had arranged all his business affairs, and sent tender messages to absent ones, who little dreamed how near their loved one stood to the grave. The tears filled my eyes more than once as I listened to those parting words. The last good-bye was spoken; then turning to me, he said: 'Now, H——, I guess you had better remove your thumb.' 'Oh, Charley! how can I,' said I. 'But it must be done, you know,' he replied. 'I thank you very much for your kindness, and now, good-bye.' He turned away his head. I raised my thumb—once more the life-current gushed forth, and in three minutes he was dead."

Having heard and seen considerable on my little pleasure trip, and my leave of absence having nearly expired, I prepared to return once more to duty, and on my way to the boat I was fortunate enough to meet with some of the Christian Commission delegates, who were going to Harrison's Landing on the same boat, and had quite a supply of good things for our sick and wounded. May God bless the Christian Commission—it is doing a noble work, not only for the sick and wounded, but for our soldiers generally.

General Howard, of Maine, that noble christian patriot of whom I have spoken in a previous chapter, was one of the speakers at the great meeting in Philadelphia, January twenty-eighth, the second anniversary of the United States Christian Commission. He delivered a most touching and appropriate address on that occasion, and as it expresses my own sentiments, both with regard to the Christian Commission and the religion of Christ generally, I will quote a portion of his speech, for the benefit of my readers who may not have read it elsewhere:

"I may be allowed to speak freely to the friends who are here to-night. Let me tell you one thing which I need not suppress if I could, and that is, that I feel in my heart a deep and abiding interest in the cause of my Redeemer. I know that this is also the cause of the Christian Commission, and therefore I love it, and identify myself with it; and I doubt not that you love it, and will do everything to sustain it, for a like reason. And now I ask you, as I am to go back to the field to take up my cross anew, and to stand up night and day, evening and morning, for the cause of Him I love, that your earnest, importunate prayers may follow me, and that God would bless the soldiers, that evil may be repressed among them, and that when they go into battle they may go without a fear, because they know in whom they have believed.

"I assert that the highest type of courage is christian courage. When your spirit yearns up to God in prayer, 'Oh, Lord, be my protector, and in this peril let me run under the shadow of thy wing,' then you will fear no evil, though you walk through the valley and the shadow of death. My friends, these things are realities with me. By the blessing of God, by his spirit, he has enabled me to have a clear conviction that should he take me away I shall go to be with him. Not because I am good, or holy, or righteous; but because I have a Saviour; an all-sufficient Saviour, who is able to save even the chief of sinners unto the utmost. Therefore, I am able to say that I can go into the battle fearing no evil. And would to God, for their sakes, that every officer in the army and every soldier in the ranks could declare, in sincerity from the depths of his heart, that God had done such great things for him! These, to me, are settled, solemn convictions; and I speak them freely and frankly, as I am encouraged to do on this auspicious occasion.

"It may seem to some that it is expressing one's feelings too publicly; but I think it well for me to bear such testimony in a work like yours, which contemplates this great and all-important result, the promotion of heart religion and the salvation of souls. And especially do I feel this in these times of excitement and terror—over the mere temporal accessories of war, the dreadful sacrifice of lives, the horrible sights of wounds, the caring for the sick and wounded, the lamentations for the dead—amid all this I fear that the still, small voice has not always been listened to; the silent and beautiful, though wonderful work of the Spirit of God has not been seen, and its importance felt as it should be in our land. This the Christian Commission is striving to accomplish; it seeks to keep alive the spirit of christianity among our soldiers. Their agency is the leaven in our armies. May they leaven the whole lump!

"It is this only that will prepare us for our liberty. This bond, the bond of christian love, is the true bond after all that shall permanently unite us. There is no other. We speak of the claims of commerce and trade, of corn and cotton, that will unite the sections of our country; but these are temporary, fluctuating, perishing links. The religion of Jesus Christ is the lasting bond that connects not only Maine with Massachusetts and Massachusetts with Connecticut, but Maine with Texas and Florida with Wisconsin.

"We boast of being an asylum for all nations. From England, Ireland, France, Germany, Russia, and almost every country beyond the ocean, come men, women and children, who settle down in our midst. How shall we cause them to assimilate to us? How shall we ever make them good and useful citizens? Will it be, think you, by merely giving them land on which to settle? Will they become one with us because they grow in material wealth and prosperity? No, no! Nothing but an education, a true education of heart and morals, such as the religion of Jesus Christ imparts, can ever truly and safely assimilate all these heterogeneous elements, and enable us to be truly one people.

"The gospel has its victories to achieve for us as well as the sword. Many of the rebels hated us worse before the war than they do now. They respect us much more than they once did, after seeing that we are not afraid to expose our bodies to be burned, if necessary, in a just cause—the cause of our country that we love; that we shrink from no sacrifice of money, time or life in order to maintain and perpetuate the beautiful Government that our fathers bequeathed to us. But this is not all. They have felt, too, the power of the spirit of kindness and love, of which the religion of Jesus has borne so many fruits in this struggle.

"They have been astonished at the kindness which has been shown to them when they have fallen into our hands. It was this that demoralized them at Vicksburg. In the West the rebels

. . . they were. When they came . . . they say they were forced to . . . mon men, and always were . . . they are coming in every day. . . . d that when General Rosecrans . . . f the Cumberland army, eight . . . ed themselves up to us. And . . . No! We have melted them . . . an kindness and love. And, my . . . ae way to disarm them. I believe, . . . emphatic assurance, that if we all . . . of the Master in our hearts we shall . . . m wherever we find them!

. . . advocate any shrinking back or . . . he terrible steeds of war. No! Fill . . . Make the next campaign more vig- . . . that has gone before it, so that it . . . e Divine help, perfectly impossible . . . o keep the field. But let us wield . . . ong with the alleviating and saving . . . e religion of Christ. Let these, as . . . e Christian Commission and in other . . . our armies everywhere, blessing . . . alike, and we shall then cause the . . . me within our lines, not only by the . . . d, but by the sixteen and sixty thou- . . . this that will ruin their cause, and . . . down their opposition."

CHAPTER XIX.

MY CONSTANT COMPANION—DISPELLING THE BLUES—GENTLE NELLIE—FACES IN THE HOSPITAL—ASLEEP AND AWAKE—MY HORSE AGAIN—AT HARRISON'S LANDING—IMPATIENT TO MOVE—DISSATISFACTION IN THE ARMY—RETREAT FROM RICHMOND—RETURN TO NEWPORT NEWS—SUSPICIOUS QUARTERS—SEARCHING THE HOUSE AND FINDING REBEL SOLDIERS—THANKS TO THE ARMY—OUR ARRIVAL AT ACQUIA CREEK.

WHILE we remained at Harrison's Landing I spent much of my time in the hospitals. Nellie was now my faithful friend and companion, my colleague when on duty, and my escort on all occasions in my rides and rambles. She was a splendid woman, and had the best faculty of dispelling the blues, dumps and dismals of any person I ever met. When we went to a hospital and found the nurses looking tired and anxious and the patients gloomy and sad, it never required more than half an hour for us to get up a different state of feeling, and dispel that "Hark-from-the-tombs-a-doleful-sound" sort of spirit, and we invariably left the men in a more cheerful mood, evidently benefited by having a little respite from that depressing melancholy so prevalent among the sick, and so often indulged by nurses.

In our own hospital we generally managed to

so assort and arrange the patients as to have all of the same temperament and disease together, so that we knew just what to do and what to say to suit each department. We had our patients divided into three classes; one was our working department, another our pleasure department, and a third our pathetic department. One we visited with bandages, plasters and pins; another, with books and flowers; and the third, with beef tea, currant wine, and general consolation. Sometimes Nellie would sit and fan the patients for hours in the latter department, and sing some soothing pieces in her soft, sweet strains, until she would have them all asleep, or quiet as babies. I think the soldiers may truly say of the gentle Nellie:

Her soothing tones with peace beguile
  The weary hours of pain,
And make the lonely sufferer smile
  And joy to come again.

Still let me often hear thy voice,
  Which gently whispers peace,
And let my troubled heart rejoice,
  And strains of sadness cease;

Still speak to me of pleasant things—
  Of faith, and hope, and joy;
Then shall I rise on lightsome wings
  Where pains no more annoy.

I used to watch with much interest the countenances of those men as they lay fast asleep, and I often thought that I could read their characters better when asleep than when awake. Some faces would grow stern and grim—they were evidently dreaming of war, and living over again those terrible battles in which they had so recently participated; some groaned over their wounds, and cursed the rebels vigorously; others grew sad, and would talk in the most pathetic tones, as if the pain borne so silently through the day revenged itself now by betraying what the man's pride concealed so well while awake. Often the roughest grew young and pleasant when sleep smoothed away the hard lines from the brow, letting the real nature assert itself. Many times I would be quite disappointed, for the faces which looked merry and pleasing when awake would suddenly grow dark and hideous, as if communing with some dark spirits of another world.

One poor fellow, whose brain was injured more than his body, would wear himself out more in an hour when asleep than in a whole day when awake. His imagination would conjure up the wildest fancies; one moment he was cheering on his men, the next he was hurrying them back again; then counting the dead around him, while an incessant stream of shouts, whispered warnings and broken lamentations would escape from his lips.

I became acquainted with a young man from Rhode Island in one of the hospitals, who was the most patient and cheerful person it has been my lot to meet under such circumstances. I find the following notice with regard to him:

"I came out here," said he, "as rough and as bad as any of them. But I had left a praying mother at home. While in camp at Poolesville I heard that she was dead. After that her image was never out of my thoughts. It seemed as if her form appeared to me as in a mirror, and always as wrestling for her wayward son. Go where I might I felt as if I saw her in her place of prayer, kneeling and putting up her petitions to God, and not even the roar of battle could drown the soft tones of her voice."

He was at the battle of Fair Oaks, and when it ceased sat down on a log, exhausted, by the wayside, and then, to use his own words, he "thought over the matter." Heaps of dead men lay on every side of him. They had fallen, but he was still unharmed. The melting words of his mother's prayer came back to his mind with new power. He thought of his own condition, and of her happy home, so far removed from the strife and agony of war. A pious soldier of his company noticed that he was very thoughtful, and inquired the reason. To this friend he opened his mind freely, and told him how he felt. They sought occasion for private conference, communed together and prayed; strength was given him to make the "last resolve," and the soldier who had been so rough and bad became a soldier in the Army of Jesus. The sainted mother had not prayed in vain. A battle had just been fought, a victory won, which was spreading joy throughout the nation; but here, too, was a triumph, a different triumph, such as cause the angels of God in heaven to rejoice.

> Just as I am, without one plea,
> But that Thy blood was shed for me,
> And that Thou bid'st me come to Thee,
> O Lamb of God! I come.

One day, while employed in the hospital assisting Nellie in some new arrangement for the amusement of the men, I received a letter from the captain to whom I had given my horse for the use of himself and three companions on the retreat from before Richmond. He and his friends had reached the James river in safety, and had been so fortunate as to get on board of one of the transports which had been sent for the wounded, and were now comfortably installed in a hospital in Washington. He also wrote that he had given my horse in charge of one of the quartermasters of General G.'s brigade, a piece of information which I was exceedingly glad to hear, for my colt was well nigh spoiled on the retreat, and if it had not been, was not fit to ride much, or indeed at all, to do it justice, for it proved to be not quite two years old.

But upon finding the quartermaster I was politely informed that he had bought and paid for the horse, and of course I could not have it. I said nothing, but went to General M.'s headquarters, stated the case, and procured an order which brought the horse in double-quick time, and no thanks to the quartermaster.

A month passed away, and everything remained quiet at Harrison's Landing and vicinity. The troops, having rested, began to grow tired of the routine of camp life, and were anxious for another brush with the enemy. The vigilant eye of McClellan noted the impatience of the men, and he daily kept urging the necessity of reinforcements, and protested against leaving the Peninsula, as retreat, in his opinion, would prove disastrous both to the army and the cause. Our commander's patience was well nigh exhausted, as the following brief despatch of July 30th indicates:

"I hope that it may soon be decided what is to be done by this army, and that the decision may be to reinforce it at once. We are losing much valuable time, and that at a moment when energy and decision are sadly needed."

About this time an order came from Washington for all the sick to be sent away, without giving any definite information with regard to the intended movements of the army.

August fourteenth orders came for the army to evacuate Harrison's Landing. None knew whither they were going, but notwithstanding every pains was taken to conceal the destination from the troops, it was evident that we were retreating; for the ominous fact that we turned our backs toward Richmond was very suggestive of a retreat. This had a demoralizing effect upon the troops, for they had confidently expected to advance upon Richmond and avenge the blood of their fallen comrades, whose graves dotted so many hillsides on the Peninsula, and whose remains would now be desecrated by rebel hands. The men were deeply moved; some wept like children, others swore like demons, and all partook in the general dissatisfaction of the movement.

On the morning of the sixteenth the whole army was *en route* for parts unknown. Our destination proved to be Newport News—a march of nearly seventy miles. It was well for us we did not know it then, or probably there would have been more swearing and less weeping among the soldiers. So far as I was personally concerned, I had a very pleasant time during that march. Mr. and Mrs. B., Dr. E., Nellie and myself, made up a small party, independent of military discipline, and rode fast or slow, just as it suited our fancy, called at the farm-houses and bought refreshments when we were hungry, and had a good time generally. Nellie rode my confiscated colt, and pronounced it a perfect gem. Dr. E. playfully said that he supposed she admired it because it was a rebel, and I suggested that he too must be a rebel, from the same premises.

Time passed away pleasantly until we drew near to Yorktown, where sad memories interrupted the animated conversation. Nellie was near her former home, with all its pleasant and sad associations. We visited the grave of Lieutenant V. I could but rejoice that he had been taken away from the evil to come. He had been saved from all those terrible marches and horrible battles, and from this distressing and humiliating retreat. We hitched our horses and remained some time there, some of the party gathering the rich, ripe fruit, which hung in abundance from the peach trees around us. Before leaving, we all bowed around the grave of our friend. Chaplain B. offered up an ardent prayer that we might all be faithful, and follow the example of our departed loved one, as he had followed Christ, and meet him where war and strife would be heard no more.

I know thou art gone to a clime of light,
  To a world of joy and love,
Beyond the reach of the sunbeam's flight,
  In the shadowless above.

And I will rejoice in thy smiles again,
  And hap'ly thy whisper hear;
Dispelling the gloom of sorrow and pain,
  When the twilight of death is near.

We stopped at a farm-house one evening during our march, and engaged lodgings for the night. The house was very large, and afforded ample accommodations. It was the first one on the Peninsula at which I had seen a strong, healthy-looking man, attending to his farm as if there was no such thing as war in the land. The lady of the house was an active, business-like sort of woman, and went to work to make us comfortable. But there was evidently something in or about that house which was not just right—and we had not been there long when I detected suspicious movements, and drew the attention of Dr. E. to the fact. The man seemed very uneasy and restless, going from one room to another, shutting the doors very carefully behind him, carrying parcels up stairs in a half frightened way which increased our suspicion. I proposed to our little party that they should remain while I rode back to the army for a detachment of the provost-guard. My proposal was agreed to, and I started back in the direction of the main column.

The family seemed alarmed, and asked a great many questions concerning my departure, to which I replied: "I am only going a short distance; I shall probably be back by the time supper is ready." I made all haste after I disappeared from view of the house, and in an hour I was on my way back again, having succeeded in finding the provost-marshal, and getting a corporal and six men to go with me. They entered the house boldly, and told the inmates that they had been informed that there were rebels concealed in the house, and they had come for the purpose of searching it; adding, that they would not disturb anything, if their suspicions were unfounded.

The lady said that she had some sick persons in the house, and did not wish them disturbed, assuring them that her family were all Union, and they would not harbor any rebels whatever. But all her excuses and pretensions did not deter the guard from accomplishing their object. So marching up stairs, they searched every room. In one room were found four rebel soldiers, or guerillas, all of whom pretended to be very ill. Dr. E. was called to examine the patients, and pronounced them well as he was. In another room were two officers; they made no excuse at all, but said that they were the landlord's sons; had been in the rebel service, and were now home on furlough. They said they had been home ever since Stuart's cavalry raid at White House, and were waiting for another such dash in order to get back again.

The provost-guard marched them all back to headquarters, which was in the saddle, and our little party thought proper to take shelter that night under the wing of the main column, instead of at a farm-house where we were not sure but that our lives would pay for that piece of information given, before morning.

The army marched on until it reached the transports. Some embarked at Yorktown, some at Newport News, and others at Fortress Monroe. The troops were literally worn out and discouraged, caring but little where they went, or what they did. They were huddled on board of transports, and were landed at Aquia Creek.

General McClellan finding his army, as he had

anticipated, much depressed and discouraged in consequence of the retreat from the Peninsula, sent the following appeal to General Halleck: "Please say a kind word to my army, that I can repeat to them in general orders, in regard to their conduct at Yorktown, Williamsburg, West Point, Hanover Court-house, and on the Chickahominy, as well as in regard to the Seven Days, and the recent retreat. No one has ever said anything to cheer them but myself. Say nothing about me; merely give my men and officers credit for what they have done. They deserve it."

The Army of the Potomac had performed an enormous amount of labor in making entrenchments, constructing roads, bridges, etc., and did it with the most gratifying cheerfulness and devotion to the interests of the service. During the entire campaign they had fought ten severely contested battles, and had beaten the enemy on every occasion, showing the most determined bravery and invincible qualities it was possible for an army to exhibit. They had submitted to exposure, sickness and death, without a murmur; and they deserved the thanks of the government and the people for their services.

On arriving at Aquia Creek, we found ourselves the victims of another rainstorm. Five of us went on board of a little steam-tug, and thus escaped a severe drenching during the night, for we had not yet seen our tents. When morning came we were treated to breakfast, and the captain was very kind indeed. We were just congratulating ourselves on our good fortune, when we discovered that all our little valuables, relics which we had brought from the Peninsula, toilet arrangements, and even our Bibles, had been stolen while we were asleep. Nellie and I were indulging in some uncharitable remarks concerning those persons upon whose hospitality we had fared sumptuously and slept comfortably, and who had so generously refused to take any remuneration in the shape of greenbacks, but who had helped themselves to things more precious to us than money, when good Chaplain B. entered just in time to catch the most unchristian-like sentence we had uttered, and forthwith gave us a lecture upon the heinous sin of ingratitude. When he had concluded, instead of saying amen, I said: "from such hospitality in future, good Lord deliver us."

We did not remain long at Aquia Creek, but were ordered to embark immediately for Alexandria, Virginia. When we arrived there, Pope's army was in danger of annihilation; and, consequently, as fast as the Army of the Potomac arrived, it was ordered to Pope's assistance; one portion in one direction, and another in another direction, until it was cut up into sections, and General McClellan was left at Washington, without an army or anything to command except his staff.

CHAPTER XX.

POPE'S ARMY—A GENERAL'S REQUEST—AGAIN A CONTRABAND—ENTERING THE REBEL LINES AS A SPY—MY ESCAPE TO THE FEDERAL LINES—IN PERIL—KEARNEY KILLED—CRAWLING THROUGH THE WOODS—BURIAL OF A PICKET—LOOKING FOR A GENERAL—MR. NEGATIVE—MC CLELLAN AND POPE—THE BATTLE OF ANTIETAM—A TOUCHING DEATH-SCENE—AN INTERESTING PATIENT—BURIAL OF A FEMALE SOLDIER.

IMMEDIATELY after arriving at Alexandria, I started for the battle-field, where a portion of McClellan's army had gone to reinforce Pope. Everything seemed to be in a confused state. There was no definite information with regard to the force of the enemy in that direction, and it seemed impossible to obtain any from reliable sources. McClellan's troops were ordered to the front, under new commanders, just as they came off the transports in which they arrived from the Peninsula, without any rest, or a proper supply of clothing, shoes, or blankets; all of which they much needed, after such a march as they had just accomplished.

While the battle raged, and the roar of cannon was reverberating over the National Capital, McClellan sent the following request to General Halleck: "I cannot express to you the pain and mortification I have experienced to-day, in listening to the distant firing of my men. As I can be of no further use here, I respectfully ask that, if there is a probability of the conflict being renewed to-morrow, I may be permitted to go to the scene of battle with my staff, merely to be with my own men, if nothing more. They will fight none the worse for my being with them. If it is not deemed best to intrust me with the command even of my own army, I simply ask to be permitted to share their fate on the field of battle."

The troops under Pope were several days in the vicinity of the Shenandoah Valley, with no rations but those they found in the fields, such as fruit, green corn, and vegetables. They certainly were in a poor condition to fight, and there was evidently a lack of that cheerful, enthusiastic spirit, which had characterized them on the Peninsula.

I was ordered by General H. to pass the rebel lines, and return as soon as possible. I took the train at Warrenton Junction, went to Washington, procured a disguise, that of a female contraband, and returned the same night. I passed through the enemy's lines in company with nine contrabands, men, women, and children, who preferred to live in bondage with their friends, rather than to be free without them. I had no difficulty whatever in getting along, for I, with several others, was ordered to headquarters to cook rations enough, the rebels said, to last them until they reached Washington.

AT REBEL HEADQUARTERS.—Page 263.

The officers generally talked in low tones, but would sometimes become excited, forget that there were darkies around, and would speak their minds freely. When I had been there a few hours, I had obtained the very information which I had been sent for. I had heard the plan of the morrow discussed, the number of troops at several important points, and the number expected to arrive during the night; and this, too, from the lips of the commanding general and his staff.

The rebel lines were guarded so strongly and so faithfully, that I did not dare to return that night, but waited anxiously for the dawn of the morrow.

Early on the following morning, while assisting the cook to carry in breakfast, I removed a coat from a camp-stool which stood in my way, and a number of papers fell from its pockets, which I instantly transferred to my own. I then hurried my arrangements in the tent, lest the documents should be missed before I could make my escape. Breakfast was announced, and I suddenly disappeared.

Going toward the picket line nearest the Federals, and seeing an old house in the distance, I went and hid myself in the cellar. Soon, firing commenced in different directions, and grew hotter and hotter, until the shot and shell began to shake the old house in which I had taken refuge, and by and by it came tumbling down around me. A part of the floor was broken down, but still I remained unharmed, and did not attempt to leave the ruins. I remembered that good old Elijah remained in the cave during the tempest, the earthquake and the fire, and afterward came the still small voice. So I waited patiently for the still small voice, and felt secure; knowing that the Lord was a sure refuge, and could protect me there as well as in a drawing-room in the quiet city.

It was not long before deliverance came, and the rebels were obliged to fall back and take a new position. When the firing ceased, I was safely within the Federal lines. I went immediately to headquarters, and reported myself as having just returned from rebeldom; gave a brief relation of my experience, and delivered the documents which I had brought from rebel headquarters. These proved to be orders intended for the different corps commanders, with instructions how and when to move, so as to act in concert with the entire plan of the morrow, and insure the capture of Washington.

During those battles and skirmishes of Pope's memorable campaign, I visited the rebel generals three times at their own camp-fires, within a period of ten days, and came away with valuable information, unsuspected and unmolested.

While the second battle of Bull Run was in progress, I was a part of the time with the Confederates, and then back again to the Federals, having made my escape while the battle raged most fiercely by concealing myself in a ravine, and watching until the rebels charged upon a battery. While they were engaged in a hand-to-hand fight, I escaped unobserved by friend or foe.

The last of these visits was made the night before the battle of Chentilla, in which the brave Kearney was killed. I was within a few rods of him when he fell, and was in the act of returning to the Union camp under cover of the extreme darkness of that never-to-be-forgotten night. I saw him ride up to the line, but supposed him to be a rebel officer until the pickets fired at him, and even then I thought they had fired at me, until I saw him fall from his horse, and heard their exclamations of joy when they discovered who he was; for the one-armed general was known throughout both armies for his bravery and brilliant career, and the name of Kearney had become a word of terror to the rebels.

When I learned who was their victim, I regretted that it had not been me instead of him, whom they had discovered and shot. I would willingly have died to save such a general to the Union army. But he was taken, while I, poor insignificant creature, was left; but left with a heart and soul as fully devoted to the Union cause as Kearney's was; only lacking the ability to accomplish the same results.

I lost no time in making good my escape, while the attention of the pickets were drawn in another direction. When I came to our lines, I found it almost as difficult to get through as I had found it on the other side. The night was so dark I could not make any sign by which the pickets could recognize me, and I was in the depths of the forest, where the rustling of the leaves and the crackling of dry branches under my feet betrayed my foot-steps as I went along. However, after crawling up pretty close to the line, and getting behind a tree to screen me from the bullets, if they should fire, I managed to make myself understood. The picket said: "All right," and I passed through in safety.

Coming within the lines, I saw a group of men kneeling on the ground digging a grave with their bayonets, with the least possible noise; for the picket lines were within half musket shot of each other. One of their comrades had been killed, and they were thus preparing his last resting-place.

> They buried him darkly at dead of night,
> The turf with their bayonets turning.

But there were no "struggling moonbeams," or glimmering stars, to shed a ray of light upon the midnight gloom of that solitary funeral—naught save the vivid flashes of lurid flame which the lightning cast upon the sad scene, lighting up for a moment the surrounding forest, and then dying away, leaving the darkness more intolerable.

We may well say of such as die at their post:

Sweet be the death of those
  Who for their country die;
Sleep on her bosom for repose,
  And triumph where they lie.

After reaching headquarters and donning another costume, I was dispatched to Washington with official documents to McClellan, who was now in command of the defenses of the Capital, and had control of all the troops who came streaming in from the disastrous battle-field. I arrived in the city just as the morning light was breaking, drenched from head to foot, and looking as if mud was my native element.

Making my way to where I supposed headquarters to be, I saw an important looking individual near by, whom I addressed, and inquired if he could tell me where General McClellan was to be found? "No, I can not." Could he tell me when he was expected at headquarters? "No." Was there any person there of whom I could inquire? "Not a person." Did he know of any place where the necessary information could be obtained? "Not a place." Could he make any suggestion, or throw the least ray of light upon the subject, which might lead to the whereabouts of the general? "Not the slightest."

Turning away in disgust, I said to the man, "Well, good-by, Mr, Negative. I hope the effort which you have made to assist me will not injure you mentally or physically;" and so saying I rode away, feeling that if I was as big as he imagined himself, and as strong as he was indifferent, I would give him a vigorous shaking before leaving him.

I went next to General H.'s headquarters. No one there could tell me anything more definite than that the general had been gone all night, carrying out General Halleck's orders and making the best possible disposition of the troops as fast as they came in, for the whole army was now in full retreat. After two hours search I found him, delivered the despatches, and returned to Washington, where I remained until the next day, being completely tired out, not having had a night's sleep for five nights previous.

On the first of September, General McClellan had an interview with the President, who requested him to use all his influence with the Army of the Potomac to insure its hearty co-operation with General Pope's army. In compliance with the President's request, McClellan sent the following despatch to General Porter: "I ask of you, for my sake, that of the country, and the old Army of the Potomac, that you and all my friends will lend the fullest and most cordial co-operation to General Pope in all the operations now going on. The destinies of our country, the honor of our arms, are at stake, and all depends upon the cheerful co-operation of all in the field. This week is the crisis of our fate. Say the same thing to my friends in the Army of the Potomac, and that the last request I have to make of them is, that, for their country's sake, they will extend to General Pope the same support they ever have to me."

Immediately after this followed the brilliant and triumphant victories at South Mountain and Antietam, which more than counterbalanced the disastrous campaign of Pope, and which sent a thrill of joy throughout the North.

But in this, as in most other instances of earthly bliss, the joy was not unmixed with sorrow—sorrow for the noble dead and wounded upon those bloody fields. At the memorable battle of Antietam there were nearly two hundred thousand men and five hundred pieces of artillery engaged during a period of fourteen hours without cessation; and at its termination two thousand seven hundred of the enemy's dead lay upon the field. The report of the Federal general in command says: "Thirteen guns, thirty-nine colors, upwards of fifteen thousand stand of small arms, and more than six thousand prisoners, were the trophies which attest the success of our army in the battles of South Mountain, Crampton's Gap, and Antietam. Not a single gun or color was lost by our army during these battles."

At the close of the battle I stood by the side of a dying officer of one of the Massachusetts regiments, who had passed through the thickest of the fight unhurt, but just at the close of the battle he was struck by a random shot which wounded him mortally. As he lay there, conscious of approaching death, the musicians of the regiment happened to pass by. He requested that they might be asked to play the "Star-Spangled Banner." They cheerfully complied with the dying man's request, and while they played the grand old tune his countenance beamed with joy. He inquired the result of the battle, and when told that it was a victory he exclaimed—"Oh! it is glorious to die for one's country at such a time as this!" Then turning to the chaplain he spoke in the most affecting manner; he said his trust was in the Redeemer; then he sent loving messages to his mother and friends at home. The chaplain read some comforting passages of Scripture and prayed with him, and soon after the happy spirit passed away.

Some one very appropriately says: "When such sacrifices are laid upon the altar of our country, we have surely new incentives to uphold the cause for which they are made, and, with God's help, not to allow the treason which has slain so many victims, to accomplish its purpose. And, through this bloody baptism, shall not our nation be purified at length, and fitted to act a nobler part in the world's history?" God grant it.

In passing among the wounded after they had

been carried from the field, my attention was attracted by the pale, sweet face of a youthful soldier who was severely wounded in the neck. The wound still bled profusely, and the boy was growing faint from loss of blood. I stooped down and asked him if there was anything he would like to have done for him. The soldier turned a pair of beautiful, clear, intelligent eyes upon me for a moment in an earnest gaze, and then, as if satisfied with the scrutiny, said faintly: "Yes, yes; there is something to be done, and that quickly, for I am dying."

Something in the tone and voice made me look more closely at the face of the speaker, and that look satisfied me that my suspicion was well founded. I went to one of the surgeons in attendance, and requested him to come and see my patient. He did so, and after a moment's examination of the wound told me that nothing could be done whatever to save him. He then left me, and I administered a little brandy and water to strengthen the wounded boy, for he evidently wished to tell me something that was on his mind before he died. The little trembling hand beckoned me closer, and I knelt down beside him and bent my head until it touched the golden locks on the pale brow before me; I listened with breathless attentention to catch every sound which fell from those dying lips, the substance of which was as follows:

"I can trust you, and will tell you a secret. I

am not what I seem, but am a female. I enlisted from the purest motives, and have remained undiscovered and unsuspected. I have neither father, mother nor sister. My only brother was killed to-day. I closed his eyes about an hour before I was wounded. I shall soon be with him. I am a christian, and have maintained the christian character ever since I entered the army. I have performed the duties of a soldier faithfully, and am willing to die for the cause of truth and freedom. My trust is in God, and I die in peace. I wish you to bury me with your own hands, that none may know after my death that I am other than my appearance indicates." Then looking at me again in that earnest, scrutinizing manner, she said: "I know I can trust you—you will do as I have requested?"

I assured her that she might place implicit confidence in me, and that I would do as she had desired me. Then I sought out a chaplain, who came and prayed with her. She was calm and peaceful. I remained with her until she died, which was about an hour. Then making a grave for her under the shadow of a mulberry tree near the battle-field, apart from all others, with the assistance of two of the boys who were detailed to bury the dead, I carried her remains to that lonely spot and gave her a soldier's burial, without coffin or shroud, only a blanket for a winding-sheet. There she sleeps in that beautiful forest where the soft southern breezes sigh mournfully through the foliage, and the little birds sing sweetly above her grave.

Her race is run. In Southern clime
She rests among the brave;
Where perfumed blossoms gently fall,
Like tears, around her grave.

No loving friends are near to weep
Or plant bright flowers there;
But birdlings chant a requiem sweet,
And strangers breathe a prayer.

She sleeps in peace; yes, sweetly sleeps,
Her sorrows all are o'er;
With her the storms of life are past:
She 's found the heavenly shore.

CHAPTER XXI.

AFTER ANTIETAM—SURGEONS ON THE FIELD—THE HOSPITALS—LIEUTENANT-COLONEL DWIGHT MORTALLY WOUNDED—A BRUTAL SURGEON—A WOUNDED CAPTAIN—AGONY FROM THIRST—CHRISTIAN SOLDIERS—PRAYING AND FIGHTING—FOPS ON THE FIELD—A REBEL PROGRAMME—PENNSYLVANIA TO BE STRIPPED—CAMP LIFE—DAILY ROUTINE—BURIAL SERVICES.

AFTER the battle of Antietam, one of the chaplains who was on the field paid a fitting tribute to the colonel commanding the regiment to which he belonged, and vividly described many scenes that came under my own observation on that day, he says:

"How faithfully many a surgeon labored! Our

own assistant surgeon was a hero; regardless of bullets in the hottest fire, he kept coolly on in his work, while near by Dr. Kendall, of the Twelfth Massachusetts, was killed. The nearest hospital, that of our own corps, was necessarily in range of the enemy's shell, which every now and then fell around and beyond. Near by were five other hospitals, all for one wing. Here were generals and privates brought together. General Mansfield I saw dying, and a few feet off, an unknown private; General Hartsuff badly wounded, and by his side a throng of others now on the same level. There is no distinction as to what body or soul needs then.

"Our own regiment helped to fill these hospitals. Our gallant dead are remembered with all the other dead of Massachusetts. But one we lost, hard to replace: Our brilliant, brave, generous, kind-hearted Lieut.-Colonel Wilder Dwight, shot mortally, but living two days. Of wonderful promise at home, cheerful, resigned, strong in faith and trust, ready to die; his only wish being to see his father and mother. While lying in the garden, moved only on a stretcher, he sent our own surgeon to relieve the wounded who were lying all around, the surgeons being occupied in amputating limbs of men in the hospitals; and again and again sent water provided for himself to the poor fellows calling for it. Yet Colonel Dwight was not free from brutal insolence. While waiting there in the night for an ambulance in which to place him, only for shelter, suddenly a harsh voice insisted on turning him out with all our men.

"I found a pompous little surgeon angry and furious. I informed him why the men were there, assured him of their good behavior, and requested permission for them to remain as we were momentarily expecting the ambulance. It was all in vain. Colonel Dwight himself was treated most harshly, although of higher rank than the brute himself; and notwithstanding I told the surgeon he was mortally wounded, he ordered the guard to turn them out at the point of the bayonet, and to prevent their return even to remove Colonel Dwight; refusing to tell his rank and even his name, until I obtained it of another party. The men were driven away while actually giving water to the wounded who had been calling in vain for help. I assured him I would take care that his conduct was made known, knowing from several scenes I had witnessed that day that he was, from brutality, pomposity and harshness, utterly unfit to be in charge of wounded men, and from gross disrespect to an officer higher in rank, unfit to be in the army. This fellow was a medical director in General Reynolds' corps, Pennsylvania Reserves," and the writer adds, "too good a corps to have such a fellow among them."

The ordinary scene which presents itself after the strife of arms has ceased, is familiar to every one. Heaps of slain, where friend and foe lie side by side, mangled bodies, shrieks and groans of the wounded and dying, are things which we always associate with the victories and defeats of war. But we seldom expect or hear of songs of praise and shouts of triumph from dying lips on the dreadful battle-field. The following account was received from the lips of a brave and pious captain in one of the Western regiments, as some friends were conveying him to a hospital from the battle-field:

"The man had been shot through both thighs with a rifle bullet; it was a wound from which he could not recover. While lying on the field he suffered intense agony from thirst. He supported his head upon his hand, and the rain from heaven was falling around him. In a short time a little pool of water collected near his elbow, and he thought if he could reach that spot he might allay his raging thirst. He tried to get into a position which would enable him to obtain a mouthful of the muddy water, but in vain; and he must suffer the torture of seeing the means of relief within sight, while all his efforts were unavailing.

"'Never,' said he, 'did I feel so much the loss of any earthly blessing. By and by the shades of night fell around us, and the stars shone out clear and beautiful above the dark field, where so many others lay wounded, writhing in pain or faint from loss of blood. Thus situated, I began to think of the great God who had given His son to die a death of agony for me, and that He was in the heavens to which my eyes were turned; that He was there above that scene of suffering and above those glorious stars; and I felt that I was hastening home to meet Him, and praise Him there. I felt that I ought to praise Him then, even wounded as I was, on the battle-field. I could not help singing that beautiful hymn—

"'When I can read my title clear
To mansions in the skies,
I'll bid farewell to every fear,
And wipe my weeping eyes.'

"'And though I was not aware of it till then,'" he continued, "'it proved there was a christian brother in the thicket near me. I could not see him, but was near enough to hear him. He took up the strain from me, and beyond him another, and another, caught the words, and made them resound far and wide over the terrible battle-field. There was a peculiar echo in the place, and that added to the effect, as we made the night vocal with our hymns of praise to God.'"

The presence of such men in the army, animated by faith in God, and conscious of serving Him in serving their country, adds materially to its elements of strength and success. "The religious element has always been acknowledged as a great power in military success. The more intelligent that principle is, the more efficient it must be in securing this result. There is every reason, natural as well as rational, why those who hold their lives in their hand should acknowledge the God of battle, and pray for themselves and their country in the midst of danger. The simplest expression of the relations of praying and fighting was, perhaps, the blunt order of the puritan chief, "Put your trust in God, and keep your powder dry." Cromwell and his praying puritans were dangerous men to meet in battle. "The sword of the Lord and of Gideon was exceeding sharp, tempered as it was by hourly prayers." Who can but admire the sublime spectacle which Gustavus Adolphus and his vast army presented on the eve of the battle of Lutzen, in which the King fell, praying on bended knees, and then chanting:

Be of good cheer; your cause belongs
To Him who can avenge your wrongs;
Leave it to Him our Lord.

The King fell, but the battle was gloriously won.

"And so," says a writer upon this subject, "unless we are untrue to our better nature, it must ever be. Before going into battle, the foolish, wicked oath is silent. With the bracing of the nerves for the shock of battle, there goes up a silent prayer for strength, and valor and deliverance. The wounded pray to be saved from death; the dying recall the words of old petitions learned in childhood, and in those broken accents commit their souls to God."

The only amusing incident after a battle is, the crowd of spectators from Washington and other places. If they are in carriages, their vehicles are sure to get smashed, and then the trouble arises, what are they to do with their baggage? Carry it, of course, or leave it behind. Even the wounded soldiers cannot help laughing at their sorry plight, gesticulations, and absurd questions.

Among all this class of individuals, there are none to be compared with government clerks for importance and absurdity. On one of these occasions I remember of a number of those pompous creatures being distressed beyond measure, because they could not return to Washington on a train which was crowded beyond description with the wounded. After the cars moved off there they stood gazing after it in the most disconsolate manner. Said one, "I came out here by invitation of the Secretary of War, and now I must return on foot, or remain here." One of the soldiers contemptuously surveyed him from head to foot, as he stood there with kid gloves, white bosom, standing collar, etc., in all the glory and finery of a brainless fop, starched up for display. "Well," said the soldier, "we don't know any such individual as the Secretary of War out here, but I guess we can find you something to do; perhaps you would take a fancy to one of these muskets," laying his hand on a pile beside him.

The clerk turned away in disgust, and disdaining to reply to the soldier, he inquired, "But where shall I sleep to-night?" The soldier replied, "Just where you please, chummy; there is lots of room all around here," pointing to a spot of ground which was not occupied by the wounded. A chaplain stepped up to him, and said: "If you wish to sleep, there is some hay you can have;" and went on to give him a brief lecture upon the impropriety of a young man, in perfect health, just fresh from the city, talking about comfortable lodgings, and a place to sleep, when so many wounded and dying lay all around him. He was horrified, and disappeared immediately.

Before the rebels attempted to cross into Maryland in force, the Richmond papers were full of editorials, of which the following is a specimen:

"Let not a blade of grass, or a stalk of corn, or a barrel of flour, or a bushel of meal, or a sack of salt, or a horse, or a cow, or a hog, or a sheep, be left wherever the Confederate troops move along. Let vengeance be taken for all that has been done, until retribution itself shall stand aghast. This is the country of the would-be-gentleman, McClellan. He has caused a loss to us, in Virginia, of at least thirty thousand negroes, the most valuable property that a Virginian can own. They have no negroes in Pennsylvania. Retaliation, therefore, must fall upon something else. A Dutch farmer has no negroes, but he has horses that can be seized, grain that can be confiscated, cattle that can be killed, and houses that can be burned."

But when they really attempted to accomplish these feats, and found with whom they had to contend, they were very glad to re-cross the Potomac, without confiscating property or burning houses, and to escape, leaving their dead and wounded on the field.

After the battle of Antietam, the army was not in a condition to follow up the rebels; but as soon as the Capital was safe, and the rebels were driven from Maryland and Pennsylvania, vigorous efforts were made to recruit, clothe, and reorganize the army. Harper's Ferry was again occupied, every weak point strengthened, and all the fords were strongly guarded. While the army thus remained inactive for a few weeks, camp duties and discipline were again strictly enforced and attended to.

I would not have my readers think that camp-life in the army is so very unpleasant, after all. I do not think so, for I have spent some of the pleasantest, happiest hours of my life in camp, and I think thousands can give the same testimony.

One of our good chaplains from the North says that even the city of New York itself can bear no favorable comparison to military life in the Army of the Potomac. "After all," he says: "New York is a humbug compared with the army. It is tattoo, as I write; what music it is, compared with the nuisance noises of those city streets!

Our candles are not brilliant; but the sight of the lights of the camps all around, is more pleasant than the glare of the city gas. The air is the pure air of heaven, not the choky stuff of the metropolis. The men are doing something noble, not dawdling away these glorious days in selling tape and ribbons. The soldier lives to some purpose, and if he dies it is a hero's death. The silks of that wealthy mart may be coveted by some; but what are the whole to our bullet-riddled old flag, which passed from the stiffening hands of one color-bearer to another, in the days of many a battle?"

To give my reader a more definite idea of the routine of camp life, I will enter into a detail of it more fully. At sunrise *reveille* beats, drum echoing to drum until the entire encampment is astir, and busy as a bee-hive. Roll-call immediately follows, which brings every man to his place in the ranks, to answer to his name. An hour later breakfast call is sounded by fife and drum, and the company cooks, who are detailed for that purpose, deal out the rations to the men as they sit or stand around the cook's quarters.

At half-past seven o'clock sick call announces to surgeons and patients that they are expected to appear at the dispensing tent—if able to go there. Then comes a general examination of tongues and pulses, and a liberal distribution of *quinine* and blue pills, and sometimes a little *eau de vie*, to wash down the bitter drugs.

Guard mounting at eight, which is an imposing affair in itself. The band marches to the usual place of dress parade and strikes up some appropriate piece, which is the signal for the regimental details to march to the place of inspection. The line is formed, arms inspected, and general appearance noted. Then the men are marched in review, and divided into three reliefs—one of which is marched to the post of each sentinel, where, after various important conferences, the old sentinel is relieved and the new one takes his place, and so on around the whole camp. The old guard is then marched to their quarters and formally dismissed, having been on duty two hours out of every six during the last twenty-four hours.

At nine o'clock the music sounds for company drill, which drill lasts an hour and a half. The bugle announces dinner at one o'clock.

At three in the afternoon battalion drill commences, which occupies an hour. At half-past four is heard the first call for evening parade, and at five o'clock comes off the great display of the day—dress parade.

Supper at six, tattoo at half past eight, and roll-call again at nine; immediately after which comes "taps" on the drum, which means "lights out."

But between all these calls drills and parades are more interesting services and duties. Away in one corner of the camp is our canvas or log meeting-house, and besides our regular preaching, we have conference and prayer meetings, debating clubs, military lectures, and numerous musical entertainments.

Then, too, comes visiting the sick in different hospitals, distribution of reading matter and delicacies, and the blessed privilege of religious conversation. And often the solemn services in connection with burying the dead. I will here give a brief description of this service:

The burial of a soldier in camp is a most solemn scene. A suitable escort is formed in two ranks opposite the tent of the deceased, with shouldered arms and bayonets unfixed. On the appearance of the coffin the soldiers present arms. The procession then forms—on each side of the coffin are the pall-bearers without muskets—and the escort moves forward with arms reversed, viz.: musket under the left arm, barrel downward, and steadied behind the back with the right hand. The band marches in front, with slow and measured tread and muffled drum they move, pouring out their melancholy wailings for the dead—a sadder dirge than which never fell upon mortal ear.

On reaching the place of interment the coffin is lowered into the grave, the soldiers leaning upon their muskets, muzzle downward, the hands clasped upon the butt of their guns, with heads uncovered and reverently bowed upon their hands. The chaplain, who has walked in the rear of the procession, conducts the burial service, at the end of which three volleys are fired over the grave, the trench is filled up, and the soldiers return to duty.

Warrior, rest! thy toils are ended:
  Life's last fearful strife is o'er;
Clarion-calls, with death-notes blended,
  Shall disturb thine ear no more!
Peaceful is thy dreamless slumber;
  Peaceful, but how cold and stern!
Thou hast joined that silent number
  In the land whence none return!

Warrior, rest! thy banner o'er thee
  Hangs in many a drooping fold;
Many a manly cheek before thee
  Stain'd with tear-drops we behold!
Thine was not a hand to falter
  When thy sword should leave its sheath;
Thine was not a cheek to alter,
  Though thy duty led to death!

Warrior, rest! a dirge is knelling
  Solemnly from shore to shore:
'T is a nation's tribute, telling
  That a patriot is no more!
And thy young bride weeps in sorrow
  That no more she hears thy tread;
That the night which knows no morrow
  Darkly veils thy laurel'd head!

Warrior, rest! we smooth thy pillow,
  For thy last, long earthly sleep;
And beneath yon verdant willow
  Storms unheard will o'er thee sweep!
There, 't is done! thy couch awaits thee!
  Softly down thy head we lay;
Here repose, till GOD translates thee
  From the dust to endless day!

CHAPTER XXII.

A MILITARY EXECUTION—THE PREPARATIONS—THE DEATH—HARPER'S FERRY—OLD JOHN BROWN—CONTRAST—ADVANCE INTO VIRGINIA—CONDITION OF THE ARMY—A DREARY RIDE—A GREEN GUARD—SEEKING SHELTER—A GUERRILLA FIGHT—MY HORSE KILLED—PLAYING POSSUM—MY POCKETS PICKED—A NARROW ESCAPE—RETURN TO CAMP—AN INTERESTING MEETING.

ABOUT this time one of those horrible and soul-revolting sights, a "military execution," took place; in other words, a soldier was shot in cold blood by his comrades. I did not witness the execution, although it occurred within a short distance of camp, and I give the particulars relating to it from the record of the chaplain who attended the unhappy man to the place of execution:

"A painful episode, the first of the kind I have witnessed, took place last Friday. It was a military execution. The person thus punished belonged to the Third Maryland, which is in our division. On Tuesday last his sentence was formally read to him. He was to be shot to death with musketry on the next Friday, between the hours of noon and four in the afternoon. He had learned the decision on the Sunday before. The day of his execution was wet and gloomy. That morning, in the midst of the provost guard, he was sitting on a bag of grain, leaning against a tree, while a sentry with fixed bayonet stood behind, never turning away from him, save as another took his place. Useless seemed the watch, for arms and feet had been secured, though not painfully, since the sentence was read. The captain of the guard had humanely done all he could, and it was partly by his request that I was there. A chaplain could minister where others would not be allowed. The rain fell silently on him; the hours of his life were numbered, even the minutes. He was to meet death, not in the shock and excitement of battle, not as a martyr for his country, not in disease, but in full health, and as a criminal. I have seen many a man die, and have tried to perform the sacred duties of my station. I never had so painful a task as this, because of these circumstances. Willingly, gladly, he conversed, heard and answered. While such a work is painful, yet it has its bright side, because of the 'exceeding great and precious promises' it is one's privilege to tell.

"When the time came for removal to the place of execution, he entered an ambulance, the chaplain accompanying him. Next, in another ambulance, was the coffin; before, behind, and on either side a guard. Half a mile of this sad journey brought him within a short distance of the spot. Then leaving the ambulance, he walked to the place selected. The rain had ceased, the sun was shining on the dark lines of the whole division drawn up in three sides of a hollow square. With guard in front and rear, he passed with steady step to the open side of the square, accompanied by the chaplain. There was a grave dug, and in front of it was his coffin. He sat upon the coffin; his feet were reconfined, to allow of which he lifted them voluntarily, and then his eyes were bandaged. In front of him the firing party, of two from each regiment, were then drawn up, half held in reserve, during which there was still a little time for words with his chaplain.

"The General (not McClellan) stood by, and the Provost Marshal read the sentence and shook hands with the condemned. Then a prayer was offered, amid uncovered heads and solemn faces. A last hand-shake with the chaplain, which he had twice requested; a few words from him to the chaplain; a lingering pressure by the hand of the condemned, his lips moving with a prayer-sentence which he had been taught, and on which his thoughts had dwelt before; and he was left alone. The word of command was immediately given. One volley, and he fell over instantly, unconscious. A record of the wounds were made by the surgeons who immediately examined him. The troops filed by his grave, and returned by the way they came. He left a mother and sister, and was twenty years of age."

Soon after I spent a night at Harper's Ferry. John Brown is still remembered there, and the soldiers go round singing "His soul goes marching on." That medley of a song does not seem so senseless after all, for the spirit of John Brown does seem to march along wonderfully fast, and our troops are becoming imbued with it to a greater extent than is generally supposed.

I also visited the court-house, where public service was held by a Massachusetts chaplain in the very room where John Brown was tried, convicted and sentenced. There was the spot where he had lain upon his litter. There in front of the judge's platform were the juror's seats. The chair which the judge had occupied was now tenanted by an abolition preacher. Oh! if old John Brown had only lived to see that day! but he is gone, and

His soul goes marching on.

On the 25th of October, the pontoon bridges being completed at Harper's Ferry and at Berlin, the army once more advanced into Virginia. The ninth corps and Pleasanton's cavalry occupied Lovettsville, a pretty little village reminding one of New England. The army was now in admirable condition and fine spirits, and enjoyed this march exceedingly, scarcely a man dropping out of the ranks for any cause whatever, but entering into the spirit of the campaign with an energy which surpassed all their former enthusiasm. As the army marched rapidly over the country from village to village, the advance guard driving the enemy's pickets from one covert to another, many thrilling adventures occurred, several of which came under my own observation, and as I am expected particularly to relate those in which I was personally concerned, I will here relate one which came very near being my last on this side the "river."

On the morning of the third day after we left Lovettsville I was sent back to headquarters, which was said to be some twelve miles in the rear. I was then with the advance guard, and when they started forward at daylight I went to the rear. In order to go more quickly I left all my traps in an ambulance—blankets, overcoat and grain, excepting enough to feed once. Then starting at a brisk canter I soon lost sight of the advancing column. I rode on mile after mile, and passed train after train, but could find no one that could tell me where McClellan's headquarters were.

On I went in this way until noon, and then found that I was six miles from headquarters. After riding a distance which seemed to me all of ten miles, I at length found the place sought for. I fed my horse, attended to the business which I had been sent to transact, and then tried to find something in the way of rations for myself, but failed utterly. Not a mouthful could I procure either at the sutler's headquarters, cook-house, or in any other place. I went to two houses and they told me they had not a mouthful in the house cooked or uncooked—but of course I believed as much of that story as I pleased.

The day had been very cold; there had been several smart showers during my ride, and now it began to snow—a sort of sleet which froze as fast as it fell. This was an October day in Old Virginia. Oh! what an afternoon I spent in the saddle on my return; hungry, wet, and shivering with cold. I traveled as fast as my horse was able to go until ten o'clock at night, with the hope of overtaking the troops I had left in the morning, but all in vain, for the whole line of march and programme for the day had been changed, in consequence of coming in contact with the enemy and having a sharp skirmish, which resulted in our troops being nearly outflanked and cut off from the main body of the army.

Of course I had no opportunity of knowing this that night, so on I went in another direction from that in which the advance guard had gone. By and by I came to some fresh troops just from the North, who had lately enlisted and been sent down to Washington, and now were on their way to join McClellan's army. They had been put on guard duty for the first time, and that too without any definite orders, their officers having concluded to remain there until the main column came up, and they scarcely knew where they were or what orders to give their men. As I rode up, one of the boys—for if boy he was, not more than sixteen summers had graced his youthful brow—stepped out in the middle of the road with his musket at a "trail arms," and there he stood till I came up close to him, and then he did not even say "halt," but quietly told me that I could not go any farther in that direction. Why not? Well, he didn't exactly know, but he was put there on guard, and he supposed it was to prevent any one from going backward or forward. Whether they have the countersign or not? Well, he did not know how that was. I then asked him if the officer of the guard had given him the countersign. Yes, but he did not know whether it was right or not.

"Well," said I, "perhaps I can tell you whether it is correct; I have just come from headquarters." He seemed to think that there could be no harm in telling me if I had been at headquarters, so he told me without any hesitation. Whereupon I proceeded to tell him of the impropriety of doing so; that it was a military offense for which he could be punished severely; and that he had no right to give the countersign to any one, not even the general in command. Then told him how to hold his musket when he challenged any one on his beat, and within how many paces to let them approach him before halting them, etc. The boy received both lecture and instructions "in the spirit of meekness," and by the time I had finished a number of the men were standing around me eager to ask questions, and especially if I knew to what portion of the army that particular regiment was to be assigned.

After passing along through these green troops I rode on till I came to a little village, which I never learned the name of, and intended to stop there the remainder of the night; but upon learning that a band of guerrillas occupied it, I turned aside, preferring to seek some other place of rest. I traveled till two o'clock in the morning, when my horse began to show signs of giving out; then I stopped at a farm-house, but not being able to make any one hear me, I hitched my horse under cover of a wood-shed, and taking the blanket from under the saddle, I lay down beside him, the saddle-blanket being my only covering. The storm had ceased, but the night was intensely cold, and the snow was about two or three inches deep. I shall always believe that I would have perished that night, had not my faithful horse lain down beside me, and by the heat of his beautiful head, which he laid across my shoulders, (a thing which he always did whenever I lay down where he could reach me,) kept me from perishing in my wet clothes.

It will be remembered that I had started at daylight the previous morning, and had never been out of the saddle, or fed my horse but once since I started, and had not eaten a mouthful myself for twenty-four hours, and had ridden all day and almost all night in the storm. In the morning my feet and hands were so chilled that they were perfectly numb, and I could scarcely stand. However, as soon as daylight came I started again. About a mile from there I went into a field where the unhusked corn stood in stacks, and fed my horse.

While employed in this manner, there came along a party of our cavalry looking after that band of guerrillas which I had passed the night before. It was known that they were in the neighborhood, and these men were sent out in search of them. I told them what I knew about it, and intimated that if I were not so hungry, I would go back with them to the village. That objection was soon removed, by supplying me with a substantial breakfast from their haversacks. We started for the village, and had gone about five miles when we were suddenly surprised and fired upon by the guerrillas. Two of our men were killed on the spot, and my horse received three bullets. He reared and plunged before he fell, and in doing so the saddle-girth was broken, and saddle and rider were thrown over his head. I was thrown on the ground violently which stunned me for a moment, and my horse soon fell beside me, his blood pouring from three wounds. Making a desperate effort to rise, he groaned once, fell back, and throwing his neck across my body, he saturated me from

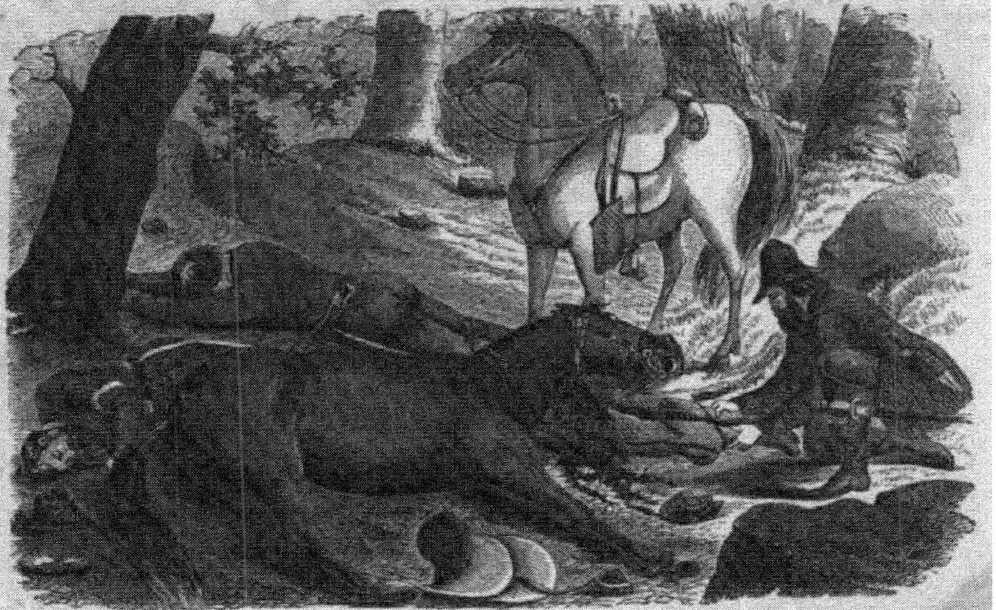

PLAYING POSSUM.—Page 295.

head to foot with his blood. He died in a few minutes. I remained in that position, not daring to rise, for our party had fled and the rebels pursued them. A very few minutes elapsed when the guerrillas returned, and the first thing I saw was one of the men thrusting his sabre into one of the dead men beside me. I was lying partially on my face; so I closed my eyes and passed for dead. The rebels evidently thought I was unworthy of their notice, for after searching the bodies of the two dead men they rode away; but just as I was making up my mind to crawl out from under the dead horse, I heard the tramp of a horse's feet, and lay perfectly still and held my breath. It was one of the same men, who had returned. Dismounting, he came up and took hold of my feet, and partially drew me from under the horse's head, and then examined my pockets. Fortunately, I had no official documents with me, and very little money—not more than five dollars. After transferring the contents of my pockets to his own, he re-mounted his horse and rode away, without ever suspecting that the object before him was playing possum.

Not long after the departure of the guerrillas, our party returned with reinforcements and pursued the rebel band. One of the men returned to camp with me, letting me ride his horse, and walked all the way himself. The guerrillas were captured that day, and, after searching them, my pocket-book was found upon one of them, and was returned to me with its contents undisturbed. It lies before me, while I write, reminding me of that narrow escape, and of the mercy of God in sparing my unprofitable life.

> A Sov'reign Protector I have,
> Unseen, yet forever at hand;
> Unchangeably faithful to save,—
> Almighty to rule and command.

After returning to camp, I found that I had sustained more injury by my fall from the horse than I had realized at the time. But a broken limb would have been borne cheerfully, if I could only have had my pet horse again. That evening we held our weekly prayer-meeting, notwithstanding we were on a march. Chaplain and Mrs. B., Nellie, and Dr. E. were present, and joined heartily in singing the following hymn:

> And are we yet alive,
> And see each other's face?
> Glory and praise to Jesus give,
> For His redeeming grace.
> Preserved by power divine
> To full salvation here,
> Again in Jesus' praise we join,
> And in his sight appear.
>
> What troubles have we seen!
> What conflicts have we past!
> Fightings without, and fears within,
> Since we assembled last!
> But out of all the Lord
> Hath brought us by His love;
> And still he doth his help afford,
> And hides our life above.

CHAPTER XXIII.

MC CLELLAN RELIEVED—HIS ADDRESS—BURNSIDE IN COMMAND—ON THE MARCH—FALMOUTH—MY RIDE—OLD BATTLEFIELDS—SAD SIGHTS—"YANKEE SKULLS"—"BONE ORNAMENTS"—SHELLING FREDERICKSBURG—PONTOON BRIDGES—OCCUPATION OF THE CITY—AIDE-DE-CAMP—DREADFUL SLAUGHTER—A GALLANT MAJOR—STRANGE SIGHTS—DARK NIGHT—DEATH OF GENERAL BAYARD—SOMEONE'S PET—RECROSSING THE RAPPAHANNOCK.

AFTER reaching Warrenton the army encamped in that vicinity for a few days—during which "Father Abraham" took the favorable opportunity of relieving the idol of the Army of the Potomac from his command, and ordered him to report at Trenton, New Jersey, just as he was entering upon another campaign, with his army in splendid condition.

After a brief address and an affecting farewell to officers and men, he hastened to comply with the order. His farewell address was as follows:

"November 7th, 1862. Officers and Soldiers of the Army of the Potomac: An order of the President devolves upon Major-General Burnside the command of this army. In parting from you I cannot express the love and gratitude I bear you. As an army you have grown up under my care. In you I have never found doubt or coldness. The battles you have fought under my command will proudly live in our nation's history. The glory you have achieved, our mutual perils and fatigues, the graves of our comrades fallen in battle and by disease, the broken forms of those whom wounds and sickness have disabled—the strongest associations which can exist among men—unite us still by an indissoluble tie. We shall ever be comrades in supporting the constitution of our country and the nationality of its people."

That was a sad day for the Army of the Potomac.

The new commander marched the army immediately to Falmouth, opposite Fredericksburg. Of the incidents of that march I know nothing, for I went to Washington, and from thence to Aquia Creek by water.

I did not return to Washington on the cars, but rode on horseback, and made a two days' trip of it, visiting all the old places as I went. The battle-ground of the first and second Bull Run battles, Centerville, Fairfax Court House, and Chentilla.

But how shall I describe the sights which I saw and the impressions which I had as I rode over those fields! There were men and horses thrown together in heaps, and some clay thrown on them above ground; others lay where they had fallen, their limbs bleaching in the sun without the appearance of burial.

There was one in particular—a cavalryman: he and his horse both lay together, nothing but the bones and clothing remained; but one of his arms stood straight up, or rather the bones and the coatsleeve, his hand had dropped off at the wrist and lay on the ground; not a finger or joint was separated, but the hand was perfect. I dismounted twice for the purpose of bringing away that hand, but did not do so after all. I would have done so if it had been possible to find a clue to his name or regiment.

The few families who still live in that vicinity tell horrid stories of the brutal conduct of the rebels after those battles.

A Southern clergyman declares that in the town where he now resides he saw rebel soldiers selling "Yankee skulls" at ten dollars apiece. And it is a common thing to see rebel women wear rings and ornaments made of our soldiers' bones—in fact they boast of it, even to the Union soldiers, that they have "Yankee bone ornaments."

This to me was a far more sickening sight than was presented at the time of the battles, with dead and wounded lying in their gore. I looked in vain for the old "brush heap" which had once screened me from the rebel cavalry; the fire had consumed it. But the remains of the Stone Church at Centerville was an object of deep interest to me.

I went from Washington to Aquia Creek by steamer, and from thence to Falmouth on horseback. I found the army encamped in the mud for miles along the Rappahannock river.

The river is very narrow between Falmouth and Fredericksburg, not more than a stone's cast in some places. I have often seen the pickets on both sides amusing themselves by throwing stones across it.

Some writer in describing the picturesque scenery in this locality says: "There is a young river meandering through its center, towards which slope down beautiful banks of mud on either side, while the fields are delightfully variegated by alternate patches of snow and swamp, and the numerous roads are in such condition that no matter which one you take you are sure to wish you had tried another instead."

All the mud and bad roads on the Peninsula could not bear the least comparison with that of Falmouth and along the Rappahannock.

It was now December and the weather was extremely cold, yet the constant rains kept the roads in the most terrible state imaginable.

On riding along the brink of the river we could see distinctly the rebel batteries frowning on the heights beyond the city of Fredericksburg, and the rebel sentinels walking their rounds within talking distance of our own pickets.

On the eleventh the city was shelled by our troops. The pontoon bridges were laid amid showers of bullets from the sharpshooters of the enemy, who were ensconced in the houses on the opposite bank. However, the work went steadily on, notwithstanding that two out of every three who were engaged in laying the bridges were either killed or wounded. But as fast as one fell another took his place.

Soon it was deemed expedient to take care of those sharpshooters before the bridges could be finished. Several companies filed into boats and rowed across in a few minutes, the men of the Seventh Michigan leading the van, and drove the rebels from the houses, killing some and taking many prisoners.

The bridges were soon completed, the troops marched over and took possession of the city. Headquarters were established in the principal building, and a church and other large buildings were appropriated for hospital purposes.

The following is an extract from my journal, written on the battlefield the second day after we crossed the river:

BATTLE-FIELD, FREDERICKSBURG, VA.,
December 13, 1862.

In consequence of one of General H.'s staff officers being ill I have volunteered to take his place, and am now aide-de-camp to General H. I wish my friends could see me in my present uniform! This division will probably charge on the enemy's works this afternoon. God grant them success! While I write the roar of cannon and musketry is almost deafening, and the shot and shell are falling fast on all sides. This may be my last entry in this journal. God's will be done. I commit myself to Him, soul and body. I must close. General H. has mounted his horse, and says Come—!

Of course it is not for me to say whose fault it was in sacrificing those thousands of noble lives which fell upon that disastrous field, or in charging again and again upon those terrible stone walls and fortifications, after being repulsed every time with more than half their number lying on the ground. The brave men, nothing daunted by their thinned ranks, advanced more fiercely on the foe—

> Plunged in the battery's smoke,
> Fiercely the line they broke;
> Strong was the saber stroke,
> Making an army reel.

But when it was proved to a demonstration that it was morally impossible to take and retain those heights, in consequence of the natural advantage of position which the rebels occupied, and still would occupy if they should fall back—whose fault was it that the attempt was made time after time, until the field was literally piled with dead and ran red with blood? We may truly say of the brave soldiers thus sacrificed—

> Their's not to reason why,
> Their's not to make reply,
> Their's but to do and die.

Among the many who fell in that dreadful battle perhaps there is none more worthy of notice than the brave and heroic Major Edward E. Sturtevant, of Keene, New Hampshire, who fell while leading the gallant Fifth in a charge upon the enemy. He was the first man in New Hampshire who enlisted *for the war.* He was immediately authorized by the Governor to make enlistments for the First New Hampshire Volunteers, and was eminently successful. He held the commission of captain in the First Regiment, and afterwards was promoted major of the Fifth.

One of the leading papers of his native State has the following with regard to him: "He was in every battle where the regiment was engaged, nine or ten in number, besides skirmishes, and was slightly wounded at the battle of Fair Oaks. He commanded the regiment most of the time on the retreat from the Chickahominy to James river. The filial affection of the deceased was of the strongest character, and made manifest in substantial ways on many occasions. His death is the first in the household, and deep is the grief that is experienced there; but that grief will doubtless be mitigated by the consoling circumstance that the departed son and brother died in a service that will hallow his memory forever. A braver man or more faithful friend never yielded up his spirit amidst the clash of arms and the wail of the dying."

I well remember the desperate charge which that brave officer made upon the enemy just before he fell, and the thinned and bleeding ranks of his men as they returned, leaving their beloved commander on the field, reminded me of the "gallant six hundred," of whom Tennyson has written the following lines:

> Stormed at with shot and shell,
> They that had struck so well
> Rode through the jaws of death,
> Half a league back again
> Up, from the mouth of hell—
> All that was left of them.

I have since had the pleasure of becoming acquainted with the bereaved family of the deceased, and deeply sympathize with them in the loss of one so noble, kind, and brave.

Major Sturtevant was the son of George W. Sturtevant, Esq., and nephew of Rev. David Kilburn—one of the pioneers of Methodism—whom thousands will remember as a faithful and efficient minister of the Gospel.

During the progress of that battle I saw many strange sights—although I had been in many a fierce battle before. I never saw, till then, a man deliberately shoot himself, with his own pistol, in order to save the rebels the satisfaction of doing so, as it would seem.

As one brigade was ordered into line of battle, I saw an officer take out his pistol and shoot himself through the side—not mortally, I am sorry to say, but just sufficient to unfit him for duty; so he was carried to the rear—he protesting that it was done by accident.

Another officer I saw there, a young and handsome lieutenant, disgrace his shoulder-straps by showing the white feather at the very moment when he was most needed.

I rode three miles with General H. to General Franklin's headquarters, the second night we were at Fredericksburg, and of all the nights that I can recall to mind that was the darkest. On our way we had numerous ditches to leap, various ravines to cross, and mountains to climb, which can be better imagined than described. It was not only once or twice that horse and rider went tumbling into chasms head first, but frequently.

As we passed along, we stopped at the headquarters of General Bayard (General of Cavalry) a few minutes—found him enjoying a cup of coffee under a large tree, which constituted his headquarters. We called again when we returned, but he was cold in death, having been struck by a stray shot, and died in a short time. He was killed just where we had left him, under the tree. He was a splendid officer, and his removal was a great loss to the Federal cause. His death cast a gloom over his whole command which was deeply felt.

Of the wounded of this battle I can say but little, for my time was fully occupied in the responsible duties which I had volunteered to perform; and so constantly was I employed, that I was not out of the saddle but once in twelve hours, and that was to assist an officer of the Seventy-ninth, who lay writhing in agony on the field, having been seized with cramps and spasms, and was suffering the most extreme pain. He was one of the brave and fearless ones, however, and in less than an hour, after having taken some powerful medicine which I procured for him, he was again on his horse, at the general's side.

On going to the Church hospital in search of Doctor E., I saw an immense shell which had been sent through the building and fell on the floor, in the centre of those wounded and dying men who had just been carried off the field, and placed there for safety. But strange to say, it did not burst or injure any one, and was carried out and laid beside the mangled limbs which had been amputated in consequence of contact with just such instruments of death. I saw the remains of the Rev. A. B. Fuller, Chaplain of the Sixteenth Massachusetts, as they were removed to the camp. He was faithful to his trust, and died at his post.

On one of my necessary rides, in the darkness of that dreadful night, I passed by a grave-yard near by where our reserves were lying—and there, in that hour of darkness and danger, I heard the voice of prayer ascend. A group of soldiers were there holding communion with God—strengthening their souls for the coming conflict. There are, scattered over the battle-fields and camping-grounds of this war, Bethels, consecrated to God, and sacred to souls who have wrestled and prevailed. This retirement was a grave-yard, with a marble slab for an altar, where that little band met to worship God—perhaps for the last time.

But among all the dead and wounded, I saw none who touched my heart so much as one beautiful boy, severely wounded; he was scarcely more than a child, and certainly a very attractive one. Some one writes the following, after he was sent to a hospital:

"Among the many brave, uncomplaining fellows who were brought up to the hospital from the battle of Fredericksburg, was a bright-eyed and intelligent youth, sixteen years old, who belonged to a northern regiment. He appeared more affectionate and tender, more refined and thoughtful than many of his comrades, and attracted a good deal of attention from the attendants and visitors. Manifestly the pet of some household which he had left, perhaps, in spite of entreaty and tears. He expressed an anxious longing for the arrival of his mother, who was expected, having been informed that he was mortally wounded, and failing fast. Ere she arrived, however, he died. But before the end, almost his last act of consciousness was the thought that she had really come; for, as a lady sat by his pillow and wiped the death-dews from his brow, just as his sight was failing, he rallied a little, like an expiring taper in its socket, looked up longingly and joyfully, and in tones that drew tears from every eye whispered audibly, 'Is that mother?' Then drawing her toward him with all his feeble power, he nestled his head in her arms, like a sleeping child, and thus died, with the sweet word, 'Mother,' on his lips."

Raise me in your arms, dear mother,
 Let me once more look
On the green and waving willows,
 And the flowing brook;
Hark, those strains of angel music
 From the choirs above!
Dearest mother, I am going,
 Truly "God is love."

A council of war was held by our generals, and the conclusion arrived at that the enterprise should be abandoned, and that the army should recross the Rappahannock under cover of darkness. Everything was conducted in the most quiet manner; so quiet, indeed, that the enemy never suspected the movement, and the retreat was accomplished, and the bridges partially removed, before the fact was discovered.

CHAPTER XXIV.

AFTER THE BATTLE—SUFFERINGS OF THE WOUNDED—GENERAL BURNSIDE'S ORDER—"STUCK IN THE MUD"—HOOKER IN COMMAND—WESTERN CAMPAIGN—CAVALRY RECONNOISSANCE—ANOTHER DISGUISE—AGAIN IN DIXIE—A WEDDING PARTY—IN A TRAP—REBEL CONSCRIPT—ON THE MARCH—A REBEL CAPTAIN—A FIERCE ENGAGEMENT—AGAIN UNDER THE OLD FLAG—PAYING A DEBT OF GRATITUDE.

AFTER the battle of Fredericksburgh the weather was very cold, and the wounded suffered exceedingly—even after they were sent to Aquia Creek, and other places—for they could not all be provided for and made comfortable immediately. Our troops returned to their old camps in the mud, and remained stationary for several weeks, notwithstanding our daily orders were to be ready to march at a moment's notice. The unnecessary slaughter of our men at Fredericksburg had a sad effect upon our troops, and the tone of the northern press was truly distressing. The wailing for the noble dead seemed wafted on every breeze, for

In the city, in the village,
In the hamlet far away,
Sit the mothers, watching, waiting,
For their soldier boys to-day.

They are coming, daily coming,
One by one, and score by score,
In their leaden casings folded,
Underneath the flag they bore.

On the twentieth of January General Burnside issued the following order to the army, which was joyfully received; for of all places for an encampment, that seemed to be the most inconvenient and disagreeable:

HEAD-QUARTERS, ARMY OF THE POTOMAC,
Camp near Falmouth, Va., Jan. 20, 1863.

GENERAL ORDERS—No. 7.

The Commanding General announces to the Army of the Potomac that they are about to meet the enemy once more. The late brilliant actions in North Carolina, Tennessee and Arkansas, have divided and weakened the enemy on the Rappahannock, and the auspicious moment seems to have arrived to strike a great and mortal blow to the rebellion, and to gain that decisive victory which is due to the country.

Let the gallant soldiers of so many brilliant battle-fields accomplish this achievement, and a fame the most glorious awaits them.

The Commanding General calls for the firm and united action of officers and men, and, under the providence of God, the Army of the Potomac will have taken the great step towards restoring peace to the country, and the Government to its rightful authority.

By command of MAJOR-GENERAL BURNSIDE.

LEWIS RICHMOND, *Assistant Adjutant-General.*

Soon after this order was issued a portion of the army did really move—but the pontoons became "stuck in the mud," and the troops returned again. In this manner the winter wore away, and a severe winter I thought it was; for in riding a distance of two miles, in two instances, I had my feet frozen.

General Hooker was now put in command of the Army of the Potomac, and Burnside, with the Ninth Army Corps, ordered to the Western department. Being desirous of leaving the Army of the Potomac, I now applied for permission to go with the Ninth Corps, which was granted. I did not go with the troops, however, but went to Washington first, and remained several days; then took the cars and proceeded to Louisville, Kentucky, and arrived there before the troops did.

The last entry in my journal, before leaving the Army of the Potomac, was as follows: "The *weather* department is in perfect keeping with the War Department; its policy being to make as many changes as possible, and every one worse than the last. May God bless the old Army of the Potomac, and save it from total annihilation."

On the arrival of the troops at Louisville, they were sent in detachments to different places—some to Bardstown, some to Lebanon, and others to guard different portions of the railroad.

The third day after my arrival I went out with a reconnoitering expedition, under command of General M. It was entirely composed of cavalry. We rode thirty-six miles that afternoon—the roads were splendid. When we were about twelve miles from our lines we changed our course and struck through the woods, fording creeks and crossing swamps, which was anything but pleasant.

After emerging from the thick undergrowth, on one occasion, we came upon an inferior force of the enemy's cavalry; a sharp skirmish ensued, which resulted in the capture of five prisoners from the rebel band, and wounding several. Three of our men were slightly wounded, but we returned to Louisville in good order, and enjoyed the luxury of a good supper at a hotel, which is a rare thing in that city.

I took the cars the next day and went to Lebanon—dressed in one of the rebel prisoner's clothes—and thus disguised, made another trip to rebeldom. My business purported to be buying up butter and eggs, at the farm-houses, for the rebel army. I passed through the lines somewhere, without knowing it; for on coming to a little village toward evening, I found it occupied by a strong force of rebel cavalry. The first house

I went to was filled with officers and citizens. I had stumbled upon a wedding party, unawares. Captain Logan, a recruiting officer, had been married that afternoon to a brilliant young widow whose husband had been killed in the rebel army a few months before. She had discovered that widow's weeds were not becoming to her style of beauty, so had decided to appear once more in bridal costume, for a change.

I was questioned pretty sharply by the handsome captain in regard to the nature of my business in that locality, but finding me an innocent, straightforward Kentuckian, he came to the conclusion that I was all right. But he also arrived at the conclusion that I was old enough to be in the army, and bantered me considerably upon my want of patriotism.

The rebel soldier's clothes which I wore did not indicate any thing more than that I was a Kentuckian—for their cavalry do not dress in any particular uniform, for scarcely two of them dress alike—the only uniformity being that they most generally dress in butternut color.

I tried to make my escape from that village as soon as possible, but just as I was beginning to congratulate myself upon my good fortune, who should confront me but Captain Logan. Said he: "See here, my lad; I think the best thing you can do is to enlist, and join a company which is just forming here in the village, and will leave in the morning. We are giving a bounty to all who freely enlist, and are conscripting those who refuse. Which do you propose to do, enlist and get the bounty, or refuse, and be obliged to go without anything?" I replied, "I think I shall wait a few days before I decide." "But we can't wait for you to decide," said the captain; "the Yankees may be upon us any moment, for we are not far from their lines, and we will leave here either to-night or in the morning early. I will give you two hours to decide this question, and in the mean time you must be put under guard." So saying, he marched me back with him, and gave me in charge of the guards. In two or three hours he came for my decision, and I told him that I had concluded to wait until I was conscripted. "Well," said he, "you will not have long to wait for that, so you may consider yourself a soldier of the Confederacy from this hour, and subject to military discipline."

This seemed to me like pretty serious business, especially as I would be required to take the oath of allegiance to the Confederate Government. However, I did not despair, but trusted in Providence and my own ingenuity to escape from this dilemma also; and as I was not required to take the oath until the company was filled up, I was determined to be among the missing ere it became necessary for me to make any professions of loyalty to the rebel cause. I knew that if I should refuse to be sworn into the service after I was conscripted, that in all probability my true character would be suspected, and I would have to suffer the penalty of death—and that, too, in the most barbarous manner.

I was glad to find that it was a company of cavalry that was being organized, for if I could once get on a good horse there would be some hope of my escape. There was no time to be lost, as the captain remarked, for the Yankees might make a dash upon us at any moment; consequently a horse and saddle was furnished me, and everything was made ready for a start immediately. Ten o'clock came, and we had not yet started. The captain finally concluded that, as everything seemed quiet, we would not start until daylight.

Music and dancing was kept up all night, and it was some time after daylight when the captain made his appearance. A few moments more and we were trotting briskly over the country, the captain complimenting me upon my horsemanship, and telling me how grateful I would be to him when the war was over and the South had gained her independence, and that I would be proud that I had been one of the soldiers of the Southern confederacy, who had steeped my saber in Yankee blood, and driven the vandals from our soil. "Then," said he, "you will thank me for the interest which I have taken in you, and for the *gentle persuasives* which I made use of to stir up your patriotism and remind you of your duty to your country."

In this manner we had traveled about half an hour, when we suddenly encountered a reconnoitering party of the Federals, cavalry in advance, and infantry in the rear. A contest soon commenced; we were ordered to advance in line, which we did, until we came within a few yards of the Yankees.

The company advanced, but my horse suddenly became unmanageable, and it required a second or two to bring him right again; and before I could overtake the company and get in line the contending parties had met in a hand to hand fight.

All were engaged, so that when I, by accident, got on the Federal side of the line, none observed me for several minutes, except the Federal officer, who had recognized me and signed to me to fall in next to him. That brought me face to face with my rebel captain, to whom I owed such a debt of gratitude. Thinking this would be a good time to cancel all obligations in that direction, I discharged the contents of my pistol in his face.

This act made me the center of attraction. Every rebel seemed determined to have the pleasure of killing me first, and a simultaneous dash was made toward me and numerous saber strokes aimed at my head. Our men with one accord rushed between me and the enemy, and warded off the blows with their sabers, and attacked them with such fury that they were driven back several rods.

The infantry now came up and deployed as skirmishers, and succeeded in getting a position where they had a complete cross-fire on the rebels, and poured in volley after volley until nearly half their number lay upon the ground. Finding it useless to fight longer at such a disadvantage they turned and fled, leaving behind them eleven killed, twenty-nine wounded, and seventeen prisoners.

The confederate captain was wounded badly but not mortally; his handsome face was very much disfigured, a part of his nose and nearly half of his upper lip being shot away. I was sorry, for the graceful curve of his mustache was sadly spoiled, and the happy bride of the previous morning would no longer rejoice in the beauty of that manly face and exquisite mustache of which she seemed so proud, and which had captivated her heart ere she had been three months a widow.

Our men suffered considerable loss before the infantry came up, but afterward scarcely lost a man. I escaped without receiving a scratch, but my horse was badly cut across the neck with a saber, but which did not injure him materially, only for a short time.

After burying the dead, Federal and rebel, we returned to camp with our prisoners and wounded, and I rejoiced at having once more escaped from the confederate lines.

I was highly commended by the commanding general for my coolness throughout the whole affair, and was told kindly and candidly that I would not be permitted to go out again in that vicinity, in the capacity of spy, as I would most assuredly meet with some of those who had seen me desert their ranks, and I would consequently be hung up to the nearest tree.

Not having any particular fancy for such an exalted position, and not at all ambitious of having my name handed down to posterity among the list of those who "expiated their crimes upon the gallows," I turned my attention to more quiet and less dangerous duties.

Then sweet thoughts of home came stealing over my mind, and I exclaimed:

> Adieu, dear land,
> With beauty teeming,
> Where first I roved a careless child;
> Of thee my heart
> Will e'er be dreaming—
> Thy snow-clad peaks and mountains wild.
> Dear land, that I cherish,
> O, long may'st thou flourish!
> My memory must perish
> Ere I forget thee.

CHAPTER XXV.

APPOINTED DETECTIVE—I VISIT LOUISVILLE—SECESH ACQUAINTANCES—SEEKING EMPLOYMENT—PEDDLING—REBEL SPIES—ACTING AS CLERK—TRAPPING SPIES—START FOR VICKSBURG—PRO-SLAVERY TROOPS—CRUELTY TO NEGROES—VISITING HOSPITALS—TOUCHING SCENES—AN ARMLESS SOLDIER—PATIENT SUFFERING—TRIUMPHANT DEATH—RALLY ROUND THE FLAG—WESTERN CHAPLAINS—SOLDIERS' TESTIMONY—EFFECT OF PRAYER IN BATTLE—CARRYING THE WOUNDED.

BEING prohibited from further explorations in that region outside of our lines, I was appointed to act as detective inside of the lines, as there were many spies in our midst who were daily giving information to the enemy, and had baffled all attempts at discovery.

I forthwith dressed in citizen's clothes and proceeded to Louisville, and there mingled freely with the citizens, visited the different places of public resort, and made many secesh acquaintances.

At length I found a merchant who was the most bitter in his denunciations of the Yankees that it has ever been my lot to meet, and I thought he would be a pretty good person to assist me in my undertakings. Stepping into his store one morning I inquired if he was in need of a clerk. He replied that he would require help in a few days, as one of his clerks was going to leave.

Then came the interrogatory process—Who was I, where did I come from, and what had brought me to that city? Well, I was a foreigner, and wishing to see a little of this great American war, I had come "down South;" and now that I was here, finding myself scarce of money, I would like to find some employment. This was literally true. I was a foreigner, and very often scarce of money, and really wished him to employ me.

He finally told me that I might come in the course of a week; but that did not suit my purpose, so I told him I would rather come at once, as I would be learning considerable before the other clerk went away; adding that he might give me just whatever he pleased for the first week's work. That seemed to suit him and I was at once set to work.

After I had been there several days, I was asked how I would like to go out to the nearest camp and sell some small articles to the soldiers. I would like it much; so was sent accordingly with an assortment of pocket knives, combs and suspenders. By the middle of the afternoon I had sold out my stock in trade, returned to the store, and gave a good account of myself and of the goods intrusted to my care.

My employer was pleased with my success and seemed interested in me, and each day brought some new proof of his confidence. Things went on this way for two weeks, in which time I had succeeded, by the good merchant's assistance, in finding a clue to three rebel spies then within our lines.

I was often questioned by my employer with regard to my political sentiments, but of course I did not know anything about politics—in fact I hardly knew how to apply the terms Federal and Confederate, and often misapplied them when talking in the store, and was frequently told that I must not call the d—d Yankees, Confederates, and all due pains were taken to instruct me, and give me a proper insight into the true state of affairs, as seen by Southern secessionists.

At last I expressed a desire to enter the Confederate service, and asked the merchant how I should manage to get through the Yankee lines if I should decide to take such a step. After a long conversation, and much planning, we at last decided that I should go through our lines the next night with a person who was considered by our troops a thorough Union man, as he had taken the oath of allegiance to the Federal Government—but who was in reality a rebel spy.

That afternoon I was sent out again to dispose of some goods to the soldiers, and while I was gone took the favorable opportunity of informing the Provost Marshal of my intended escape the following night together with my brother spy.

After telling him that I might not be able to leave the store again with any more definite information without incurring suspicion, and that he had better send some one to the store at a certain hour the next day to purchase some trifle, so that I might inclose in the parcel the necessary information, I went back to the store, and my clever employer told me that I had better not trouble myself any more about anything, but get ready for my journey. Having but little preparation to make, however, I soon returned to the store.

Not long after a gentleman came in, to whom I was introduced, and was told that this was the person who proposed to conduct me through the lines He was not announced in his true character, but I understood at once that this gentlemanly personage was no less than the spy before referred to. He questioned me pretty sharply, but I being "slow of speech," referred him to the merchant, whose eloquence had convinced me of my duty to the Southern confederacy.

My employer stood beside me and gave him a brief history of our acquaintance and of his confidence in me; also of his own peculiar faculty of impressing the truth upon unprejudiced minds.

The spy evidently took me for a poor green boy whom the merchant had flattered into the idea of becoming a soldier, but who did not realize the responsibility of my position, and I confirmed him in that opinion by saying—"Well, I suppose if I don't like soldiering they will let me go home again?"

The Provost Marshal himself came in during the day, and I had my document ready informing him what time we would start and what direction we were to take.

The night came, and we started about nine o'clock. As we walked along toward the rebel lines the spy seemed to think that I was a true patriot in the rebel cause, for he entertained me with a long conversation concerning his exploits in the secret service; and of the other two who were still in camp he said one of them was a sutler, and the other sold photographs of our generals.

We were pursuing our way in the darkness, talking in a low, confidential tone, when suddenly a number of cavalry dashed upon us and took us both prisoners. As soon as we were captured we were searched, and documents found on my companion which condemned him as a spy. We were then marched back to Louisville and put under guard. The next morning he was taken care of, and I was sent to General M.'s head-quarters.

The next thing to be done was to find the other two spies. The sutler was found and put under arrest, and his goods confiscated, but the dealer in photographs had made his escape.

I never dared go back to Louisville again, for I had ample reason to believe that my life would pay the penalty if I did.

About this time the Ninth Army Corps was ordered to Vicksburg, where General Grant had already commenced his siege. While the troops waited at the depot for transportation a little incident occurred which illustrates the spirit of the Kentucky soldiers on the slavery question.

Two of our Kentucky regiments were stationed as guards at the depot, and on this occasion were amusing themselves by throwing stones at every poor negro who had occasion to pass within a stone's throw of them.

A Michigan regiment marched into the depot on its way to Vicksburg, and along with it some smart, saucy darkies, in the capacity of servants. The native soldiers began the same game with them, by throwing stones at and abusing them; but the Michigan men informed them that "if they did not stop that kind of business immediately they would find more work on hand than they could attend to," as they considered their servants a necessary part of their regiment, and would not permit them to be abused or insulted any more than if they were white men.

This gave rise to a warm discussion between the troops, and ended in the Kentuckians forbidding and prohibiting the different regiments from taking a negro with them from the State under any circumstances. Of course this incensed our patriotic troops, and in five minutes they were in line of battle arrayed against their pro-slavery brethren in arms. But before blood was shed the commander of the post was informed, and hastened to the spot to prevent further mischief. When the case was fully made known to him he could not settle the matter, for he was a Kentuckian by birth, and his sympathies were with the native troops—yet he knew if he should decide in their favor that a bloody fight would be the consequence, as the troops still remained in line of battle awaiting the decision of the commander. He finally told them that they must remain there until he telegraphed to the headquarters of the department and received an answer. Consequently the troops were detained two days waiting for the despatch that would decide the contest. The men became tired of the fun and marched back to camp.

In consequence of this affair the poor negroes fared worse than ever, and the troops had no sooner gone back to camp than the Kentuckians swore they would hang every "nigger" that came into their camp.

During the day I was passing through the depot, and saw a little black urchin selling cakes and pies, who had no sooner made his appearance than the guards took his basket away from him. The boy commenced to cry, when four of the soldiers took hold of him, each one taking hold of a hand or foot, and pulled him almost limb from limb—just as I have seen cruel schoolb[illegible] frogs.

When they threw him on the ground he could neither speak, cry, nor walk, but there he lay a little quivering, convulsive heap of pain and misery.

The telegram came at last, and the troops were permitted to depart in peace—taking with them their colored friends, to the chagrin of the Kentucky guards.

Before reaching Vicksburg I visited several hospitals where the wounded had been brought from those terrible battles preceding the siege of Vicksburg, where thousands lay, with all conceivable sorts of wounds.

Several I saw without either arms or legs, having been torn and mangled by shell so that it was impossible to save even a single limb—and yet they lived, and would probably recover.

One handsome young man lay on one of the hospital boats who had lost both arms—a most noble specimen of the patient, cheerful, suffering soldier.

Of this young man the Rev. Mr. Savage writes: "There he lay upon his cot, armless, and knowing that this must be his condition through life; but yet with a cheerful, happy countenance, and not a single word of complaint. I ministered to his wants, and as I cut up fruit in mouthfuls, and put them in his mouth, he would say, 'Well, now, how good that is! How kind of you! The Lord will bless you for it. I don't see why you are so kind to me. As if any one could be too kind to a man who had suffered such a loss in defense of his country. His soul seemed to be resting peacefully upon Jesus amid all his great sufferings. One thing touched me exceedingly: As I spoke of his feelings, the tears coursed down his cheeks and lay upon them. He had no hands with which even to wipe away the tears from his own face; and as I took a handkerchief and tenderly performed this office, that beautiful passage of scripture occurred to me with a force it never did before: 'and God shall wipe away all tears from their eyes.'"

Near by lay another young man, an officer, mortally wounded—fast breathing his life away—he seemed unconscious of his dying state. I asked the nurse, in a low whisper, if he knew he was dying, but before the nurse could reply, he looked up with a smile, and said: "Yes, yes, I know it. Praise God! there is not a cloud between my soul and Jesus. I am waiting—I—waiting——." These were his last words. A few moments more and his tongue was silent in death.

> But he's gone to rest in heaven above,
> To sing his Saviour's praise.

One of the military agents at Nashville relates a most thrilling incident, which he witnessed in a hospital at that place. He says:

"Last evening, when passing by the post hospital, my attention was arrested by the singing, in rather a loud voice, of 'Rally round the flag, boys,' by one of the patients inside. While listening to the beautiful music of that popular song, I observed to a nurse standing in the door-way, that the person singing must be in a very merry mood, and could not be very sick. 'You are mistaken, sir,' said he; 'the poor fellow engaged in singing that good old song is now grappling with death—has been dying all day. I am his nurse,' he continued, 'and the scene so affected me that I was obliged to leave the room. He is just about breathing his last.'

"I stepped into the ward, and true enough, the brave man was near his end. His eyes were already fixed in death. He was struggling with all his remaining strength against the grim monster, while at the same time there gushed forth from his patriotic soul incoherently the words: 'Rally round the flag, boys,' which had so often cheered him through his weary march, and braced him up when entering the field of blood in defense of his country. Finally he sank away into his death-slumber, and joined his Maker's command, that is marching onward to that far-off, better land. The last audible sound that escaped his lips was, 'Rally boys, rally once again!' As his eyes were closing, some dozen of his comrades joined in a solemn, yet beautiful hymn, appropriate to the occasion. Take it altogether, this was one of the most affecting scenes I have ever witnessed in a hospital. It drew tears copiously from near one hundred of us. It occurred in the large ward which occupies the entire body of the church on Cherry street. The deceased was an Illinoisan, and had been wounded in one of the recent skirmishes."

I noticed in the Western department that the chaplains were much more faithful to their trust, and attentive to the sick and wounded, than the chaplains in the Army of the Potomac—taking them as a class.

One man in speaking of his chaplain, said: "He is one of the best men in the world; he has a temperance meeting once a week, a prayer meeting twice a week, and other meetings as he is able to hold them; and then he labors personally among the men. He also comforts the sick and dying. I saw him with one of our comrades before he died, watching and praying with him; and when he died, he closed his eyes and prepared him for the grave with his own hands."

Another said: "Over at Frederickstown, as our lines were beginning to give way, and many thought the day was lost, our chaplain stepped right out from the ranks, between us and the enemy's lines, knelt down upon the ground, and lifted up his voice in most earnest prayer to God for divine help in that hour of need. I never felt so in all my life as I did at that moment. An inspiration, as from God, seemed to seize us all; we rallied, charged, drove the enemy before us, and gained the important victory at Fredrickstown, which perhaps has saved to us the State of Mississippi."

And yet another soldier gave testimony like the following, with regard to a chaplain who had followed his regiment through every battle in which it had participated. Said he: "He was with us day after day, and as soon as a man fell wounded, he would take him up in his arms and carry him out where the surgeon could take care of him; and the last day I saw him, his clothes, from head to foot, were literally dripping with the blood of dead and wounded men that he had carried from the battle-field."

This noble chaplain reminds me of a brave soldier in the Army of the Potomac, who was in the hottest of the battle at Antietam, where the bullets were sweeping like death-hail through the ranks. The line wavered; there were strong symptoms of falling back on the part of his regiment. This man rushed toward the color-bearer, who stood hesitating, seized the standard and advanced with firm and rapid step several paces in front of the foremost man; then thrusting down the flag-staff into the ground he looked up at the banner, then at the wavering line, and said—"There, boys, come up to that!"

CHAPTER XXVI.

A UNIONIST FROM THE REBEL ARMY—HIS TESTIMONY—SOUTHERN HOSPITALS—PATRIOTISM—FEMALE RECRUITING—CRINOLINE—"SWEET LITTLE MAN"—CONFEDERATE SYSTEM—NORTH AND SOUTH CONTRASTED—REBEL IMPRESSMENT—BROTHERS' CRUELTY—DYING FOR THE UNION—FATE OF A TENNESSEE PATRIOT—ON THE MISSISSIPPI—INVISIBLE ATTRACTION—AN IMPORTANT QUESTION—MORAL SUBLIMITY—CONTRABAND'S JUBILEE.

AT one of the hospitals near Vicksburg I met a man who had served a year in the Confederate army, having been conscripted by the rebels, and remained that length of time before he found an opportunity to escape.

He was an educated, and highly intelligent young man, and it was deeply interesting to listen to his account of the Southern side of this rebellion. He told me that the Southern people, and especially the ladies, were much more patriotic than the people of the North.

After a battle, the citizens, both men and women, come with one accord to assist in taking care of the wounded; bringing with them, gratuitously, every article of comfort and convenience that their means will admit, and their patriotism suggest.

Farmers come to the hospitals with loads of provisions, and the women come with fruits, wines, jellies, etc., and cheerfully submit to the hardships and fatigue of hospital labor without the slightest remuneration. Said he: "The women down South are the best recruiting officers—for they absolutely refuse to tolerate, or admit to their society, any young man who refuses to enlist; and very often send their lovers, who have not enlisted, skirts and crinoline, with a note attached, suggesting the appropriateness of such a costume unless they donned the Confederate uniform at once."

I have often thought of this trait of the Southern ladies' character, and contrasted it with the flattering receptions so lavishly bestowed upon our able-bodied "home guards," by the New-England fair ones who profess to love the old flag and despise its enemies. And I have wondered if an extensive donation of "crinoline" would not be more effectual in filling up our ranks, than graceful bows and bewitching smiles. And I would mildly suggest that each package of crinoline be accompanied by the following appropriate lines:

Now, while our soldiers are fighting our battles,
  Each at his post to do all that he can,
Down among rebels and contraband chattels,
  What are *you* doing, my sweet little man?

All the brave boys under canvas are sleeping,
  All of them pressing to march with the van,
Far from their homes where their sweethearts are weeping;
  What are *you* waiting for, sweet little man?

You, with the terrible warlike mustaches,
  Fit for a colonel or chief of a clan,

You with the waist made for sword-belts and sashes,
  Where are your shoulder-straps, sweet little man?

We send you the buttonless garments of woman!
  Cover your face lest it freckle or tan;
Muster the apron-string guards on the common—
  That is the corps for the sweet little man.

All the fair maidens about him shall cluster,
  Pluck the white feathers from bonnet and fan,
Make him a plume like a turkey-wing duster—
  That is the crest for the sweet little man.

Give him for escort a file of young misses,
  Each of them armed with a deadly rattan,
They shall defend him from laughter and hisses
  Aimed by low boys at the sweet little man.

And now, while I am contrasting the conduct of the North and South, I may as well give another testimony in favor of the confederate system.

The following testimony comes from one who has served in the rebel army in the capacity of surgeon. He says: "The confederate military authorities have complete control of the press, so that nothing is ever allowed to appear in print which can in any way give information to the North or prove a clue to Southern movements. In this it appears to me that they have an unspeakable advantage over the North, with its numberless papers and hundreds of correspondents in the loyal army. With what the correspondents tell and surmise, and what the Confederates find out through spies and informers of various kinds, they are able to see through many of the plans of the Union forces before they are put into execution.

No more common remark did I hear than this as officers were reading the Northern papers: 'See what d—d fools those Yankees are. General A—— has left B—— for C——. We will cut him off. Why the Northern generals or the Secretary of War tolerate this freedom of news we cannot imagine.'"

And he further adds: "Every daily paper I have read since I came North has contained information, either by direct statement or implication, by which the enemy can profit. If we meant to play into the hands of the rebels, we could hardly do it more successfully than our papers are doing it daily. Sure am I that if a Southern paper contained such information of their movements as do the Northern of ours, the editor's neck would not be safe an hour. But some will say: 'We often see information quoted from the Southern papers of their movements.' Never, until the movement has been carried out. It is always safe to conclude, if you see in a Southern paper any statement with regard to the movement of troops, or that the army is about to do a certain thing, that it will not be done, but something different."

Freedom of opinion and of the press is certainly a precious boon, but when it endangers the lives of our soldiers and frustrates the plans of our Government, surely it is time to adopt measures to control it, just as much as it is necessary to arrest the spies who come within our lines.

Another relates the following touching incident of the Southern style of increasing their army, and punishing offenders: "When the rebels were raising a force in Eastern Tennessee, two brothers by the name of Rowland volunteered. A younger brother was a Union man, and refusing to enlist, was seized and forced into the army. He constantly protested against his impressment, but without avail. He then warned them that he would desert the first opportunity, as he would not fight against the cause of right and good government. They were inexorable, and he was torn from his family and hurried to the field. At the battle of Fort Donaldson, Rowland escaped from the rebels in the second day's fight, and immediately joined the loyal army. Though now to fight against his own brothers, he felt that he was in a righteous cause, and contending for a worthy end. In the battle of Pittsburg Landing he was taken prisoner by the very regiment to which he had formerly belonged. This sealed his fate. On his way to Corinth several of his old comrades, among them his two brothers, attempted to kill him, one of them nearly running him through with a bayonet. He was, however, rescued by the guard, and brought to camp. Three days after the retreating army had reached Corinth, General Hardee, in whose division was the regiment claiming this man as a deserter, gave orders to have Rowland executed. About four o'clock in the afternoon, the same day, some ten thousand Tennessee troops were drawn up in two parallel lines, facing inward, three hundred yards apart. The doomed man, surrounded by the guard, detailed from his own regiment to shoot him, marched with a firm step into the middle of the space between the two lines of troops. Here his grave was already dug, and a black pine coffin lay beside it. No minister of religion offered to direct his thoughts to a gracious Saviour. The sentence was read, and he was asked if he had anything to say why it should not be executed. He spoke in a firm, decided tone, in a voice which could be heard by many hundreds, and nearly in the following words: 'Fellow-soldiers, Tennesseeans—I was forced into Southern service against my will, and against my conscience. I told them I would desert the first opportunity I found, and I did it. I was always a Union man, and never denied it; and I joined the Union army to do all the damage I could to the Confederates. I believe the Union cause is right, and will triumph. They can kill me but once, and I am not afraid to die in a good cause. My only request is, that you let my wife and family know that I died in supporting my principles. My brothers there would shoot me if they had a chance, but I forgive them. Now shoot me through the heart, that I may die instantly.'

"After Rowland had ceased to speak, he took off hat, coat and neck-tie, and laying his hand on his heart, he said, "Aim here." The sergeant of the guard advanced to tie his hands and blindfold him. He asked the privilege of standing untied, but the request was not granted. His eyes were bandaged, he knelt upon his coffin and engaged in prayer for several minutes, and then said he was ready. The lieutenant of the guard then gave the word, 'Fire!' and twenty-four muskets were discharged. When the smoke lifted, the body had fallen backward, and was still. Several bullets had passed through his head, and some through his heart. His body was tumbled into the rough pine box, and was buried by the men who shot him."

Such was the fate of a Tennessee patriot, who was not afraid to declare his love for the Union, and his faith in its final triumph, in the very presence of some of the leading traitors, and of thousands of his rebellious countrymen, a moment before sealing his patriotism with his blood.

On board of a transport, on the Mississippi river, as we glided toward our destination, I sat quietly listening to the variety of topics which was being discussed around me, until a peculiarly sweet voice caused me to turn and look in the direction from whence it proceeded.

Reader, has your heart ever been taken by storm, in consequence of the mere intonations of a voice—ere you beheld the individual who gave them utterance? On this occasion, I turned and saw "one of God's images cut in ebony." Time had wrinkled his face, and the frosts of four-score winters had whitened his woolly locks, palsied his limbs, and dimmed his vision. He had been a slave all his life, and now, at the eleventh hour, when "the silver cord was almost loosed, and the golden bowl well nigh broken," he was liberated from bondage, and was rejoicing in freedom from slavery, and in that freedom wherewith Christ makes His children free.

By some invisible attraction, a large crowd gathered around this old, decrepid slave, and every eye was fixed upon his sable withered face, as he gave a brief and touching history of his slave life.

When he had finished, the soldiers eagerly began to ask questions—but suddenly the old colored man turned querist, and raising himself up, and leaning forward toward the crowd, he asked, in a voice strangely thrilling and solemn, "Are any of you soldiers of the Lord Jesus Christ?"

One looked at another with evident embarrassment; but at length some one stammered out—"We don't know exactly; that is a hard question, Uncle." "Oh no," said he, "dat is not a hard question—if you be soldiers of Christ you *know* it, you must know it; de Lord does not do His work so poorly dat His people don't know when it's done. Now jes' let me say a word more: Dear soldiers—before eber you lebe dis boat—before eber you go into anoder battle—enlist for Jesus;

become soldiers ob de blessed Redeemer, and you are safe; safe when de battle rages, safe when de chills ob death come, safe when de world 's on fire."

One of the men, desirous of changing the conversation, said: "Uncle, are you blind?" He replied: "Oh no, bless de Lord, I am not blind to de tings ob de spirit. I see by an eye ob faith my blessed Saviour sitting at de right hand ob God, and I'll soon see Him more clearly, for Jesus loves dis old blind darkie, and will soon take him home."

Now, when we talk of moral sublimity we are apt to point to Alexander conquering the world, to Hannibal surmounting the Alps, to Cæsar crossing the Rubicon, or to Lawrence wrapping himself in the American flag and crying "Don't give up the ship!" But in my opinion here was a specimen of moral sublimity equal to anything that ever graced the pages of history or was ever exhibited upon a battle-field—a poor old, blind, palsied slave, resting upon the "Rock of Ages," while the waves of affliction dashed like mountains at his feet; yet, looking up to heaven, and trusting in the great and precious promises, he gave glory to God, and triumphed over pain and disease, rejoicing even in tribulation.

While the old slave was talking to the soldiers a number of young darkies came forward, and when the conversation ceased they all struck up the following piece, and sang it with good effect:

Oh, praise an' tanks! De Lord he come
To set de people free;
An' massa tink it day ob doom,
An' we ob jubilee.
De Lord dat heap de Red Sea waves,
He jes' as strong as den;
He say de word—we las' night slaves,
To-day de Lord's free men.

CHORUS—De yam will grow, de cotton blow,
We'll hab de rice an' corn,
O nebber you fear if nebber you hear
De driber blow his horn.

Ole massa on his trabbles gone
He lebe de land behind;
De Lord's breff blow him furder on,
Like corn-shuck in de wind.
We own de hoe, we own de plow,
We own de hands dat hold;
We sell de pig, we sell de cow,
But neber chile be sold.

CHORUS—De yam will grow, etc,

We know de promise nebber fail,
An' nebber lie de Word;
So, like de 'postles in de jail,
We waited for de Lord.
An' now He open ebery door,
An' trow away de key,
He tink we lub Him so before,
We lub Him better free.

CHORUS—De yam will grow, etc.

Then a collection was taken up among the soldiers and presented to the old blind colored man, who wept with delight as he received it, for said he—"I hab no home, no money, an' no friend, but de Lord Jesus."

CHAPTER XXVII.

ARRIVAL AT VICKSBURG—ITS SURROUNDINGS—GRANT'S ARMY—ASSAULT ON THE REBEL WORKS—THE SEVEN COLOR-BEARERS—PEMBERTON'S HARANGUE—IN THE TRENCHES—SUFFERINGS OF THE WOUNDED—PEMBERTON'S PROPOSED CAPITULATION—GRANT'S REPLY—TERMS OF SURRENDER—OCCUPATION OF THE CITY—LOSS OF THE ENEMY—COMPLIMENTARY LETTER—GRANT'S SUCCESS—ATTACHMENT OF HIS SOLDIERS—"FIGHTING DICK"—GOLD LACE—REBEL SUFFERINGS—SIGHTS IN VICKSBURG—INCIDENTS OF THE SIEGE—CAVE LIFE.

OUR troops at length joined General Grant's army near Vicksburg, where those veterans had been digging and fighting so many weeks.

The city of Vicksburg is nestled among numerous terraced hills, and would under other circumstances present a magnificent and romantic appearance; but I could not at that time realize its beauty, for the knowledge of the sufferings and distress of thousands within its walls detracted materially from its outward grandeur.

The enemy's works had consisted of a series of redoubts extending from Haines' Bluff to the Warrenton road, a distance of some ten miles. It was a vast plateau, upon which a multitude of little hills seemed to have been sown broadcast, giving the enemy a position from which it could sweep every neighboring crest and enfilade every approach. But the rebels had already been driven from this position after a severe struggle.

On the twenty-second of May, at two o'clock in the morning, heavy guns were opened upon the rebel works, and continued until ten o'clock, when a desperate assault was made by three corps moving simultaneously. After a severe engagement and heavy loss the flag of the Seventh Missouri was planted on one of the rebel parapets, after seven color-bearers had been shot down.

After this contest the rebel general, Pemberton, addressed his men as follows: "You have heard that I was incompetent and a traitor, and that it was my intention to sell Vicksburg. Follow me, and you will see the cost at which I will sell Vicksburg. When the last pound of beef, bacon and flour, the last grain of corn, the last cow and hog, horse and dog shall have been consumed, and the last man shall have perished in the trenches, then, and not till then, will I sell Vicksburg."

It became evident that the works could not be carried by assault, and that nothing but a regular siege could reduce the fortifications.

While the sige was in progress our soldiers endured hardships, privations and sufferings which words can but inadequately express. Our men were closely packed in the trenches, often in water to the knees, and not daring to lift their heads above the brow of the rifle pits, as the rebel sharpshooters lost no time in saluting every unfortunate head which made its appearance above ground.

The sufferings of the wounded were extreme. Those who were wounded during the day in the trenches nearest the city could not be removed until the curtain of night fell upon the scene and screened them from the vigilant eye of the enemy.

General Grant steadily approached the doomed city by means of saps and mines, and continued to blow up their defenses, until it was evident that another day's work would complete the capture of the city.

Such was the position of affairs on the third of July, when General Pemberton proposed an armistice and capitulation.

Major General Bowen, of the Confederate army, was the bearer of a despatch to General Grant, under a flag of truce, proposing the surrender of the city, which was as follows:

HEADQUARTERS, VICKSBURG,
July 3d, 1863.

Major General Grant, commanding United States forces:

GENERAL—I have the honor to propose to you an armistice for — hours, with a view of arranging terms for the capitulation of Vicksburg. To this end, if agreeable to you, I will appoint three commissioners to meet a like number to be named by yourself, at such place and hour to-day as you may find convenient. I make this proposition to save the further effusion of blood, which must otherwise be shed to a frightful extent, feeling myself fully able to maintain my position for a yet indefinite period. This communication will be handed to you, under flag of truce, by Major General James Bowen.

Very respectfully, your obedient servant,

J. C. PEMBERTON.

To which General Grant replied:

HEADQUARTERS, DEPARTMENT OF TENNESSEE,
In the Field, near Vicksburg,
July 3*d*, 1863.

Lieutenant General J. C. Pemberton, commanding Confederate forces, etc.:

GENERAL—Your note of this date, just received, proposes an armistice of several hours for the purpose of arranging terms of capitulation, through commissioners to be appointed, etc. The effusion of blood you propose stopping by this course can be ended at any time you may choose by an unconditional surrender of the city and garrison. Men who have shown so much endurance and courage as those now in Vicksburg will always challenge the respect of an adversary, and, I can assure you, will be treated with all the respect due them as prisoners of war. I do not favor the proposition of appointing commissioners to arrange terms of capitulation, because I have no other terms than those indicated above.

I am, General, very respectfully, your obedient servant,

U. S. GRANT.

Then the following document was made out by General Grant, and submitted for acceptance:

General—In conformity with the agreement of this afternoon, I will submit the following proposition for the surrender of the city of Vicksburg, public stores, etc. On your accepting the terms proposed, I will march in one division, as a guard, and take possession at eight o'clock to-morrow morning. As soon as paroles can be made out and signed by the officers and men, you will be allowed to march out of our lines, the officers taking with them their regimental clothing, and staff, field and cavalry officers, one horse each. The rank and file will be allowed all their clothing, but no other property. If these conditions are accepted, any amount of rations you may deem necessary can be taken from the stores you now have, and also the necessary cooking utensils for preparing them; thirty wagons also, counting two two-horse or mule teams as one. You will be allowed to transport such articles as cannot be carried along. The same conditions will be allowed to all sick and wounded officers and privates as fast as they become able to travel. The paroles for these latter must be signed, however, whilst officers are present authorized to sign the roll of prisoners.

After some further correspondence on both sides this proposition was accepted, and on the fourth of July the Federals took possession of the city of Vicksburg.

A paragraph from General Grant's official despatch will best explain the result of his campaign, together with the surrender of Vicksburg: "The defeat of the enemy in five battles outside of Vicksburg, the occupation of Jackson, the capital of the State of Mississippi, and the capture of Vicksburg and its garrison and munitions of war, a loss to the enemy of thirty-seven thousand prisers, among whom were fifteen general officers, at least ten thousand killed and wounded, and among the killed Generals Tracy, Tilghman and Green, and hundreds, perhaps thousands, of stragglers, who can never be collected and organized. Arms and munitions of war for an army of sixty thousand have fallen into our hands, besides a large amount of other public property, consisting of railroads, locomotives, cars, steamboats, cotton, etc., and much was destroyed to prevent our capturing it."

On the thirteenth of July the President sent an autograph letter to General Grant, of which the following is a copy:

EXECUTIVE MANSION, WASHINGTON,
July 13*th*, 1863.

To Major General Grant:

MY DEAR GENERAL—I do not remember that

you and I ever met personally. I write this now as a grateful acknowledgment for the almost inestimable service you have done the country. I wish to say a word further. When you first reached the vicinity of Vicksburg I thought you should do what you finally did—march the troops across the neck, run the batteries with the transports, and thus go below; and I never had any faith, except a general hope that you knew better than I, that the Yazoo Pass expedition and the like could succeed. When you got below and took Port Gipson, Grand Gulf and vicinity, I thought you should go down the river and join Banks; and when you turned northward, east of the Big Black, I feared it was a mistake. I now wish to make a personal acknowledgment that you were right and I was wrong.

Yours, very truly,

A. LINCOLN.

It is stated on good authority that at the time the news of Grant's success reached the President, there were several gentlemen present some of whom had just been informing Mr. Lincoln that there were great complaints against General Grant with regard to his intemperate habits. After reading the telegram announcing the fall of Vicksburg, the President turned to his anxious friends of the temperance question and said:

"So I understand Grant drinks whiskey to excess?"

"Yes," was the reply.

"What whiskey does he drink?"

"What whiskey?" doubtfully queried his hearers.

"Yes. Is it Bourbon or Monongahela?"

"Why do you ask, Mr. President?"

"Because if it makes him win victories like that at Vicksburg, I will send a demijohn of the same kind to every general in the army."

It is also stated on the same authority that General Grant is strictly temperate.

His men are almost as much attached to him as are the Army of the Potomac to General McClellan. He is a true soldier, and shares all the hardships with his men, sleeping on the ground in the open air, and eating hard bread and salt pork with as good a grace as any private soldier.

He seldom wears a sword, except when absolutely necessary, and frequently wears a semi-military coat and low crowned hat.

The mistakes which people used to make, when coming to headquarters to see the general, often reminded me of a genuine anecdote which is told of General Richardson, or "Fighting Dick," as we familiarly called him. It occurred when the troops were encamped near Washington, and was as follows:

The general was sauntering along toward a fort, which was in course of erection not far from headquarters, dressed in his usual uniform for fatigue, namely: citizen's pants, undress coat, and an old straw hat which had once been white, but was now two or three shades nearer the general's own complexion.

Along came one of those dashing city staff officers, in white gloves, and trimmed off with gold lace to the very extreme of military regulations. He was in search of General Richardson, but did not know him personally. Reining up his horse some little distance from the general, he shouted: "hallo, old fellow! can you tell me where General Richardson's headquarters are?"

The general pointed out the tent to him, and the young officer went dashing along, without ever saying "thank you." The general then turned on his heel and went back to his tent, where he found the officer making a fuss because there was no orderly to hold his horse. Turning to General R., as he came up, he said: "Won't you hold my horse while I find General R.?" "Oh yes, certainly," said he.

After hitching the horse to a post near by for that purpose, the general walked into the tent, and, confronting young pomposity, he said in his peculiar twang, "Well, sir, what will you have?"

When the Federal troops marched into Vicksburg, what a heart-sickening sight it presented; the half-famished inhabitants had crawled from their dens and caves in the earth, to find their houses demolished by shell, and all their pleasant places laid waste.

But the appearance of the soldiers as they came from the entrenchments covered with mud and bespattered with the blood of their comrades who had been killed or wounded, would have touched a heart of stone.

The poor horses, and mules, too, were a sad sight, for they had fared even worse than the soldiers—for there was no place of safety for them—not even entrenchments, and they had scarcely anything at all to eat for weeks, except mulberry leaves.

One man, in speaking of the state of affairs in the city, during the siege, said: "The terror of the women and children, their constant screams and wailings over the dead bodies of their friends, mingled as they were with the shrieks of bursting shell, and the pitiful groans of the dying, was enough to appall the stoutest heart." And others said it was a strange fact that the women could not venture out of their caves a moment without either being killed or wounded, while the men and officers walked or rode about with but little loss of life comparatively.

A lady says: "Sitting in my cave, one evening, I heard the most heart-rending shrieks and groans, and upon making inquiry, I was told that a mother had taken her child into a cave about a hundred yards from us, and having laid it on its little bed, as the poor woman thought, in safety, she took her seat near the entrance of the cave. A mortar-shell came rushing through the air, and fell upon the cave, and bursting in the ground entered the cave; a fragment of the shell mashed the head of the little sleeper, crushing out the young life, and leaving the distracted mother to pierce the heavens with her cries of agony."

How blightingly the hand of war lay upon that once flourishing city! The closed and desolate houses, the gardens with open gates, and the poor, starving mules, standing amid the flowers, picking off every green leaf, to allay their hunger, presented a sad picture.

I will give the following quotation as a specimen of cave life in Vicksburg: "I was sitting near the entrance of my cave about five o'clock in the afternoon, when the bombardment commenced more furiously than usual, the shells falling thickly around us, causing vast columns of earth to fly upward, mingled with smoke. As usual, I was uncertain whether to remain within, or to run out. As the rocking and trembling of the earth was distinctly felt, and the explosions alarmingly near, I stood within the mouth of the cave ready to make my escape, should one chance to fall above our domicile.

"In my anxiety I was startled by the shouts of the servants, and a most fearful jar and rocking of the earth, followed by a deafening explosion, such as I had never heard before. The cave filled instantly with smoke and dust. I stood there, with a tingling, prickling sensation in my head, hands and feet, and with confused brain. Yet alive! was the first glad thought that came to me—child, servants, all here, and saved!

"I stepped out and found a group of persons before my cave, looking anxiously for me, and lying all around were freshly-torn rose bushes, arbor-vitæ trees, large clods of earth, splinters, and pieces of plank.

"A mortar-shell had struck the corner of the cave; fortunately, so near the brow of the hill, that it had gone obliquely into the earth, exploding as it went, breaking large masses from the side of the hill—tearing away the fence, the shrubbery and flowers—sweeping all like an avalanche down near the entrance of my poor refuge.

"On another occasion I sat reading in safety, I imagined, when the unmistakable whirring of Parrott shells told us that the battery we so much dreaded had opened from the entrenchments. I ran to the entrance to call the servants in. Immediately after they entered a shell struck the earth a few feet from the entrance, burying itself without exploding.

"A man came in, much frightened, and asked permission to remain until the danger was over. He had been there but a short time when a Parrott shell came whirling in at the entrance and fell in the center of the cave before us, and lay there, the fuse still smoking.

"Our eyes were fastened upon that terrible missile of death as by the fascination of a serpent, while we expected every moment that the terrific explosion would take place. I pressed my child closer to my heart and drew nearer the wall. Our fate seemed certain—our doom was sealed.

"Just at this dreadful moment, George, a negro boy, rushed forward, seized the shell, and threw it into the street, then ran swiftly in the opposite direction.

"Fortunately the fuse became extinguished and the shell fell harmless to the ground, and is still looked upon as a monument of terror."

CHAPTER XXVIII.

WESTERN GIBRALTAR—THE "LEAD MINERS"—THE PALMETTO EXCHANGED FOR THE STARS AND STRIPES—ENTHUSIASM OF TROOPS—SUFFERINGS FORGOTTEN—I AM ATTACKED BY FEVER—UNFIT FOR DUTY—"VICKSBURG IS OURS"—SPIRIT YEARNINGS—"ROCK ME TO SLEEP MOTHER"—IMPOSITION OF STEAMBOAT OFFICERS—GRANT'S CARE FOR HIS MEN—BURSTING OF A SHELL IN CAMP—CONSEQUENCES—SPEECHLESS AGONY—I AM RELEASED FROM DUTY—MY TRIP TO CAIRO—MISS MARY SAFFORD—ARRIVAL AT WASHINGTON.

IT was a proud day for the Union army when General U. S. Grant marched his victorious troops into the rebel Sebastopol—or "the western Gibraltar," as the rebels were pleased to term it.

The troops marched in triumphantly, the Forty-fifth Illinois, the "lead miners," leading the van, and as they halted in front of the fine white marble Court House, and flung out the National banner to the breeze, and planted the battle-worn flags bearing the dear old stars and stripes—where the "palmetto" had so recently floated—then went up tremendous shouts of triumphant and enthusiastic cheers, which were caught up and re-echoed by the advancing troops until all was one wild scene of joy; and the devastated city and its miserable inhabitants were forgotten in the triumph of the hour.

This excitement proved too much for me, as I had been suffering from fever for several days previous, and had risen from my cot and mounted my horse for the purpose of witnessing the crowning act of the campaign. Now it was over, and I was exhausted and weak as a child.

I was urged to go to a hospital, but refused; yet at length I was obliged to report myself unfit for duty, but still persisted in sitting up most of the time. Oh what dreary days and nights I passed in that dilapidated city! A slow fever had fastened itself upon me, and in spite of all my fortitude and determination to shake it off, I was each day becoming more surely its victim.

I could not bear the shouts of the men, or their songs of triumph which rung out upon every breeze—one of which I can never forget, as I heard it sung until my poor brain was distracted, and in my hours of delirium I kept repeating "Vicksburg is ours," "Vicksburg is ours," in a manner more amusing than musical.

I will here quote a few verses which I think are the same:

Hark! borne upon the Southern breeze,
As whispers breathed above the trees,
Or as the swell from off the seas,
In summer showers,
Fall softly on the ears of men
Strains sweetly indistinct, and then—
Hist! listen! catch the sound again—
"Vicksburg is ours!"

O'er sea-waves beating on the shore,
'Bove the thunder-storm and tempest o'er,
O'er cataracts in headlong roar,
High, high it towers.
O'er all the breastworks and the moats
The Starry Flag in triumph floats,
And heroes thunder from their throats
"Vicksburg is ours!"

Spread all your banners in the sky,
The sword of victory gleams on high,
Our conquering eagles upward fly,
And kiss the stars;
For Liberty the Gods awake,
And hurl the shattered foes a wreck,
The Northern arms make strong to break
The Southern bars.

All honor to the brave and true
Who fought the bloody battles through,
And from the ramparts victory drew
Where Vicksburg cowers;
And o'er the trenches, o'er the slain,
Through iron hail and leaden rain,
Still plunging onward, might and main,
Made Vicksburg ours.

I think I realized, in those hours of feverish restlessness and pain, the heart-yearnings for the touch of a mother's cool hand upon my brow, which I had so often heard the poor sick and wounded soldiers speak of. Oh how I longed for one gentle caress from her loving hand! and when I would sometimes fall into a quiet slumber, and forget my surroundings, I would often wake up and imagine my mother sat beside me, and would only realize my sad mistake when looking in the direction I supposed her to be, there would be seen some great bearded soldier, wrapped up in an overcoat, smoking his pipe.

The following lines in some measure express my spirit-longings for the presence of my mother in those nights of torturing fever and days of languor and despondency:

Backward, turn backward, O Time, in your flight;
Make me a child again, just for to-night!
Mother, O come from the far-distant shore,
Take me again to your heart as of yore;
Over my slumbers your loving watch keep—
Rock me to sleep, mother, rock me to sleep.

* * * * * * *

Backward, flow backward, O tide of the years!
I am so weary of toils and of tears,
Toil without recompense—tears all in vain—
Take them, and give me my childhood again.
I have grown weary of warfare and strife,
Weary of bartering my health and my life,
Weary of sowing for others to reap—
Rock me to sleep, mother, rock me to sleep.

After the fall of Vicksburg a large proportion

of the soldiers in that vicinity, who had fought so bravely, endured so many hardships, and lain in the entrenchments so many weary weeks during the siege, were permitted to visit their homes on furlough.

In view of this General Grant issued a special order forbidding steamboat officers to charge more than five dollars to enlisted men, and seven dollars to officers, as fare between Vicksburg and Cairo. Notwithstanding this order the captains of steamers were in the habit of charging from fifteen to thirty dollars apiece.

On one occasion one of those steamers had on board an unusually large number of soldiers, said to be over one thousand enlisted men and nearly two hundred and fifty officers, *en route* for home on leave of absence; and all had paid from twenty to twenty-five dollars each. But just as the boat was about to push off from the wharf an order came from General Grant requiring the money to be refunded to men and officers over and above the stipulated sum mentioned in a previous order, or the captain to have his boat confiscated and submit himself to imprisonment for disobedience of orders. Of course the captain handed over the money, and amid cheers for General Grant, sarcastic smiles, and many amusing and insinuating speeches and doubtful compliments to the captain, the men pocketed the recovered "greenbacks," and went on their way rejoicing.

When the General was told of the imposition practiced by the boatmen on his soldiers, he replied: "I will teach them, if they need the lesson, that the men who have periled their lives to open the Mississippi for their benefit cannot be imposed upon with impunity."

A noble trait in the character of this brave general is that he looks after the welfare of his men as one who has to give an account of his stewardship, or of those intrusted to his care.

I remained in my tent for several days, not being able to walk about, or scarcely able to sit up. I was startled one day from my usual quietude by the bursting of a shell which had lain in front of my tent, and from which no danger was apprehended; yet it burst at a moment when a number of soldiers were gathered round it—and oh, what sad havoc it made of those cheerful, happy boys of a moment previous! Two of them were killed instantly and four were wounded seriously, and the tent where I lay was cut in several places with fragments of shell, the tent poles knocked out of their places, and the tent filled with dust and smoke.

One poor colored boy had one of his hands torn off at the wrist; and of all the wounded that I have ever seen I never heard such unearthly yells and unceasing lamentations as that boy poured forth night and day; ether and chloroform were alike unavailing in hushing the cries of the poor sufferer. At length the voice began to grow weaker, and soon afterwards ceased altogether; and upon making inquiry I found he had died groaning and crying until his voice was hushed in death.

The mother and sister of one of the soldiers who was killed by the explosion of the shell arrived a short time after the accident occurred, and it was truly a most pitiful sight to see the speechless grief of those stricken ones as they sat beside the senseless clay of that beloved son and brother.

All my soldierly qualities seemed to have fled, and I was again a poor, cowardly, nervous, whining woman; and as if to make up for lost time, and to give vent to my long pent up feelings, I could do nothing but weep hour after hour, until it would seem that my head was literally a fountain of tears and my heart one great burden of sorrow. All the horrid scenes that I had witnessed during the past two years seemed now before me with vivid distinctness, and I could think of nothing else.

It was under these circumstances that I made up my mind to leave the army; and when once my mind is made up on any subject I am very apt to act at once upon that decision. So it was in this case. I sent for the surgeon and told him I was not able to remain longer—that I would certainly die if I did not leave immediately.

The good old surgeon concurred in my opinion,

and made out a certificate of disability, and I was forthwith released from further duty as "Nurse and Spy" in the Federal army.

The very next day I embarked for Cairo, and on my arrival there I procured female attire, and laid aside forever (perhaps) my military uniform; but I had become so accustomed to it that I parted with it with much reluctance.

While in Cairo I had the pleasure of seeing the celebrated Miss Mary Safford, of whom so much has been said and written.

One writer gives the following account of her, which is correct with regard to personal appearance, and I have no doubt is correct throughout:

"I cannot close this letter without a passing word in regard to one whose name is mentioned by thousands of our soldiers with gratitude and blessing.

"Miss Mary Safford is a resident of this town, whose life, since the beginning of this war, has been devoted to the amelioration of the soldier's lot and his comfort in the hospital.

"She is a young lady, *petite* in figure, unpretending, but highly cultivated, by no means officious, and so wholly unconscious of her excellencies and the great work that she is achieving, that I fear this public allusion to her may pain her modest nature.

"Her sweet young face, full of benevolence, her pleasant voice and winning manner, install her in every one's heart directly; and the more one sees of her the more they admire her great soul and noble nature.

"Not a day elapses but she is found in the hospitals, unless indeed she is absent on an errand of mercy up the Tennessee, or to the hospitals in Kentucky.

"Every sick and wounded soldier in Cairo knows and loves her, and, as she enters the ward, every pale face brightens at her approach. As she passes along she inquires of each one how he had passed the night, if he is well supplied with books and tracts, and if there is anything she can do for him. All tell her their story frankly—the old man old enough to be her father, and the boy in his teens, all confide in her.

"For one she must write a letter to his friend at home; she must sit down and read at the cot of another; must procure, if the surgeon will allow it, this or that article of food for a third; must soothe and encourage a fourth who desponds and is ready to give up his hold on life; must pray for a fifth who is afraid to die, and wrestle for him till light shines through the dark valley; and so on, varied as may be the personal or spiritual wants of the sufferers.

"Surgeons, nurses, medical directors, and army officers, are all her true friends, and so judicious and trustworthy is she, that the Chicago Sanitary Commission have given her *carte blanche* to draw on their stores at Cairo for anything she may need in her errands of mercy in the hospitals.

"She is performing a noble work, and that too in the most quiet and unassuming manner."

From Cairo I went to Washington, where I spent several weeks, until I recovered from my fever and was able to endure the fatigue of traveling. Then after visiting the hospitals once more, and bidding farewell to old scenes and associations, I returned to my friends to recruit my shattered health.

CHAPTER XXIX.

REVIEW OF HOSPITAL AND CAMP LIFE—QUESTIONS ANSWERED—BEHIND THE SCENES—BLESSED EMPLOYMENT—LIVING PAST SCENES OVER AGAIN—MY MOST IMPORTANT LABORS—MOTHER AND SON—STRANGE POWER OF SYMPATHY—HERO'S REPOSE—OFFICERS AND MEN—THE BRAVEST ARE KINDEST—GENERAL SEDGWICK—BATTLE SCENES—MR. ALVORD'S DESCRIPTION—VOLUNTEER SURGEONS—HEART SICKENING SIGHTS—AN AWFUL PICTURE—FEMALE NURSES—SENTIMENTAL—PATRIOTIC—MEDICAL DEPARTMENT—YOUNG SURGEONS—ANECDOTES.

SINCE I returned to New England there have been numerous questions asked me with regard to hospitals, camp life, etc., which have not been fully answered in the preceding narrative, and I have thought that perhaps it would not be out of place to devote a chapter to that particular object.

One great question is: "Do the soldiers get the clothing and delicacies which we send them—or is it true that the surgeons, officers and nurses appropriate them to their own use?"

In reply to this question I dare not assert that all the things which are sent to the soldiers are faithfully distributed, and reach the individuals for whom they were intended. But I have no hesitation in saying that I have reason to believe that the cases are very rare where surgeons or nurses tamper with those articles sent for the comfort of the sick and wounded.

If the ladies of the Soldiers' Aid Societies and other benevolent organizations could have seen even the quantity which I have seen with my own eyes distributed, and the smile of gratitude with which those supplies are welcomed by the sufferers, they would think that they were amply rewarded for all their labor in preparing them.

Just let those benevolent hearted ladies imagine themselves in my place for a single day; removing blood-clotted and stiffened woollen garments from ghastly wounds, and after applying the sponge and water remedy, replacing those coarse, rough shirts by nice, cool, clean linen ones, then dress the wounds with those soft white bandages and lint; take from the express box sheet after sheet, and dainty little pillows with their snowy cases, until you have the entire hospital supplied and every cot looking clean and inviting to the weary, wounded men—then as they are carried and laid upon those comfortable beds, you will often see the tears of gratitude gush forth, and hear the earnest "God bless the benevolent ladies who send us these comforts."

Then, after the washing and clothing process is gone through with, the nice wine or Boston crackers are brought forward, preserved fruits, wines, jellies, etc., and distributed as the different cases may require.

I have spent whole days in this blessed employment without realizing weariness or fatigue, so completely absorbed would I become in my work, and so rejoiced in having those comforts provided for our brave, suffering soldiers.

Time and again, since I have been engaged in writing this little narrative, I have thrown down my pen, closed my eyes, and lived over again those hours which I spent in ministering to the wants of those noble men, and have longed to go back and engage in the same duties once more.

I look back now upon my hospital labors as being the most important and interesting in my life's history. The many touching incidents which come to my mind as I recall those thrilling scenes make me feel as if I should never be satisfied until I had recorded them all, so that they might never be forgotten. One occurs to my mind now which I must not omit:

"In one of the fierce engagements with the

rebels near Mechanicsville, a young lieutenant of a Rhode Island battery had his right foot so shattered by a fragment of shell that on reaching Washington, after one of those horrible ambulance rides, and a journey of a week's duration, he was obliged to undergo amputation.

"He telegraphed home, hundreds of miles away, that all was going on well, and with a soldier's fortitude composed his mind and determined to bear his sufferings alone. Unknown to him, however, his mother—one of those dear reserves of the army—hastened up to join the main force. She reached the city at midnight, and hastened to the hospital, but her son being in such a critical condition, the nurses would have kept her from him until morning. One sat by his side fanning him as he slept, her hand on the feeble, fluctuating pulsations which foreboded sad results. But what woman's heart could resist the pleading of a mother at such a moment? In the darkness she was finally allowed to glide in and take the nurse's place at his side. She touched his pulse as the nurse had done. Not a word had been spoken; but the sleeping boy opened his eyes and said: 'That feels like my mother's hand! Who is this beside me? It is my mother; turn up the gas and let me see mother!' The two loving faces met in one long, joyful, sobbing embrace, and the fondness pent up in each heart wept forth its own language.

"The gallant fellow underwent operation after operation, and at last, when death drew near, and he was told by tearful friends that it only remained to make him comfortable, he said he 'had looked death in the face too many times to be afraid now,' and died as gallantly as did the men of the Cumberland."

> When a hero goes
> Unto his last repose,
> When earth's trump of fame shall wake him no more;
> When in the heavenly land
> Another soul doth stand,
> Who perished for a Nation ere he reached the shore;
> Whose eyes should sorrow dim?
> Say, who should mourn for him?
>
> Mourn for the traitor—mourn
> When honor is forsworn;
> When the base wretch sells his land for gold,
> Stands up unblushingly
> And boasts his perfidy,
> Then, then, O patriots! let your grief be told
> But when God's soldier yieldeth up his breath,
> O mourn ye not for him! it is not death!

Another question is frequently asked me—"Are not the private soldiers cruelly treated by the officers?" I never knew but a very few instances of it, and then it was invariably by mean, cowardly officers, who were not fit to be in command of so many mules. I have always noticed that the bravest and best fighting officers are the kindest and most forbearing toward their men.

An interesting anecdote is told of the late brave General Sedgwick, which illustrates this fact:

"One day, while on a march, one of our best soldiers had fallen exhausted by fatigue and illness, and lay helpless in the road, when an officer came dashing along in evident haste to join his staff in advance.

"It was pitiable to see the effort the poor boy made to drag his unwilling limbs out of the road. He struggled up only to sink back with a look that asked only the privilege of lying there undisturbed to die.

"In an instant he found his head pillowed on an arm as gentle as his far-away mother's might have been, and a face bent over him expressive of the deepest pity.

"It is characteristic of our brave boys that they say but little. The uncomplaining words of the soldier in this instance were few, but understood.

"The officer raised him in his arms and placed him in his own saddle, supporting the limp and swaying figure by one firm arm, while with the other he curbed the step of his impatient horse to a gentler pace.

"For two miles, without a gesture of impatience, he traveled in this tedious way, until he reached an ambulance train and placed the sick man in one of the ambulances.

"This was our noble Sedgwick—our brave general of the Sixth Corps—pressed with great anxieties and knowing the preciousness of every moment. His men used to say: 'We all know that great things are to be done, and well done, when we see that earnest figure in its rough blouse hurrying past, and never have we been disappointed in him. He works incessantly, is unostentatious, and when he appears among us all eyes follow him with outspoken blessings.'"

I have often been asked: "Have you ever been on a battle-field before the dead and wounded were removed?" "How did it appear?" "Please describe one."

I have been on many a battle-field, and have often tried to describe the horrible scenes which I there witnessed, but have never yet been able to find language to express half the horrors of such sights as I have seen on those terrible fields.

The Rev. Mr. Alvord has furnished us with a vivid description of a battle-field, which I will give for the benefit of those who wish a true and horrifying description of those bloody fields:

"To-day I have witnessed more horrible scenes than ever before since I have been in the army. Hundreds of wounded had lain since the battle, among rebels, intermingled with heaps of slain—hungering, thirsting, and with wounds inflaming and festering. Many had died simply from want of care. Their last battle was fought! Almost every shattered limb required amputation, so putrid had the wounds become.

"I was angry (I think without sin) at your volunteer surgeons. Those of the army were too few, and almost exhausted. But squads of volunteers, as is usual, had come on without instruments, and without sense enough to set themselves at work in any way, and without any idea of dressing small wounds. They wanted to see amputation, and so, while hundreds were crying for help, I found five of these gentlemen sitting at their ease, with legs crossed, waiting for their expected reception by the medical director, who was, of course, up to his elbows in work with saw and amputating knife. I invited them to assist me in my labors among the suffering, but they had 'not come to nurse'—they were 'surgeons.'

"The disgusting details of the field I need not describe. Over miles of shattered forest and torn earth the dead lie, sometimes in *heaps* and *winrows*—I mean literally! friend and foe, black and white, with distorted features, among mangled and dead horses, trampled in mud, and thrown in all conceivable sorts of places. You can distinctly hear, over the whole field, the hum and hissing of decomposition. Of course you can imagine shattered muskets, bayonets, cartridge-boxes, caps, torn clothing, cannon-balls, fragments of shell, broken artillery, etc. I went over it all just before evening, and after a couple of hours turned away in sickening horror from the dreadful sight. I write in the midst of the dead, buried and unburied—in the midst of hospitals full of dying, suffering men, and weary, shattered regiments."

This is a very mild illustration of some battle-fields, and yet it presents an awful picture.

O God! this land grows rich in loyal blood
  Poured out upon it to its utmost length!
The incense of a people's sacrifice—
  The wrested offering of a people's strength.

It is the costliest land beneath the sun!
  'Tis purchaseless! and scarce a rood
But hath its title written clear, and signed
  In some slain hero's consecrated blood.

And not a flower that gems its mellowing soil
  But thriveth well beneath the holy dew
Of tears, that ease a nation's straining heart
  When the Lord of Battles smites it through and through.

Now a word about female nurses who go from the North to take care of the soldiers in hospitals. I have said but little upon this point, but could say much, as I have had ample opportunity for observation.

Many of the noble women who have gone from the New England and other loyal States have done, and are still doing, a work which will engrave their names upon the hearts of the soldiers, as the name of Florence Nightingale is engraved upon the hearts of her countrymen.

It is a strange fact that the more highly cultivated and refined the ladies are, they make all the better nurses. They are sure to submit to inconvenience and privations with a much better grace than those of the lower classes.

It is true we have some sentimental young ladies, who go down there and expect to find everything in drawing-room style, with nothing to do but sit and fan handsome young mustached heroes in shoulder-straps, and read poetry, etc.; and on finding the *real* somewhat different from the *ideal*, which their ardent imaginations had created, they become homesick at once, and declare that they "cannot endure such work as washing private soldiers' dirty faces and combing tangled, matted hair; and, what is more, won't do it." So after making considerable fuss, and trailing round in very long silk skirts for several days, until everybody becomes disgusted, they are politely invited by the surgeon in charge to migrate to some more congenial atmosphere.

But the patriotic, whole-souled, educated woman twists up her hair in a "cleared-for-action" sort of style, rolls up the sleeves of her plain cotton dress, and goes to work washing dirty faces, hands and feet, as if she knew just what to do and how to do it. And when she gets through with that part of the programme, she is just as willing to enter upon some new duty, whether it is writing letters for the boys or reading for them, administering medicine or helping to dress wounds. And everything is done so cheerfully that one would think it was really a pleasure instead of a disagreeable task.

But the medical department is unquestionably the greatest institution in the whole army. I will not attempt to anwer all the questions I have been asked concerning it, but will say that there are many true stories, and some false ones, circulated with regard to that indispensable fraternity.

I think I may freely say that there is a shadow of truth in that old story of "whiskey" and "incompetency" which we have so often heard applied to individuals in the medical department, who are intrusted with the treatment, and often the lives of our soldiers.

There is a vast difference in surgeons; some are harsh and cruel—whether it is from habit or insensibility I am not prepared to say—but I know the men would face a rebel battery with less forebodings than they do some of our worthy surgeons.

There is a class who seem to act upon the principle of "no smart no cure," if we may be allowed to judge from the manner in which they twitch off bandages and the scientific twists and jerks given to shattered limbs.

Others again are very gentle and tender with the men, and seem to study how to perform the necessary operations with the least possible pain to the patients.

But the young surgeons, fresh from the dissecting room, when operating in conjunction with our old Western practitioners, forcibly reminded me of the anecdote of the young collegian teaching his grandmother to suck an egg: "We make an incision at the apex and an aperture at the base;

then making a vacuum with the tongue and palate, we suffer the contained matter to be protruded into the mouth by atmospheric pressure." "La! how strange!" said his grandmother; "in my day we just made a hole in each end, and then sucked it without half that trouble."

I once saw a young surgeon amputate a limb, and I could think of nothing else than of a Kennebec Yankee whom I once saw carve a Thanksgiving turkey; it was his first attempt at carving, and the way in which he disjointed those limbs I shall never forget.

CHAPTER XXX.

CLOSING INCIDENTS—PROFESSOR LOWE'S BALLOON—FITZ JOHN PORTER'S ADVENTURE—HIS UPWARD FLIGHT—RECONNOITERING FROM A DANGEROUS POSITION—COOL COURAGE—ENTHUSIASTIC GREETING—AN EARNEST INQUIRER—A BAPTISM IN THE ARMY—PREACHING BY MOONLIGHT—A MAGNIFICENT SCENE—A WEDDING IN CAMP—GAY TIMES—A CONTRAST—HOSPITAL IN WINCHESTER—SPIRIT OF REVENGE—SABLE HEROINE—A WHITE DARKEY—COLORED SOLDIERS—CONCLUSION.

IN looking back over the events of the two years which I spent in the army, I see so much worthy of record I scarcely know where to stop.

A most thrilling incident occurs to my mind at this moment in connection with Professor Lowe and his balloon, which I must relate before closing.

It took place while McClellan's army was in front of Yorktown.

General Fitz John Porter having been in the habit of making frequent ascensions in company with Professor Lowe, learned to go aloft alone.

One morning he stepped into the car and ordered the cable to be let out with all speed. We saw with surprise that the flurried assistants were sending up the great straining canvas with a single rope attached. The enormous bag was only partially inflated, and the loose folds opened and shut with a sharp report like that of a pistol. Noisily, fitfully, the great yellow mass rose toward the sky, the basket rocking like a feather in the breeze. Presently a sound came from overhead like the explosion of a shell—the cable had snapped asunder, and the balloon was adrift.

All eyes were turned toward the receding car, where General Porter sat in his ærial castle, being borne heavenward as fast as if on eagle wings, without the power either to check or guide his upward flight.

The whole army was agitated by this unwonted occurrence, and the rebel army evidently partook in the general excitement.

Lowe's voice could be heard above the confusion and tumult shouting to the soaring hero—"Open—the—valve! Climb—to—the—netting—and—reach—the valve—rope!"

"The valve—the valve!" repeated a multitude

of voices, but all in vain, for it was impossible to make him hear.

Soon the signal corps began to operate, and at last the general was made to understand by signals when it was impossible to reach him by the human voice.

He appeared directly over the edge of the car, and then clambered up the netting and reached for the cord, but he was so far above us then he looked no bigger than a great black spider.

It was a weird spectacle—that frail, fading object floating in the azure sky, with the miniature boat swinging silently beneath, looking no bigger than a humming-bird's nest; and a hundred thousand brave hearts beneath beating with the wildest excitement and warmest sympathy, yet powerless to render the least assistance to their exalted brother-in-arms.

"Had the general been floating down the rapids of Niagara he could not have been farther from human assistance."

We at length saw him descend from the netting and reappear over the edge of the basket, and he seemed to be motioning to the breathless crowd below the story of his failure.

Soon after the balloon began slowly to descend, and when we next saw him it was with spyglass in hand, reconnoitering the rebel works. Shouts of joy and laughter went up from the long lines of spectators as this cool procedure was observed.

For a moment it seemed doubtful in which direction the balloon would float; it faltered like an irresolute being, and at length moved reluctantly toward Fortress Monroe. Bursting cheers, half uttered, quivered on every lip. All eyes glistened, and many were dim with tears. But the wayward canvas now turned due west, and was blown rapidly toward the confederate works.

Its course was fitfully direct, and the wind seemed to veer often, as if contrary currents, conscious of the opportunity, were struggling for the possession of the daring navigator.

The south wind held the mastery for awhile, and the balloon passed the Federal front amid groans of despair from the soldiers. It kept right on, over sharpshooters, rifle-pits, etc., until it stood directly over the rebel fortifications at Yorktown. The oool courage, either of heroism or despair, seemed to seize the general, for turning his tremendous glass upon the ramparts and masked batteries below, he viewed the remote camps, the beleaguered town, the guns of Gloucester Point, and distant Norfolk. Had he been reconnoitering from a secure perch on the top of the moon he could not have been more vigilant; and the Confederates probably thought this some Yankee device to peer into their sanctum in spite of ball or shell. None of their large guns could be brought to bear upon the balloon, but there were some discharges of musketry, which seemed to have no effect whatever, and finally even these demonstrations ceased.

Both armies were gazing aloft in breathless suspense, while the deliberate general continued to spy out the land.

Suddenly another change of position, and the air craft plunged and tacked about, and steered rapidly for the Federal lines again. Making a desperate effort to catch the valve-rope, the general at length succeeded, and giving it a jerk, the balloon came suddenly to the ground; fortunately, however, it struck a tent as it descended, which perhaps saved the general from any serious injuries from the fall.

By the time the crowd had reached the spot, Porter had disentangled himself from the folds of oiled canvas, and was ready to greet his anxious friends; and amid hearty congratulations and vociferous cheers, he was escorted to his quarters.

As this chapter is devoted to incidents in camp, I will try to illustrate the variety of interesting events with which our camps abound.

After one of the most severe battles ever fought in Virginia, and while our troops were still rejoicing over their victory, a young soldier sought the chaplain for the purpose of religious conversation. Said the chaplain: "The tears were in his eyes, and his lips trembled with emotion. I knew that he was in earnest. We knelt down together and I prayed with him, and he prayed for himself. In this manner we spent several hours, pleading with God in his behalf, until light broke through the darkness, and he arose from his knees praising God."

Wishing to manifest by some outward sign his consecration to God and to His service, he requested the chaplain to baptize him by immersion. The next day being the Sabbath his request was complied with, in the presence of thousands of his comrades.

The scene was a most solemn one, and after the ordinance was administered there was scarcely a dry eye in the company to which he belonged.

In the evening one of the delegates of the Christian Commission preached to an immense congregation of grim warriors seated on the ground—a little pine grove for a church, the great blue dome of heaven for galleries, and the clear, bright moon for a chandelier.

The scene was a magnificent one. A little to the right lay a cloud of white canvas tents shining in the moonlight, and just below, in plain sight, were the transports dotting the water, with their gleaming lights and star-spangled banners floating in the evening breeze. All combined to make the scene beautiful and interesting.

The discourse was excellent and well chosen, and the men listened with profound attention, and I have no doubt with much profit. Then was sung

Lord, dismiss us with thy blessing,

and the benediction being pronounced, the vast assembly marched to their quarters as solemnly as if going from a funeral.

Next came a wedding! Yes; a real wedding in camp. You must know that when military necessity prevents our young heroes from going home to fulfill their engagements to their devoted fair ones, it is the privilege of the waiting damsels, in war times, to remove all unnecessary obstacles, and facilitate matters by declaring themselves in favor of the *union*, and claiming their lovers on the field.

This wedding was a grand affair, and took place in a camp which was very prettily decorated, being picturesquely arranged among pine trees—just the most romantic place imaginable for such an event.

A little before noon the guests began to arrive in large numbers. Among them were Generals Hooker, Sickles, Carr, Mott, Hobart, Ward, Revere, Bartlett, Birney, and Berry.

The troops, looking their very best, formed a hollow square, in the center of which a canopy was erected, and an altar formed of drums.

As the generals marched into the square—General Hooker leading the van—and grouped themselves on each side of the altar, the bands struck up "Hail to the Chief," and on the appearance of the bridal party the "Wedding March" was played.

The day was cold and windy, with a few snowflakes interspersed, which made the ladies in attendance look very much like "blue noses"; but the blushing bride bore the cold and the admiring glances of the soldiers like a martyr, and retained her dignity and self-possession throughout the ceremony worthy of a heroine, as she was.

To add to the dramatic effect of the scene, a line of battle was formed by the remaining troops in that section, a short distance from camp, to repel an expected attack of the enemy.

The ceremony having been performed, dinner was announced, and all partook of the good things provided for the occasion.

After dinner, came numerous toasts, speeches, songs, and music from the bands, and, to close up the day in good style, a regular military ball was held, and fireworks exhibited in the evening—"and on the whole," a newspaper correspondent says, "it entirely eclipsed an opera at the Academy of Music."

I have before alluded to the vindictive spirit manifested by the women of Virginia toward our soldiers. I will illustrate this fact by an incident which took place in one of the hospitals just after a severe battle.

Many wounded soldiers, both Union and Confederate, were brought into the town of Winchester, and placed in the churches and court-house side by side.

The ladies (beg pardon, ladies, I mean females) of that place brought into the hospital many things to nourish and tempt the appetites of the sufferers, but they gave all these delicacies to the Confederate soldiers: our men were passed by as unworthy of notice or sympathy.

One day a lady, who had been a constant visitor, brought in a supply of fragrant tea. She went from one cot to another of her friends, but had no eye or heart of pity for others.

One of our wounded men, who lay near his end, longed for a cup of this tea as he saw it handed to those around him, and requested the chaplain, who stood by his side, to ask the lady for a little of the tea.

He did so in a very polite manner, at the same time telling her how ill the man was, and that it was the soldier himself who wished him to make the request.

"No," said she, and her face flushed with anger; "not a drop of it; this tea is all for our suffering martyrs."

The chaplain replied: "Madam, I looked for no other answer. I beg pardon for having seemed for a moment to expect a different one."

A few moments afterwards, as the poor disappointed man lay there seeing the delicious tea passed on all sides of him and could not procure a drop of it, an old lame negro woman came limping up the aisle with a large basket on each arm.

Coming up to where the chaplain stood, she laid down the baskets and addressed him thus:

"Massa, I'se a slave—my husban' and chil'en is slaves. Will you 'cept dese tings for de poor men?"

Then taking up a roll of stockings, she said: "Dem I knit wid my own hands for de soldiers, when all sleep, in my cabin. We know'd dis war was comin' long 'fore you Yankees did. We see it 'proaching, an' we began to prepare for it."

Then taking packages of tea, cans of fruit, pears and peaches, lint, linen for bandages, and pocket-handkerchiefs, she said: "Massa, permit me to give you dese for de poor men. I have not stole 'em. My own hands have earned 'em over de washtub. I wish to do something for de Union soldiers, Lord bless 'em!"

"As she talked," says the chaplain, "she grew more earnest, and looking around on the mutilated men the tears rolled down her black face, and fell on her hands, as she lifted the treasures out of the baskets and handed them to me."

Our sick men looked with wonder and admiration on the old colored woman, and soon a hundred voices cried out "God bless you, aunty! You are the only white woman we have seen since we came to Winchester."

Some people assert that colored people have no souls. Which, think you, acted most as if lacking soul—the black or the white woman in the hospital at Winchester?

The devotion of the negro woman, as manifested in the hospital, is a perfect sample of the devotion of the contrabands, male and female, to the Union cause.

And now that the time has come when the colored men are permitted, by the laws of the land, to assume the privileges of rational beings, and to go forth as American soldiers to meet their cruel oppressors on the bloody field, there is evidently as great, if not greater, enthusiasm and true patriotism manifested by them, as by any troops in the United States army.

And still further—it has been proved satisfactorily within the last twelve months that the colored troops endure fatigue as cheerfully and fight as well (and get less pay) as any of the white troops. Thank God, this is one great point gained for the poor down-trodden descendants of Africa.

I imagine I see them, with their great shiny eyes and grinning faces, as they march to the field, singing—

Oh! we're de bully soldiers of de "First of Arkansas,"
We are fightin' for de Union, we are fightin' for de law,
We can hit a rebel furder dan a white man eber saw,
As we go marchin' on:
Glory, glory, hallelujah, etc.

See dar! above de center, where de flag is wavin' bright;
We are goin' out of slavery; we are bound for freedom's light;
We mean to show Jeff. Davis how de Africans can fight!
Glory, glory, hallelujah,
Glory, glory, hallelujah,
Glory, glory, hallelujah,
As we go marching on.

And now, what shall I say in conclusion? The war still continues—our soldiers are daily falling in battle, and thousands are languishing in hospitals or in Southern prisons; and I for months past have not given even a cup of cold water to the sufferers. I am ashamed to acknowledge it! But when I look around and see the streets crowded with strong, healthy young men who ought to be foremost in the ranks of their country's defenders, I am not only ashamed, but I am indignant!

To prove to my friends that I am not ambitious of gaining the reputation of that venerable general (Halleck) whose "pen is mightier than his sword," I am about to return to the army to offer my services in any capacity which will best promote the interests of the Federal cause—no matter how perilous the position may be.

And now I lay aside my pen, hoping that after "this cruel war is over," and peace shall have once more shed her sweet influence over our land, I may be permitted to resume it again to record the annihilation of rebellion, and the final triumph of Truth, Right, and *Liberty*.

O Lord of Peace, who art Lord of Righteousness,
Constrain the anguished worlds from sin and grief,
Pierce them with conscience, purge them with redress,
AND GIVE US PEACE WHICH IS NO COUNTERFEIT!

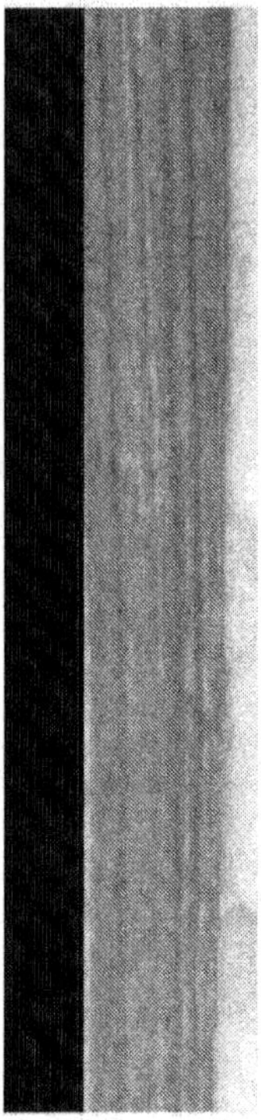

CPSIA information can be obtained
at www.ICGtesting.com
Printed in the USA
LVOW13*1222220817
545790LV00012BA/352/P

9 781296 604509